**Multiple Echo**

# Multiple Echo

*Explorations in Theology*

CORNELIUS ERNST O.P.

*Edited by Fergus Kerr O.P.
and Timothy Radcliffe O.P.*

*Foreword by Donald MacKinnon*

Wipf & Stock
PUBLISHERS
*Eugene, Oregon*

Wipf and Stock Publishers
199 W 8th Ave, Suite 3
Eugene, OR 97401

Multiple Echo
Explorations in Theology
By Ernst, Cornelius
Copyright©1979 Darton, Longman & Todd
ISBN 13: 978-1-59752-992-1
ISBN: 1-59752-992-3
Publication date 10/5/2006
Previously published by Darton, Longman & Todd, 1979

## Contents

| | |
|---|---|
| Acknowledgements | vi |
| Original Sources | vii |
| Abbreviations | ix |
| Foreword | xi |
| Introduction | 1 |
| 1 Thomas Aquinas | 7 |
| 2 Words, Facts and God | 13 |
| 3 World Religions and Christian Theology | 28 |
| 4 The *Concilium* World Congress: Impressions and Reflections | 41 |
| 5 A Theological Critique of Experience | 47 |
| 6 Metaphor and Ontology in *Sacra Doctrina* | 57 |
| 7 Theological Methodology | 76 |
| 8 Holy, Holy, Holy | 87 |
| 9 Acts of Christ: Signs of Faith | 97 |
| 10 Mary: Sign of Contradiction or Source of Unity? | 115 |
| 11 Philosophy in the Seminary | 126 |
| 12 The Significance for Ecclesiology of the Declaration on non-Christian Religions and the Decree on Missions of Vatican II | 137 |
| 13 The Significant Life of a Dominican House of Studies | 149 |
| 14 Priesthood and Ministry | 158 |
| 15 The Primacy of Peter | 171 |
| 16 How to See an Angel | 187 |
| 17 Wrestling with the Word | 202 |
| 18 The Necessity of the Church in the Context of non-Christian Religions | 210 |
| 19 The Vocation of Nature | 225 |
| Index of Names | 239 |
| Analytic Index of Subjects | 243 |

# Acknowledgements

Thanks are due to the following for permission to quote from copyright sources:

Faber and Faber: An excerpt from 'Asides on the Oboe' by Wallace Stevens

The Hogarth Press: An excerpt from 'The Second Elegy' taken from 'The Duino Elegies' by R. Rilke, translated by Leishman.

# Original Sources

1. Thomas Aquinas
   Radio 3 talk, published in *The Listener*, 10 October 1974
2. Words, Facts and God
   Lecture on St Thomas's day, Nijmegen University, 1963
3. World Religions and Christian Theology
   Text of a Spalding Lecture given at the University of Sussex, 1969
4. The *Concilium* World Congress: Impressions and Reflections
   Published in *New Blackfriars*, 1970
5. A Theological Critique of Experience
   Lecture given on various occasions in 1972
6. Metaphor and Ontology in *Sacra Doctrine*
   Published in *The Thomist*, 1974
7. Theological Methodology
   Contributed to *Sacramentum Mundi*, ed. Karl Rahner. Burns & Oates 1970
8. Holy, Holy, Holy
   Review of *Honest to God* in *Life of the Spirit*, 1963
9. Acts of Christ: Signs of Faith
   Paper at the Maynooth Summer School, 1963. First published in *Sacraments*, ed. D. O'Callaghan. Gill & Son 1964
10. Mary: Sign of Contradiction or Source of Unity?
    Published in *The Clergy Review*, 1964
11. Philosophy in the Seminary
    Paper given to the Priests' Philosophical Group, 1964
12. The Significance for Ecclesiology of the Declaration on Non-Christian Religions and the Decree on Missions of Vatican II
    Paper to conference of Dominican theologians concerned with revising curriculum of theological studies. First published in *Angelicum*, 1966
13. The Significant Life of a Dominican House of Studies

Inaugural lecture as Regent of Studies, Blackfriars, Oxford, 1966
14. Priesthood and Ministry
    Paper given to the Clerical Students Conference, Spode House, 1967
15. The Primacy of Peter: Theology and Ideology
    Published in *New Blackfriars*, 1969
16. How to See an Angel
    Edited from tape recording of a talk at the Summer School of Theology, Spode House, 1967
17. Wrestling with the Word
    Sermon preached in 1970, with reflections on its composition
18. The Necessity of the Church in the Context of non-Christian Religions
    Paper to a missiological congress in India, 1971. First published in *Documenta Missionalia*, Rome 1972
19. The Vocation of Nature
    Lecture at the Institute of Contemporary Arts, published in *The Limits of Human Nature*, edited by Jonathan Benthall, Allen Lane, 1973

Chapters 2, 3, 4, 11, 13, 14, 15 and 17 first appeared in *New Blackfriars*.

Thanks are due to the publishers and periodicals cited above for permission to reproduce previously published material.

# Abbreviations

Denz   H. Denzinger, *Enchiridion Symbolorum Definitionum et Declarationum de Rebus Fidei et Morum* (1952)
DS     The above, edited by A. Schönmetzer (1965)
LCL    Loeb Classical Library (1912 ff.)
LTK    *Lexikon für Theologie und Kirche* (1957–67)
PG     *Patrologia Graeca*, ed. J. P. Migne
PL     *Patrologia Latina*, ed. J. P. Migne
RAC    *Reallexikon für die Antike und Christentum* (1950 ff.)
RGG    *Die Religion in Geschichte und Gegenwart* (1957–65)

# Foreword

I first met Father Cornelius Ernst when in May 1952 at the invitation of the then Prior, Father Ian Hislop (later Provincial), I delivered a lecture on moral philosophy at Hawkesyard, then the Dominican philosophy house. Later, in 1958, he contributed to *Blackfriars* a critical notice of my book on ethics, *A Study in Ethical Theory*, that was at once deeply understanding of its aims and method and searchingly critical of its fundamental weaknesses. It was a criticism of a kind for which any author must be permanently grateful. We met occasionally across the years, and he gave me valuable help in a letter in the early '60s when I was engaged in revising the Aquinas prescription for Part III, Section 5 of the Cambridge Theological Tripos (advanced philosophy of religion).

From his occasional writings I knew he was a theologian of exceptional promise. There was a report that he hoped one day to write a major study of the theology of the Fourth Gospel, and the sensitivity and range of concern he showed in matters theological combined with the fact that he had studied philosophy at Cambridge in the days of Wittgenstein made me hope I should live to read this work, having been long convinced that the interpretation of the Fourth Gospel called for the very rare combination of biblical scholarship, poetic sensibility, rigorous philosophical self-discipline and constructive theological power. *Sed Deo aliter visum*.

What we have is this collection of papers, very well entitled *Multiple Echo*. They are varied in style as well as in subject matter. The opening piece on St Thomas Aquinas is a brilliant lecture, appreciative of the great achievement of the Angelic Doctor, defining his central inspiration as the intelligibility of being, leaving the reader (or in the first case, the listener) to give contemporary cash-value to the expression Fr Cornelius has used. But as one reads on, one realizes that maybe Fr Cornelius was in fact exploiting the extreme difficulty inherent in deciding what precisely

Aquinas (and indeed Aristotle, his master, on whose *Metaphysics* Thomas wrote one of his best Aristotelian commentaries) meant by being, to suggest his own conviction that there was nothing mentionable in a complete inventory of the things that there are, through which and by which and in which the outskirts of God's ways could not be traced. The range, the restlessness, of Fr Cornelius' mind bears witness to his impatience with the suggestion, characteristic of post-Kantian German *Religionsphilosophie* from Schleiermacher to Otto, that we can isolate in human experience some identifiable *Anknüpfungspunkt* between men and God: or in the manner of champions of the argument to design (even of the intellectual power of F. R. Tennant in his *Philosophical Theology*) lay hold on certain isolatable features of the human environment that are in a special way evidence of its origin. Against this, in practice Fr Cornelius warns his readers against supposing that, e.g., work in set theory, the study of the foundations of mathematics, is not of genuine, if highly elusive relevance in the intellectual pilgrimage of one who would seek to seek in assimilable human terms the name of Him 'whom all men call God'.

Fr Cornelius' master in the Order was the late Fr Victor White O.P., best remembered for his studies of the relation of Christian theology and religion to the psychology of C. G. Jung in his volume *God and the Unconscious* (Harvill Press). But there is work possibly of greater value in his other collection of papers *God and the Unknown* (Harvill Press) which show him as a theologian of very considerable power. Although Fr Victor died in 1960, before the second Vatican Council had met, he was a considerable oecumenist. In 1938, following the publication of the report *Doctrine in the Church of England*, the work of an intellectually powerful commission established as far back as 1921, he published in *Blackfriars* for March/April of that year two articles on the Report which superbly pinpointed its strengths and its weaknesses. Although hardly remembered today, they are of permanent value, and something in these wide-ranging, yet never soft-centred papers of Fr Victor's pupil recalled them to me. One cannot read long without realizing that part of Fr Cornelius is (like Fr Victor) a very tough-minded theologian, widely read, sharply critical, aware of the ultimately mysterious, yet never finding in that awareness an excuse for relapsing into the sort of radical subjectivism that makes believing the measure of what is believed. He knows the limitations of theology; his astringent remark to the effect that, since the 17th century, we have had no genuinely creative philosophical moves from clerical sources shows sense of those limitations. He writes excellently on Wittgenstein and is at home in the worlds of Lévi-

Strauss, Paul Ricoeur, Gadamer, etc. He is well aware that one can penetrate deeper in *res divinas* by reflection on *Antigone*, the *Women of Trachis*, *Medea*, *Lear*, or by the close reading of great poetry, than by reading a great many professional theological treatises. Yet he is of the Order of the author of the *Summa*; and though theology is not everything, it is a vitally important something, its concern the ultimate mystery of God's decisive self-involvement with the human race, in which his most secret, most ultimate being is involved. So it must be taken very seriously. But what *is* proper seriousness here?

At first one regrets the inconclusive, unfinished character of these astonishingly wide-ranging essays. Then one realizes that therein lies a part of their worth. For they beckon the reader imperiously on to undertake himself the work whose sheer demand in intellectual energy they advertise.

*Donald MacKinnon*
*5 April 1979*

# Introduction

> Ultimately, I cannot accept the framework of experience demanded and presupposed by the orthodox ecclesiastical tradition. I think I must face this, with consequences I can't foretell. I have another tradition to which I am almost equally respectful – in some ways more so – the tradition of the human heart: novels, art, music, tragedy. I cannot allow that God can only be adored in spirit and in truth by the individual introverted upon himself and detached from all that might disturb and solicit his heart. It must be possible to find and adore God in the complexity of human experience.

These lines from a notebook, written in 1972, suggest why some of Cornelius Ernst's essays are difficult. It could not always be easy to take seriously the complexity of human experience and to find there the secret purpose of the hidden God. The theologian can mediate the God who creates and renews, and who raised Jesus from the dead to new life, only by submitting himself to a discipline that transforms and renews and brings to light new possibilities of experience and meaning.

This concern with transformation, perhaps his most characteristic word, exhibits Cornelius Ernst's conviction that we are in the midst of a profound shift in our philosophical presuppositions. Almost from the beginning, the Catholic theological tradition has been dependent upon a Greek philosophy of *being*. This seems no longer to satisfy our requirements. We can be loyal to the multiplicity of ways in which man today attempts to make sense of himself and his world only in terms of a philosophy of *meaning*.

In his little book on grace (*The Theology of Grace*, Dublin and Cork: The Mercier Press, 1974), Cornelius Ernst defined meaning as follows (page 68):

> meaning is that praxis, that process and activity, by which the world to which man belongs becomes the world which belongs

to man. ... We transform the world to which we belong by taking it up into the world of the games we play. Meaning, that is to say, is historical: it assumes a world prior to man into a world of human communication, by work, play, dance, travel, love, conversation, reflection – the totality of human life and death, in the continuity of a humanity which inwardly transforms the biological into the historical order.

But if such language, in a way only too familiar to English philosophers of religion, displays a certain debt to the later writings of Ludwig Wittgenstein, it must be added immediately that, for Cornelius Ernst, the importance of the later writings of Martin Heidegger was precisely that they seemed, however opaquely, to maintain the *ontological* commitments of the theological tradition in which St Thomas Aquinas represents the classical moment.

For, in this collection of essays, there are three major formative thinkers whose influence is pervasive: Wittgenstein, Heidegger and St Thomas Aquinas.

It is not the Wittgenstein who, as he himself feared, has only sown a crop of jargon, which has bloomed academically in many ways but particularly as a well-meaning branch of philosophy of religion. The Wittgenstein that Cornelius Ernst respected was the iconoclastic and destructive questioner whose work would have put an end to the kind of philosophy that even now appropriates his name to prolong its existence. Heidegger is the other great philosopher of our time who has sought to make an end of philosophy. In very different ways, therefore, they each focus the problem of rewriting Christian theology in a non-metaphysical perspective and mode.

It is characteristic of the writer of these essays that he could never have adopted only one way of doing philosophy. For him, one way could be travelled only in the light of another. From the conflict of styles, and from the difference of perspectives, the illumination would come, and no other way.

What he envied, in St Thomas, on the other hand, was that 'view of the world in which the world effortlessly shows itself for what it is, flowers into the light' (page 11). He sought 'that intuition of *claritas*, transparent radiance, which was Thomas's original and originating vision'. It was only that, with Thomas's medieval world now so remote from us, with Plato and Aristotle and the whole of European metaphysics displaced, with Catholic Christianity itself temporarily in question, and with the whole of the West cast into solution, 'any vision of the world will have to provide for the simultaneous and successive manifestation of multiple worlds'.

It follows that these essays must be read, not so much as disciplined studies on theological topics, but more as we might read a collection of poems. We must allow the play between the different perspectives upon which they draw to transform our experience through their multiple echo.

\* \* \*

Cornelius Ernst was born in Ceylon (as it then was) on 16th October, 1924. His parents were descendants of the Dutch settlers who ruled the island until the British took over. He was sent to England, to go to school at St Paul's, but was at home when war broke out in 1939. Later, as a student at the University of Ceylon, he belonged to a generation who were among the first to call for an end to British rule. He became a sympathizer-member of the local communist party and played a very active part for two years, instructing groups in the doctrines of dialectical materialism, and assuring them of the cultural importance of Soviet Russia. His break with the Party came, characteristically enough, when he was asked to review a novel by Ilya Ehrenburg which had won the Stalin Prize. He found it such a bad novel that he wrote a very severe review, which the Party officials refused to print. His sense of truth was outraged.

In 1944 he returned to England, as an undergraduate at Magdalene College, Cambridge. As he wrote some years later: 'I shall always be grateful to Cambridge for what I learned there. If I were to try to sum it up in a phrase, I might say that I began to learn there how to reconcile freedom of the spirit with tradition. I read the works of the Danish Protestant Kierkegaard and the Russian Orthodox Berdyaev, and began to glimpse something of the uniqueness of faith and also to recognize that *Christians too were capable of intellectual exploration*' (his own emphasis).

Thus, after years of atheism, he began to think of himself again as an Anglican. But within weeks he recognized that 'Christian doctrine needed definition and authority'. While reading Newman's *Apologia*, of which he had received a copy quite accidentally from a Jewish friend, he was, as he said, 'like so many others, deeply moved by Newman's complete intellectual honesty and his purity of mind'. A week or so later, on 8th May, 1946, 'it became quite simply and luminously clear to me that I had to be a Catholic'. On the same day, without knowing much about them, he decided to become a Dominican friar.

Ordained priest in 1954, he soon found himself teaching at Hawkesyard Priory in Staffordshire, then the philosophy house of the English Province of the Dominican Order. In intervals between teaching, he translated the first volume of Karl Rahner's *Theological Investigations* (published in 1961). He was thus enabled to enter early into the unexpectedly radical shift in Roman Catholic consciousness which found expression at the Second Vatican Council.

Many of his essays reflect, and contribute to, that change of theological perspective. The papers on the sacraments (chapter 9), on the Virgin Mary (chapter 10), and on natural theology (chapters 2 and 11), all date from this period, and, although now some fourteen or fifteen years old, contain lines of thought that have not yet by any means been exhausted.

In 1966 he returned to Blackfriars, Oxford, as Regent of Studies, and as a member of the Theological Faculty of the University. His inaugural lecture (chapter 13) testifies to his acute sense of the *loss* as well as of the gains in the great upheaval of Vatican II. His distaste for certain more recent developments in Catholic theology may be sampled in his wry picture of the 'World Congress' organized by the editorial board of *Concilium* (chapter 4). But his deep commitment to the reshaping of Catholic doctrine comes out clearly in his papers on the Apostolic ministry and on the Petrine office (chapters 14 and 15). The missionary dimension of the Church, in the context particularly of non-Christian religions, remained a permanent focus of reflection (chapters 3, 12 and 18).

Questions about the method of theological reflection preoccupied him a great deal. They recur throughout his essays but are treated more systematically, if very diversely, particularly in chapters 5 and 7 of this book. Beyond this, however, the attempt to bring to bear upon theological studies something of the insights of poetry and the creative imagination led him to the most difficult, and certainly the most radical, confrontations between St Thomas and Pseudo-Dionysius on the one hand (chapter 6), and St Thomas and William Blake on the other hand (chapter 19). These interrogations of the nature of *symbol* and of the nature of *nature* return to the question about the relationship of language to reality, and thus the question about the meaning of being, with which Cornelius Ernst was always concerned.

The talk on angels, transcribed from a recording, has been left unedited, so as to communicate something of the difference between his writing and his discourse (chapter 16). The echo of his voice may also be heard, more personally and subjectively, in the account of how he prepared himself to preach a sermon (chapter 17).

However much he owed to Wittgenstein and Heidegger, and (on a quite different level) to Karl Rahner, Evans-Pritchard and many others, not forgetting his Dominican master, Victor White, it was always St Thomas Aquinas who set his standard of theological seriousness and integrity (chapter 1). But in the end it is perhaps in his critique of Bishop Robinson's *Honest to God*, one of the earliest essays printed here, that we come nearest to the central conviction of his own Christian experience (chapter 8): 'the very grace-life in us is a conformation to the death and resurrection of Jesus Christ' (page 95).

Throughout his years in Oxford, he carried a heavy burden of teaching, in lectures and tutorials, never finding the time to write much, until, at his own request, he moved in the summer of 1975 to the peace and quiet and solitude enjoyed by the chaplain to the Dominican contemplative nuns at Carisbrooke on the Isle of Wight. Quite unexpectedly, he died a few weeks after his fifty-third birthday, on 17th November, 1977.

There is one last point. Professional theologians, like many other professionals, tend to lose contact, as they work, with the living realities with which they are concerned. The mystery tends to disappear behind the problems whose very existence depends upon the mystery itself. This is not a reproach which can be made against the writer of these essays. They manifest throughout a pressure and an urgency which come only from living contact with the mystery of Christ, and which explain, at least in part, the density of the writer's language. But theologians ought to bear inscribed on their hearts these words of St Augustine:

> And what have I now said, my God, my life, my holy joy?
> For what does any man say, when he speaks of Thee?
> Yet woe to those who keep silent about Thee,
> since those who talk most are dumb. *Confessions* 1,4

28th January 1979  Fergus Kerr O.P.
Blackfriars  Timothy Radcliffe O.P.
Oxford

# 1

# Thomas Aquinas (1225–1274)

It isn't without some misgivings that one embarks upon a commemoration of the famous dead, especially when the commemoration in question marks the seven hundredth anniversary of a medieval theologian, the Dominican St Thomas Aquinas, who died, like his Franciscan contemporary, St Bonaventure, in 1274. What is more, until quite recently, Thomas used to be presented as very much an ecclesiastical figure, whose philosophical and theological teachings were supported by the canonical sanctions of the Roman Catholic Church. Perhaps after the Second Vatican Council and the revaluation of theological tradition which has followed it, we are now in a better position to assess the significance of Thomas's work.

There are two major difficulties in our way when we try to reassess Thomas's significance. The more obvious of these is that he was a Christian thinker, what we might call today a Christian theologian. The second difficulty, of a more general sort, is that as a thinker he belonged to what is in fact a remote past, that he inhabited a different world. Of course this last difficulty meets us whenever we try to come to terms with a thinker of the past, or with a thinker from a non-European culture. I shall try to suggest later that it is just this difference of worlds, this discontinuity of experience, which should make Thomas more interesting to us, provided that we can discover the deeper continuity which makes him accessible to us at all.

But first let us consider Thomas as a Christian thinker. Is the phrase 'Christian thinker' in fact an appropriate category? Nowadays we have theologians (a somewhat discredited class of academic, certainly), philosophers (respected, perhaps, but not taken much notice of), scientists (less admired than they used to be), sociologists and psychologists (again less the intellectual arbiters they used to be even two or three years ago), poets, holy men and so on. The trouble is that Thomas was all of these at once, even a poet, since he has left us three or four excellent poems which get into the anthologies of medieval Latin poetry. The word 'thinker' is meant to suggest someone who doesn't fit into our modern academic categories, someone who lies behind them; the trouble is that this suggests someone *of our own times* who doesn't fit into the categories, an amateur, a publicist, a diagnostician of our times, a crank. Thomas was eminently a professional, trained in the strictest University disciplines of his time, who spent most of his life teaching in a University context. That University context, that universe of discourse, was dominated by law, medicine and above all theology – that is to say, disciplined reflection, engaging every available intellectual resource, upon the tradition of the Christian revelation of God. In that universe of discourse Thomas was original enough to have some of his views condemned both in the University of Paris and at Oxford by his fellow-Dominican, Robert Kilwardby, then Archbishop of Canterbury. In this sort of intellectual context, a theologian was a rather different figure from his modern counterpart – hence the phrase 'Christian thinker'.

But this still doesn't meet the real difficulty. What is a Christian thinker supposed to think about, and how do Christian thinkers differ among themselves? The answer is simple enough for Thomas and his contemporaries: it was the job of Christian thinkers, of doctors of theology, to think about *everything*, to think about the whole of truth, including the truth of Christian revelation. To be more precise, to allow the truth of Christian revelation and all other truth mutually to illuminate each other, so that truth should show itself as a whole which had its unity in God and Christ. No doubt such an intellectual goal was less ridiculously presumptuous in the thirteenth century than it would be today; and no doubt this is why the modern theologian is an ambiguous figure in the academic setting of a modern University – someone who by his historical origins is supposed to be able to show how he holds the key to all truth, and quite unable in fact to make any such claim good, if he even dared to make it.

Today it isn't easy to maintain that reality as a whole might have a single key, it isn't easy to maintain that reality is a whole anyway, in any useful sense; and it is still less easy to suggest that Christianity is the possessor of this hypothetical key. The diversification of academic roles – theologian, philosopher, physicist, psychologist and so on – reflects a differentiation of knowledge, a complexity of the real to be known, which seems to defy any possibility of a unified vision, or even the possibility of alternative visions of the whole.

According to Thomas, it is the business of the wise man to set things in order, speculatively or practically. For Thomas as a theologian, the source and end of the order into which reality as a whole can be shown and seen to fall, is God; so Thomas's first major and decisive option as a constructive theologian is to hold that God is the subject of theology, so Thomas has to make this presupposition explicit. Hence what have been called the Five Ways, five argumentative readings of primary human experience intended to exhibit the dependence of the experienced world on a source and end which all men, vaguely and confusedly, call 'God'. But this argumentation only makes explicit the God who is the presupposition of theology and of all possible human experience of the world; what is unique to Christianity is its disclosure of God, source and end, in God become man, man assumed into God, in Jesus Christ. God is not only the background and the presupposition of human experience; he is the foreground, the personally accessible sense in human terms of the human search for the absolute beginning and the absolute end: the ultimate meaning of what it is to be human at all, an ultimate meaning inscribed once and for all on the human face of Jesus Christ.

Supposing that these are indeed the steps Thomas took to disclose the order implicit in human experience, how in rather more detail did he actually take them? Supposing that the job of a Christian thinker or theologian might be described in Thomas's terms as an ordering of the whole in relation to God in Christ, what conceptual equipment did he deploy in the verbal, literary construction of the order? Here we meet the second difficulty I mentioned earlier, the difficulty of coming to terms with a thinker from a different world. Thomas was heir to the classical philosophy of Greece; like all medieval thinkers, he reached intellectual consciousness through the diverse Neo-Platonisms of St Augustine and the Pseudo-Dionysius; he criticized their assumptions with the help of the newly-discovered and newly-translated writings of Aristotle (especially the physical works); and, again like all medieval thinkers, was forced by his acquaintance with the Bible to take what account he could of the process of human history. Finally, like all scholastic thinkers of the thirteenth and later centuries, his style was closely analytic and argumentative, the product of the discipline of a sophisticated logical grammar.

This analytic, argumentative style takes a little getting used to; but it is important to realize that it depends for its cogency on a web of concepts which haven't themselves been acquired in any purely logical way. In his theological ordering of truth as a whole, Thomas proceeded as a metaphysician, so that his theological order exhibits not only the surface structure of a formal, logical kind, but also a deeper order of a metaphysical kind.

We can make use here of a distinction proposed some years ago by Professor P. F. Strawson between 'descriptive' and 'revisionary' metaphysics. Roughly speaking, the revisionary metaphysician says: 'That's how things *look,* may be; but really they aren't like that. We need to look at things like *this*, and then we shall see things as they really are.' The descriptive metaphysician says: 'Things look like this, as everyone admits; now how is it that they look like this, what makes them look like this?' Of course the distinction isn't watertight; someone who intends simply to disclose and analyse the implications of the way things look may either begin by seeing things queerly or end by persuading us that we've been seeing things queerly or both; and someone who is convinced that we need to look at things differently, to revise our way of looking at things, may very well succeed in convincing us that our everyday way of looking at things is just a bad habit which we must learn to discard. But the primary intention does count for something; and certainly Thomas's primary intention as a metaphysical thinker was descriptive, not revisionary. Things do show themselves for what they are; there is in principle no abrupt discontinuity between appearance and reality. So it is in principle possible to scrutinize the way things look and discover what they really are; and what things really are is capable of being understood as an intelligible order, an order of subordinate orders.

Perhaps it is worth pointing out that a genuine and quite fundamental option is involved here. Most of us today, I think, take it for granted in a confused and unreflective way that the world we see isn't what it seems. Isn't the physical world really sub-atomic particles or waves, aren't our free choices really determined symptoms of unconscious drives, individual or environmental, isn't politics merely the expression of economic forces? We take it for granted that appearances are deceptive, that our lives are schizoid; we might even deliberately induce a more real world of dreams or make the absurd our point of departure so that the sense we find is always and only the sense we have already arbitrarily imposed. So it is strange to find an entire order of thought which claims only to render in an explicit form the implicit and yet manifest order of the world. For Thomas the fundamental categories of our thought and speech are the fundamental categories of the disclosed world: truth is prior to illusion and falsehood possible, truth is the revelation of being.

This may be naivety or innocence, but it certainly isn't some insipid common-sensism. Because below (or above) the surface rigour of the argument – and yet showing through it; below (or above) even the metaphysical web of concepts – and yet showing through them – Thomas's writings do attempt, fairly successfully, to realize in their own actual texture the purity of an intuition: the fine perception of the mystery of the intelligibility of being. How do we make sense *at all*, not this or that sense; how do we make mistakes, pretend or lie; how does a mask mis-represent a face, how can a face be a mask? Only because, ultimately, things show themselves for what they *are*, to *be* is ultimately to *be true*.

Thomas's genuine and permanent originality was to display the internal consistency of a view of the world in which the world effortlessly shows itself for what it is, flowers into the light. We may appreciate his originality more clearly if we compare his basic intuition with what in its many current forms can conveniently be labelled here 'structuralism', best known, perhaps, in the writings of Lévi-Strauss. The comparison relies on the common ground that knowledge involves some kind of re-presentation, some alternative version of what is known, some genesis of likeness without total identity. All the advanced sophistication of structuralist interpretation seems to me to rest on the basic assumption that the only sort of re-presentation, the only sort of likeness there can be, is likeness of structure: a one-to-one correspondence of analysable parts each of which in isolation lacks meaning. Language is coding, we understand a language by cracking the code. Thomas is archaic enough to rely, implicitly and explicitly, on the pre-Socratic assumption that 'like is known by like'. His real and permanent originality, so it seems to me, is not his theory of concepts, for which likeness is generated primarily between elements of structures – a primitive semantics, as it were, opposed to a sophisticated syntax. What makes Thomas permanently valuable is his recognition that likeness is generated at all, that being, truth and meaning are indefinitely diverse and yet (this is the ultimate mystery) that being does disclose itself in meaning.

Now I don't want to suggest that Thomas's intuition and vision of the world are best kept alive and active in our consciousness today by being transmitted through the machinery of a philosophical or theological school, some so-called 'Thomism' competing for our assent with other schools and -isms. I don't even think his view of the world can be appropriated by us except through the exercise of historical sympathy. In fact it seems essential to any right understanding of Thomas to begin by acknowledging his remoteness from our world, by undergoing the acute discontinuity between his world and ours, rather like the social anthropologist making a field study of a preliterate society. There doesn't seem to be much future for the kind of warmed-up scholasticism which one still finds today and which still seems to attract enthusiasm and even deference. Thomas's world was very remote from our world or worlds. If we want today to recover a disciplined innocence of vision, a transparency to the light, it can't be by a sort of infantile regression. At the very least we have to come to terms with all that is involved in the human construction of meaning and the human genesis of worlds in the process of history. I doubt whether we can ever again allow ourselves to submit to a unique, a metaphysical rendering of the world: any vision of the world will have to provide for the simultaneous and successive manifestation of multiple worlds. But just as it would be inept for any modern philosopher to ignore Plato or Aristotle, so it would be inept for any modern Christian thinker to be ignorant of Thomas. It ought to be possible for someone, sometime, in the not too distant future, to recover in a new idiom that intuition of *claritas*, transparent radiance, which was Thomas's original and originating vision. Perhaps I might make my point about Thomas and the future best by recalling part of the poem, 'Asides on the Oboe', by the American poet Wallace Stevens, with its ironic balance of nostalgia and hope, its imagery of light, remembering that the oboe of the title is one of Stevens' instruments of poetic transfiguration.

> In the end, however naked, tall, there is still
> The impossible possible philosophers' man,
> The man who has had the time to think enough,
> The central man, the human globe, responsive
> As a mirror with a voice, the man of glass,
> Who in a million diamonds sums us up.
> He is the transparence of the place in which
> He is and in his poems we find peace.

# 2

## Words, Facts and God[1]

A traveller from a far country has the obligation to entertain his hosts with tales of strange customs and mythical monsters, heroes and spells. The country of which I am to tell you today is a very strange one indeed. I do not know if President de Gaulle ever became acquainted with English philosophy during his stay in England, but certainly it would entirely justify his claim that England does not, today, at least, belong to Europe. Perhaps, however, as a middleman of ideas, I shall be permitted here to enter the intellectual Common Market; fortunately there are no tariffs on ideas, though as we all know only too well, there are more serious barriers to communication, cultural, existential, confessional – and linguistic.

It is the strangest of paradoxes that the philosopher who was perhaps more influential than any other in giving modern English philosophy its character and stance was an Austrian, Ludwig Wittgenstein. Wittgenstein was more utterly dedicated to philosophy than anyone I have ever met; and I think the main benefit I gathered from his lectures, most of which I did not understand when I heard them as an undergraduate at Cambridge in the academic year 1946–7, was the encounter with a living example of philosophical depth and integrity, a standard of seriousness, by which I could, and can now, measure my own deficiencies. It is, I believe, important to remember that he was a kind of philosophical 'primitive', a Douanier Rousseau of philosophy, who came to philosophy by way of engineering and the mathematical logic of Frege and Russell. Like all young Austrians of his time, no doubt, he had read Schopenhauer and been deeply impressed by him; but his acquaintance with the great philosophers of the past was

[1] The substance of a paper read before the University on St Thomas's day 1963, at the Albertinum, Nijmegen. I have deliberately retained the style of an address to a Continental audience, since this itself is part of the communication I should wish to make *here*.

extremely fragmentary. In what follows I shall try to indicate certain features of his thought, with particular reference to the problems it sets for metaphysical theology. My purpose is not historical scholarship, or even interpretation, but an attempt to raise certain problems in our thinking about God, in the hope that these may be of interest even to those not engaged in the disputes of an offshore island.

In the Preface to the *Tractatus Logicus-Philosophicus*, Wittgenstein says:

> Thus the aim of the book is to set a limit to thought, or rather – not to thought, but to the expression of thoughts; for in order to be able to set a limit to thought, we should have to find both sides of the limit thinkable (i.e., we should have to be able to think what cannot be thought). It will therefore only be in language that the limit can be set, and what lies on the other side of the limit will simply be nonsense.

This notion of a limit, *Grenze*, to thought and language is fundamental to Wittgenstein's views in the *Tractatus*. It should be noticed that he fully recognizes the strangeness of the attempt to draw a limit, a boundary, round what can be said or thought. For in order to draw a boundary round something, we must be able to stand *outside* it; now since we are here proposing to draw a limit to thought by drawing a limit to language, what we say will be nonsense, *Unsinn*, since we are trying to be simultaneously inside and outside language. At the end of the *Tractatus* Wittgenstein says:

> My propositions serve as elucidations in the following way: anyone who understands me eventually recognizes them as nonsensical (*unsinnig*), when he has used them – as steps – to climb up beyond them. (He must, so to speak, throw away the ladder after he has climbed up it.) He must transcend these propositions, and then he will see the world aright. What we cannot speak about we must consign to silence. *Wovon man nicht sprechen kann, darüber muss man schweigen.*

Thus Wittgenstein's efforts are directed to showing the *internal* structure of language in such a way that once we have seen it we realize the limitation which this structure imposes on our speech and thought. In doing so he necessarily has to use language in a way which on his own theory must be called nonsensical; but once we have *seen* what it is he is trying to say, we can forget about these 'nonsensical' statements and henceforth confine ourselves to meaningful utterance, not be misled by the superficial grammar and logic of our language into supposing that we can step over the true boundaries of language and talk about simply anything. We seem to be able to talk about all sorts of things – about logic, ethics, the beautiful, God; once we have seen what our language is really like then we shall realize that most of what we say is nonsense, though not necessarily unimportant nonsense because much of what we talk about nonsensically, although it cannot really be said, can be seen, for it shows itself, *sich zeigt*. The most important of these things which can 'show' themselves, become apparent or manifest, is the logic of our language; and once this has been seen, then it will be seen that, for example, God too belongs to this large realm of what Wittgenstein calls 'the mystical', *das Mystische,* what can be seen but cannot be said.

The limit, *Grenze,* then, of what can be said marks off what can be said from what can (only) be seen, what shows itself, *sich zeigt*. We may now try to see more closely how Wittgenstein thought of this limit. He says (5.6 s.):

> The limits of my language mean the limits of my world. Logic pervades the world: the limits of the world are also its limits. . . . We cannot think what we cannot think; so what we cannot think we cannot *say* either. . . . The world is *my* world: this is manifest (*das zeigt sich*) in the fact that the limits of language (of that language which I alone understand) mean the limits of *my* world . . . I am my world. (The microcosm.) There is no such thing as the subject that thinks, *das denkende, vorstellende Subjekt*. . . . The subject does not belong to the world: rather it is a limit of the world. Where *in* the world is a metaphysical subject to be perceived (*merken*)? You will say that this is exactly like the case of the eye and the visual field. But really you do *not* see the eye. And nothing *in the visual field* allows you to infer that it is seen by an eye.

This is a particularly interesting example. Wittgenstein uses it primarily to show that the eye is not in its own visual field, nor the 'I' in its 'world'. But we may extend his use of it and point out that the eye is not *outside* its visual field either, at least in the sense in which inside and outside are found within the visual field. I mean that with our eyes we can *see* tea inside a cup and the cup outside the tea; but we cannot 'see' with our eyes the way in which the eye is not inside the visual field. The limit of the visual field cannot be represented by a visual boundary. The boundary between inside and outside *within* the visual field is not the same kind of boundary as the boundary between what is inside and outside the visual field. That is to say: (1) we cannot make a picture of the visual field but only a picture *within* the visual field; (2) the negation represented by a boundary within the visual field is not the same as the negation expressing the boundary between what is within the visual field and what is outside it: this latter negation cannot be 'represented', we cannot make a picture of it. I believe that it is important to recognize these two sorts of negation, which we may perhaps call horizontal and vertical negation. The limit, *Grenze,* of language, which separates what can from what cannot be said, is in this terminology a vertical negation.

We must now try to see what Wittgenstein meant by 'world'. The *Tractatus* begins:

> The world is all that is the case. The world is the totality of facts, not of things. The world is determined by the facts, and by their being all the facts. For the totality of facts determines what is the case, and also what is not the case. The facts in logical space are the world. The world divides into facts.

The notion of logical space may be explained in three steps. The first step is to point out that for Wittgenstein space is thought of as capable of being represented in a system of co-ordinates. In its simplest terms, the notion is that if, for example, all space were in the plane of a blackboard, then any configuration on this blackboard could be uniquely determined by reference to a set of co-ordinates. We think the configuration through the co-ordinates; and if all space were exhausted by the plane of the blackboard, then we could not think any configuration except through these co-ordinates. Any point *not* on the plane of the blackboard would not be thinkable, would not belong to the world defined by the system of co-ordinates. We cannot think a spatial fact unless we think spatially.

The second step in explaining the notion of logical space is to notice that in the geometrical space we considered in our first step, relationships of similarity hold; that is, one configuration can be the picture, *Bild,* of another configuration. If geometrical space can be thought through with reference to a co-ordinate system, then any given configuration must be capable of being repeated at a different location in the co-ordinate system; the *generality* of the co-ordinate system consists in the possibility of comparison. For a co-ordinate system is a means of expressing comparison numerically. It is this picturing relationship, *abbildende Beziehung,* which obsessed Wittgenstein in the *Tractatus,* and which he used as the model for his picture theory of language. If we stretch our imaginations by considering the relationships between figures on different planes, as is done in projective geometry, we may better understand Wittgenstein's obsession; and we may extend the idea of projective relationships still further, as Wittgenstein did, when we consider the relationship between the music played by an orchestra, the groove on the gramophone record, and the marks on the musical score, or again electronic transformations (what do we 'see' when we use an electron microscope): all these possess an 'inner similarity' to each other, by which each can serve as the 'picture' of the other, each being related to the other by a law of projection, within a logic of depiction, *Logik der Abbildung*.

And this brings us to the third and most important step in our explanation of 'logical space'. For the possibility of *comparison* which we found to be implicit in our thinking of geometrical space implies also the possibility of *correct* and *incorrect* picturing of one configuration by another. For one figure to be capable of picturing another, it is not sufficient that each should be capable of being repeated as a different location; comparison implies the possibility of being *unlike* as well as being *like*. We can only call one figure a picture of another if it is capable of *not* being a picture of it. Thus logical space necessarily includes the possibility of *negation*, the negation I have called 'horizontal'; logical space is what has been called by a Finnish commentator on the *Tractatus* a 'Yes-No' space.

For Wittgenstein the notion of logical space is not merely a metaphorical one, as though geometrical space were merely a kind of illustration which could be forgotten after it had served its purpose. On the contrary, geometrical space is an *instance* of logical space. Every geometrical picture is *also* a logical picture; but there are logical pictures which are not geometrical pictures. A sentence, for instance, is such a logical picture, which is not at the same time a geometrical picture; when properly analysed, a sentence must reveal in its physical structure the combination of objects in the world which constitutes a fact; for the sentence itself is a fact, *Tatsache*, which is a non-geometrical projection of the physical fact, isomorphic with it. Thus any properly analysed proposition merely pictures the fact in logical space which it refers to; if it is a true proposition it pictures a positive fact, if it is a false proposition it pictures a negative fact, in both cases at the same place in logical space. We cannot think any fact unless we think logically.

The important point for our purposes here is that the laws of logical structure themselves, the projective relationship, cannot be pictured; they can only be instanced. The musical score, for example, is only another embodiment of the projective relationship which holds between the symphony played by an orchestra and the groove on the gramophone record.

It will of course be understood that the account I have given here of Wittgenstein's views in the *Tractatus* is a highly simplified one, but I hope I have given some slight indication of their power and elegance. If the relationship between words and facts is the kind of picturing relationship which we often vaguely take it to be – and Wittgenstein's theory is only a rigorous, logically systematized statement of our vague idea – then his views about what can be said and what, while it cannot be said, can at best become manifest, are impregnable; and theology vanishes into the ineffable. As he himself said: 'God does not show himself *in* the world.'

We may now turn to a brief examination of St Thomas's account of negation, so far as this is relevant to our talk about God. It may be said in general that this account depends upon an insight into the connaturality between the human mind and the physical world, the world of Nature and natures. St Thomas seems to envisage two sorts of negation, one which discriminates essences from each other, such that anything of a definite kind is *not* of another kind; and a second negation which discriminates existences from each other, such that individuals even within a distinct kind are discriminated from one another by being different subsistents. Corresponding to these two modes according to which variety and distinction are manifested in the world of Nature, there are two modes of intelligent apprehension of variety, called by St Thomas *abstractio* and *separatio*. In either case, the intrinsic distinctness of things, whether natures or individual beings, provides the permanent ground of our insight into their distinction. We can negate because *things* are distinct, because they are *not* each other.

Thus *unum*, the concrete unity of each thing, is the intellectual negation of multifariousness which identifies the given being as a self-identity. This identification is presupposed in any statement we may make; we may say that to Wittgenstein's points in logical space, his logical indivisibles, there correspond in St Thomas's thought the intrinsic unities of *substances*. St Thomas's metaphysics may be regarded as an examination of the presuppositions of our language, at least of our subject-predicate language. The logic of our language is a revelation of the logic, the intelligibility, of Being. It is this intuition into the intelligibility of Being which explains the pervasive influence on St Thomas of Aristotle's *Posterior Analytics*. Existence has a logic, a *structure* of intelligibility, which can be 'shown' in a demonstration, *epideixis* (compare Wittgenstein's ineffable *Sich-zeigen*); and the fundamental principle which governs this 'analytic' demonstration, *resolutio,* is the principle of unity, of non-contradiction. For Aristotle and St Thomas the demonstrative syllogism can reveal the inner structure of intelligibility of Being. The logic of Being is ont-ology.

Two points should be borne in mind here, first as regards what we may call *essential* negation, corresponding to the differentiation of essences, and secondly as regards *existential* negation, corresponding to the differentiation of existents. It seems that for St Thomas essential differentiation is not found on one level but establishes a hierarchy of grades or levels of being, from inanimate matter upwards. And as regards existential differentiation, it is true that in the world of corporeal nature, individual existents are differentiated from each other by their bodily shape and size. The existence of an individual existent reveals its uniqueness through its physical, bodily, quantitative differentiation; but this does not exclude the possibility that in some other, non-physical world, existents may be differentiated from each other simply by being distinct existences, e.g., for St Thomas, the angels.

In his striking book, *Der Gott der neuzeitlichen Metaphysik,* Walter Schulz describes as characteristic of the medieval idea of God its formulation by St Anselm in *comparative* terms. God is thus supreme only in the sense that he occupies the summit of a hierarchy, and thus is still contained within a totality, and thus analogically related to lower levels of the hierarchy. In a very familiar and very characteristic passage, the *Quarta Via,* St Thomas seems to provide clear evidence of the correctness of this estimate. He seems to be comparing God as maximum within the *magis* and *minus* of being, good, truth and so on to fire in hot things, and so seems to be suggesting that the transcendence of God is merely a supremacy depending upon a universal immanence. The remarkable thing here is that he refers to Bk II ($a$) of Aristotle's *Metaphysics,* where a maximum of degree, like that of fire causing heat in bodies made up of the elements, is contrasted with something which transcends degree, like the sun causing heat in this nether world, *aliquid amplius quam calidissimum,* as St Thomas puts it in his commentary on the passage. What we have to see is that for St Thomas the transcendence of God is defined ultimately by *existential* negation. God is the maximum not merely essentially but existentially; St Thomas always finds it convenient to use the Platonist terminology of transcendence but always with the explicit or implicit proviso that it must be interpreted in his own existentialist sense. I realize of course that this interpretation of St Thomas would need detailed justification; but let me simply say here that for St Thomas God is not only the supreme case of a perfection immanent in finite things. He is the existentially separate cause of the immanence itself, he is both sun and fire.

The importance of this conclusion for our present enquiry is that it offers a way of thinking limits from *outside* the limits. The feature which Wittgenstein has in common with most modern thinkers from Nicholas of Cusa to Heidegger is to think limits from *within,* as it were to describe a circle round oneself. What is characteristic of St Thomas's approach is that it locates man and his thought within the unlimited without at the same time limiting the unlimited by making it merely a supreme case, a maximum in a Platonist sense. But of course our difficulty is that we too are 'modern', we would prefer our thought to be located in the unlimited, not by way of our human nature but by way of our experience of our own finitude, whether this is defined in Wittgenstein's terms or Heidegger's. One embarrassment this involves us in is that when we attempt to define our limitations from within, theism and atheism differ only by a hairsbreadth: the *docta ignorantia* may be sustained either by a pure faith or by a Dionysian affirmation of Life or simply a humanist agnosticism – this latter course is usual in England. The resolute acceptance of one's own finitude can be made to seem the highest wisdom. Any attempt to place this finitude from without, to apply an external measure to it, can be presented as a childish mistake about the nature of our limitation, a hangover from the days of the closed cosmos.

We seem to be faced with a dilemma. *Either* we affirm a God who, although he is not merely supreme among beings, yet confronts us as an Infinite to which we ascend by way of the world, a world which has now become alien to us or from which we have become alienated, by our very act of knowing about it – an objectified world. *Or* we resort to *das Mystische,* the God behind my shoulder, the shadow, who is indistinguishable from a Nothing: a nameless Void.

Now it may seem that Wittgenstein's later views offer us a way out of this dilemma, though the cure may seem worse than the disease. It is certain that Wittgenstein was his own severest critic, and that the *Philosophical Investigations* are a radical re-thinking of many of the problems of the *Tractatus;* common to both is a passionate concern for the problem of meaning, in such a way that all philosophical problems need to be seen as aspects of the central problem of meaning, even if they then appear to be merely pseudo-problems, mistakes and muddles of meaning.

In general we may say that the basis of Wittgenstein's later views is the awareness of meaning as a common and public world, since language has a bearer, the community or tribe, and thus is active as a form of the life of that community: a language, he says, is a form of life, a *Lebensform*. Hence language and meaning are as various as life: the profound error of all previous philosophers, and especially the author of the *Tractatus*, was to assume that a unique and uniquely general relationship obtained between language and reality; the picturing relationship is the clearest instance of such a uniquely general relationship. The most satisfactory model for language is the games we play. There is no uniquely absolute essence 'Game,' but we play or can recognize others playing games of indefinite variety, from the child playing by himself to team games to chess. Consider the multiplicity of language-games in the following examples (I, 23):

> Giving orders, and obeying them – describing the appearance of an object, or giving its measurements – constructing an object from a description (a drawing) – reporting an event – speculating about an event – forming and testing a hypothesis – presenting the results of an experiment in tables and diagrams – making up a story, and reading it – play-acting – singing catches – guessing riddles – making a joke; telling it – solving a problem in practical arithmetic – translating from one language into another – asking, thanking, cursing, greeting, praying.

And he comments: 'It is interesting to compare the multiplicity of the tools in language and of the way they are used, the multiplicity of kinds of word and sentence, with what logicians have said about the structure of language.'

The reference to 'tools' will not have escaped attention. The special importance of this comparison, as also of the conception of language-games, is that language, in all its multiplicity, no longer confronts the world: it is no longer what Wittgenstein called in the *Tractatus* 'the great mirror'. If chess is conceivable without chess-men, language is inconceivable outside a world of things and actions. The standard metre in Paris, for example, is part of our language of measurement; and it is an especially interesting part because precisely owing to its role as a means of representation it appears to possess a kind of necessary existence. 'What looks [he says] as though it had to exist is part of the language.'

If the whole picture-theory of language collapses in this way (what is wrong with it is precisely that it fails to allow for the variety of different ways in which we can *apply* pictures), the old notions of negation and limit collapse with it. About negation he says:

Negation: a 'mental activity'. Negate something and observe what you are doing. Do you perhaps inwardly shake your head? And if you do – is this process more deserving of our interest than, say, that of writing a sign of negation in a sentence? Do you know the *essence* of negation? (I, 457).

We have here a very characteristic pattern of the *Investigations*: a polemic against the linking of 'essence' and 'mental activity', using a kind of shock-technique of examples which force out into the open vague images and pictures which so often exercise a hidden domination over our thinking. 'My aim [he says] is to teach you to pass from a piece of disguised nonsense to something that is patent nonsense' (I, 464). '*Essence* is expressed by grammar' (I, 371), i.e., by the pattern of use of a word in a community. He goes on:

> We should like to say: The sign of negation is our occasion for doing something – possibly something very complicated. But what? That is not said. It is as if it only needed to be hinted at; as if we already knew (I, 549). Negation, one might say, is a gesture, *Gebärde*, of exclusion, of rejection. But such a gesture is used in a great variety of cases! (I, 550).

Here is a clue to what Wittgenstein is alluding to. Consider, for instance, the *great variety* of cases in which one shakes one's head, not just 'inwardly' but in the ordinary public way, refusing a request, for instance, or expressing doubt or qualification. Or consider again what Wittgenstein points out: that if our normal way of expressing negation were by the gesture of shaking our heads, a double negation would not be an affirmation but only perhaps a strengthened negation. We must be on our guard against the temptation to reject examples like these because they are more 'crude' and more 'primitive' than the sophisticated games we have learnt to play, relying perhaps on some pure essence of negation which we find in the textbooks of logic. By the criterion of human intelligibility, of the meaning which is embodied in the human life of a community, the 'pure' negation is only one member of a large family, a member which has its special uses, e.g., in mathematics, but not in others. If we want to know what we 'mean' by negation, all we have to do is to look at the variety of different ways in which we use our different signs and gestures of negation. 'Nothing is hidden', as Wittgenstein says. Our trouble only starts when we ask. 'What is negation?', and start scratching our heads. For surely something unique must correspond to this word 'not' which we find everywhere? It must be something in our heads, or something deep in things. And we must answer: 'The picture of something in our heads – or in our minds – the picture of something deep, is quite a useful picture, in certain circumstances; but the real question is the *application* of the picture; and we can only learn the proper application of the picture by examining our *use* (*Gebrauch*) of the sentences in which the sign occurs, the *Praxis* of the language; and this use is very various.'

Similarly the notion of boundary or limit (*Grenze*). I quote:

> To say, 'This combination of words makes no sense,' excludes it from the sphere of language and thereby bounds the domain of language. But when one draws a boundary it may be for various kinds of reason. If I surround an area with a fence or a line or otherwise, the purpose may be to prevent someone getting in or out; but it may also be a part of a game and the players be supposed, say, to jump over the boundary; or it may shew where the property of one man ends and that of another man begins; and so on. So if I draw a boundary line that is not yet to say what I am drawing it for (I, 499).

So the notion we found in the *Tractatus* of a unique boundary or limit separating sense from nonsense also vanishes: it is part of the old metaphysical search for a unique essence of language. There is, for example, a perfectly good use for nonsense in certain songs; an *Alleluia,* for instance, despite its Hebrew etymology, is really used by us as significant nonsense – Wittgenstein insists that there is a closer relationship between a sentence and a musical theme than we ordinarily like to think. Or take again the 'Ha! Ha!' which is probably still being used in cheap English books to indicate the sound made by someone laughing; is it a word, and then a nonsense word, or is it not a word at all but a sort of musical notation? We don't know what to say; there isn't a clear boundary.

Yet another metaphysical concept to be dissolved by this new style of philosophizing is the concept of the self, the subject, the I. We have seen that in the *Tractatus* Wittgenstein regarded the subject as the limit of the world, separated from it by what I called vertical negation. Now, by way of an analysis of the conceptual grammar of psychological words – thinking, intending, expecting, pain and so on – Wittgenstein shows that the feeling of the privacy of the self depends on yet another of those pictures which have their real application but whose application is restricted. As we have seen already, what 'goes on inside my head' is such a picture, the picture of 'processes in the head'. The language of the privacy of the self is one kind of language-game which has to be learned just like any other kind of language-game; that is to say, our privacy is dependent upon the common public world of language-games embodied in the life of the community. We cannot be more private to ourselves than the common life of language will let us; every 'exploration of our depths' is an extension of the possibility of *other* people's privacy. 'Depth' is a picture the application of which we have to learn; to 'explore our depths' is to enlarge the language-game of depth, something we see going on in novels or poetry, say. We have to learn to say 'I', and some people, mental defectives, never learn it. 'Nothing is hidden', even the techniques of language for hiding ourselves from each other, e.g., lying. Do we suspect the baby in its cot of only *pretending* to smile at us? (This is perhaps the point at which to observe that a very common reaction to meeting Wittgenstein's kind of thinking for the first time is to be made very angry– 'What is he going on about? Does he really. . . .' He asks himself in the *Investigations*: 'What is your aim in philosophy?' His answer is: 'To show the fly the way out of the fly-bottle' (I, 309).

One thing should at least be clear by now; and that is that together with 'pure' logic, 'pure' essence, 'pure' negation, absolute limits and the absolute self, God too has vanished from the scene: or more accurately, he only appears as part of the picture of pure logic, the absolute self and so on. God is indeed mentioned four or five times in the *Investigations,* but the role he plays there is only as a 'metaphysical' guarantee of a mistake about the meaning of meaning. He is not even the nameless Void: he is only the memory of a feeling of a void which arose from a confusion about language, like the memory of pain we once had long ago. The realm of *das Mystische* has vanished. 'Nothing is hidden.'

And our dilemma vanishes too. The compulsion we seemed to have, that we should be able to sense God's transcendence from within an experience of our own finitude, has been shown to rest upon the misapplication of a picture. But unfortunately the other horn of our dilemma, the God who seems to be irrelevant because it is merely a cosmic world which he transcends, is no more readily acceptable now that we have been shown the way out of the fly-bottle of the Absolute. For the finitude which is presented to us in the *Investigations* is no longer opposed to any sort of transcendence; it is merely one aspect of the Indefinite, the indefinite variety of human life. Not even agnosticism is significant any longer: nothing is hidden.[2]

---

[2] I need hardly say that I am only concerned with what seem to be the consequences of Wittgenstein's published writings, not with his personal convictions.

What are we to say now? This is of course a real question, not just a rhetorical one. I hope no one is expecting me to produce a solution from up my sleeve. What I shall offer here are only observations on a problem, not a solution of it.

First as regards my interpretation of the late Wittgenstein. This would almost certainly be challenged by many English philosophers. They would say: 'You have absurdly falsified the picture by presenting Wittgenstein outside his own proper context, just as though he were a Continental philosopher. His philosophy is a method of philosophizing, without doctrinal implications; it is a therapy, a technique. You would not expect swimming or riding a bicycle to be theistic or agnostic; why are you upset when philosophizing turns out to be neither too?' To which my answer is that if philosophy becomes nothing more than a method, if it ceases to be its function to make substantive statements at all, then my interpretation is already justified: just this aseptic methodological professionalism constitutes an existential stance. Certainly the method can be applied to all sorts of language-games, including religious ones – Wittgenstein has a parenthetical note which says simply 'Theology as grammar' (I, 373), and a good deal of well-meaning discussion goes on in England today about the 'grammar of religious language'. But the point is that at best this method of philosophizing is a technique for analysing *other people's* convictions; even one's own convictions have to be put into something like phenomenological brackets, hence the invisible inverted commas which this technique of linguistic philosophy must always sketch in the air, since it constitutes itself as philosophy, and differentiates itself from sociology or natural science, by seeing all things *sub specie verbi*, which is as it were its act of self-generation. On this view philosophy may help to clarify one's convictions, but never to state, utter and declare them; it could clarify the grounds for the convictions one already has, but never itself supply the grounds (cf. I, 121). This impartial neutrality is indeed very like swimming; but swimming does not teach one to put one's feet on the ground. A philosophy which defines itself methodologically severs its ontological roots; it becomes either parasitic on constructive philosophy or merely trivial. Mr Peter Winch, in an excellent book on the significance of Wittgenstein's later philosophy for social studies, makes my point for me admirably in a remark about the task of philosophy as 'uncommitted enquiry':

> In performing this task the philosopher will in particular be alert to deflate the pretensions of any form of enquiry to enshrine the essence of intelligibility as such, to possess the key

to reality. For connnected with the realization that intelligibility takes many and varied forms is the realization that reality has no key (*The Idea of a Social Science*, p. 102).

Secondly, isn't the whole theory an enormous mistake? Doesn't it rest on a fundamental error? We must be very cautious about an objection like this; philosophies are not like scientific theories which are at least *supposed* to be easily falsifiable. If the philosophical error is a *fundamental* one, then it ceases in a way to be just an error: plain errors are superficial. But isn't the starting-point of the whole view wrongly chosen? Philosophy, we must reply, doesn't choose a starting-point arbitrarily: the philosophical starting-point is the vanishing-point of a perspective, the tonic of a key. Everything in our experience may go to show that *there*, where I am not yet but trying to reach, is the only point from which my experience falls into an order, a harmony. If the public world of human behaviour in language shows itself to Wittgenstein as a perspective defining a point of origin, then this is something important about the way things are: if we can, to some extent, think Wittgenstein's thoughts, then those thoughts are thinkable. It would be childish to say that the point of origin was wrongly chosen, unless we could indicate a perspective with its point of origin which *included* the perspective of the *Investigations*. As regards God, for instance, it is important that he is philosophically problematic, not merely as 'object' but as vanishing-point of a perspective (note that we are hovering round a *picture*, the picture of 'perspective'); it tells us something about God that we can to some extent recreate a perspective which is neutral in respect to him. Any perspective of our own which did not allow for this neutral perspective, say by merely disqualifying it as 'bad will', would be misleading over-simplification. We need a negative theology which not only allows for God's presence-in-absence in the world of Nature but also for his presence-in-absence in the world of human history.

Thirdly, is there any way of indicating this wider, more inclusive perspective? As a Christian, a Catholic and a disciple of St Thomas, I believe that it must be *possible* to do so, not in 1963 perhaps, but perhaps in 2000. I have some suggestions. I am constantly struck by what seems to me a kinship (a 'family-relationship') between Wittgenstein and Heidegger, say the Heidegger who writes about Hölderlin's '*dichterisch wohnet der Mensch auf der Erde*'. Heidegger claims to disclose a more 'original', *ursprünglich,* bond between man and language than the use of linguistic tools: language is the event of truth which manifests the sacred transcendence of the 'Earth', that is, 'Being', *Sein*, in the forms of the gods. I do not think that Heidegger's transcendence or his gods can satisfy the theist: his gods are too much like the faces we see in the clouds, and his transcendence too much like an Indefinite than an Infinite. But I am sure that the original genesis of meaning as constituting a human essence is an important clue: *the nativity of the word,* which is a very traditional notion. And we may find analysis as well as intuition of this notion in Continental writers like Merleau-Ponty, Caruso and Buytendijk. We may try to use this paradigm to grasp in an analogical unity the variety of ways of life and language-games studied by social anthropologists; and there is no doubt that Wittgenstein is methodologically valuable for students of primitive religion. We may wish to try to do all this in the properly theological perspective of the *Deus absconditus,* the God of the *mysterion,* whose transcendence is revealed in *history,* and made concrete in a *personal* revelation of the Father in the incarnate Son, and re-presented in the linguistic community of the Church. But these are only suggestions: the gaps are obvious.

# 3

# World Religions and Christian Theology

It seems to me only fair to begin this paper by inquiring whether the topic indicated by the title actually exists in any serious sense, or whether it has simply been conjured up by a trick of language within the general and familiar process of academic over-production and waste-making. The fact that a considerable literature more or less concerned with the topic does undoubtedly exist provides no guarantee of the existence of a genuine problem; for some at least of this literature tends to heighten one's suspicions rather than to assuage them.

The title is, at any rate, 'World Religions and Christian Theology', not 'World Religions and Christianity'. By 'world religions' I understand those religions which have not been confined to a particular ethnic or political unit but are found in more or less diversified forms remote from their place of origin. It is clear enough that Christianity is one of these world religions, in so far as we allow ourselves to use the word 'religion' with an appropriate looseness; we need do no more than declare 'religion' a family-word, where the different items all to be called *religions* need not share a single definition but form an irregular network. Now this paper does not attempt to consider the place of Christianity among world religions. This is not only because my own equipment for such a task would be wholly inadequate, but also because I suspect that no one's equipment would be.

For consider what this task would involve, if it could be envisaged at all. It would mean analysing the whole irregular network of religions in terms of features shared by only some of them and accounting for the lack of shared features when they are not present. Christianity and religion A might have feature $\alpha$ in common, Christianity and religion B have feature $\gamma$ in common, religions A and B have feature $\beta$ in common. The hermeneutic standpoint of an investigator who terminated his analysis at this point, after merely establishing these common features would be a queer one.

For he would need to have been guided in his analysis by some indistinct sense of comparable features, at the very least by some hypothesis of structural frames or of human possibilities; and whatever his analysis has established will have to be expressed as a confirmation or a qualification of his hypothesis, and this again in some language of ordinary human concern. I do not see how ordinary human concern could come to an end with the establishment of the features constituting an irregular network, though I admit that there is a strong trend in current studies of all kinds to claim that this sort of investigation is desirable and therefore possible.

The claim seems even less plausible when we cease to consider the formal model and turn to the actual business of investigation. What in our case of Christianity among world religions would actually constitute shared or comparable features is a good deal more complex than the model would suggest. There would always be the possibility that such a shared feature, once extracted from the two ways of life thought of as having the feature in common, would become a feature merely in a third context which was a way of life for no one. At best this third context might serve as a dialectical stage in a progressive attempt to achieve a unified and differentiated consciousness of two ways of life. Certainly it is difficult to see how a really serious attempt to achieve such a consciousness could hope in any significant way to embrace the whole field of world religions. For the sake of example, I need merely mention that 'feature' in Christianity which is ordinarily called God. A serious attempt to achieve a communicating consciousness of God in Christianity and some feature in another religion thought to be comparable would seem to be a lifelong task, not easily combined with an attempt to achieve this communicating consciousness of God in respect of a third religion or of, say, Salvation in respect of this third religion. It would have to be an attempt which did not confine itself to a comparison of Scriptures or of written traditions but included an effort to enter into a lived tradition. It would have to recognize that such an effort to share the lived tradition must have as its consequence a shift of consciousness in which the Christian God-feature itself underwent modification.

This last point seems to me of special importance; at any rate it suggests interesting ambiguities. I wonder if it would be unfair to describe a good deal of the literature of comparative religion, whether from Christian or non-Christian practitioners, as a sort of genteel theosophy. What such a description implies positively is that the comparative study of religions can be serious enough to go beyond the systematic analysis of a referential network but in such a way that, negatively, it proposes in the disguise of an academic exercise some enlargement and stimulus of religious experience. There is a tendency for the study of religions itself to become an independent religious mode, not simply a religion, because this study rarely allows itself to accept that wider discipline which would regulate a whole way of life; perhaps it could be called 'religion in the head', the study of religions as a surrogate for religion.

The boundary between this sort of vicarious religiosity and the sort of evolving communion in religious life envisaged earlier is not easy to draw, partly because it is a shifting one; after all, theosophy can be a serious affair, and theology can be intellectually and humanly trivial. But the possibility of a distinction, if it is admitted, allows me to indicate what I take this paper to be about, namely, world religions and Christian *theology*. By 'theology', in this context, at any rate, I mean the activity of *self*-understanding, *Selbstverständnis*, the exploratory, continually renewed effort within the Christian tradition to examine the implications of that tradition where it is continually being interrogated by the conjunctures of historical change; the diversification of human experience by factors which are not themselves at the very least explicitly given in that tradition. The entrance of world religions into the course of European history forms one series of such factors of diversification. The thesis proposed in this paper is simply that the genesis of Christianity itself out of its contemporary Jewish-Hellenistic environment is the paradigm case for the self-understanding of Christian theology as the response of Christianity to its interrogation by world religions.

But before going on to argue this thesis it would be as well to say a little more about the notion of theology just indicated. Firstly and more generally, by self-understanding, *Selbstverständnis*, is understood that process by which from some preliminary, more or less implicit, understanding, *Vorverständnis*, some creative and constructive advance is made, in the course of which the one who understands is himself reconstituted as an identity, if only provisionally. The process, that is, is intrinsically open to further development, not only in the sense of being open to an unforeseeable future but also in the sense of actually reinterpreting the whole sense of past, present and future; on this view time is not merely endured but also constituted as history. Christian theology as self-understanding in this sense involves the acceptance of responsibility for a particular sequence of constructive historical moments, identified by a series of monuments of self-understanding. It involves then the acceptance by the individual theologian of membership of an identifiable society considered not only synchronically but also diachronically. If any thinker must at least indistinctly accept responsibility for the whole of humanity, in its prior history as well as its unforeseeable future, the theologian must accept as a defining condition of that responsibility the interpretative value of an identifiable sequence of human history, the figure in the carpet.

Secondly and more particularly, any self-understanding of Christian theology in response to the interrogation of Christianity by world religions would tend to be trivial if it were not also responding at the same time to the interrogation of Christianity by other movements of ideas and sentiments which come to light historically. It cannot for instance be irrelevant to the Christian theologian that an important stage in the interrogation of Christianity by world religions began at the end of the eighteenth century. Henceforth the Romantic relativization of eighteenth-century rationalism and *Aufklärung* would provide the medium through which Oriental religions would be presented to the European reader. The recognition that a peculiarly narrow view of the human mind as rational or empiricist has become a recurrent stance of European consciousness since the eighteenth century has generated a complementary receptiveness to other styles of consciousness which in certain modes offer themselves as a saving gnosis. It is not an accident that Robert Graves should write a preface to Mr Idries Shah's book on *The Sufis*, that Professor Zaehner should associate Proust, Rimbaud and Richard Jeffries with the Upanishads, and that the Oxford University Press should be reprinting Evans-Wentz's Tibetan translations in paperback for the readers of R. D. Laing and the *International Times*. The theological response to world religions must take into account the historical forms through which they have been mediated, and this requires some sense of the other historical factors which have helped to shape the mediating forms. Certainly in our own time political disillusionment, the discrediting of established Christianity (as sentiment and idea as well as institution), in England the obscurantist professionalism of philosophy, the recurrence of mechanistic accounts of man in sophisticated cybernetic versions, all these have helped to create a mode in which world religions other than Christianity find among some a ready acceptance. A Christian theology which responded to world religions without remaining critically alert to other calls upon its self-understanding would (and in fact sometimes does) float in a faint haze of absorbed self-intoxication.

If I formulate the requirements for a theological response to world religions in such demanding terms, it must be obvious that I see myself falling short of them too, and of others which I have not formulated or have failed to see the necessity for formulating. On the other hand, my own inability to fulfil the requirements will have to serve as an excuse for restricting this paper to a fairly narrowly-conceived exercise in Christian self-understanding. For I shall not attempt what is quite beyond my powers, the Christian interpretation of world-religions (supposing that this were possible at all and were not an impertinence). All I shall propose is a version of Christian self-understanding which seems to me to respond to some part of the interrogation of Christianity by world religions and to be in that sense open to them, leaving it to those who have a deeper insight into one or other of those religions to take up the offered dialogue by evaluating what is offered.

\* \* \*

In a recent book on *The Earliest Christian Confessions,* Vernon H. Neufeld proposes, more or less as a matter of course, that the two most 'primitive' forms of Christian confession were *Iesous Christos,* Jesus is the Christ, the Messiah, and *Kurios Iesous,* Jesus is Lord. We shall return to this notion of a 'primitive' confession in a moment. First we may note that these two formulae do in fact embody the central tension in any Christian theology: the identification of a particular historical individual, Jesus, as someone who transcends the historical process. Or to put it differently, the two questions relevant to establishing identity, 'Who is he?' and 'What is he?' receive answers the compatibility of which it is the permanent business of Christian theology to vindicate.

The term *Christos,* Messiah, clearly makes sense only within the special history of Israel; the term *Kurios,* Lord, whatever the precise scholarly standpoint adopted in its controversial interpretation, would at least have made sense in a Hellenistic context. If some fairly recent discussion among Christian theologians, under the rubric of 'the Jesus of history and the Christ of faith', has served any positive purpose at all, it has been to show that the identification of Jesus as Christ and Lord is the central affirmation of Christian faith; and we may also see that this identification implies an interpretation of the historical traditions which supplied the terminology in which such an affirmation could be made. For it is clear on the one hand that the affirmation would have been meaningless unless the terminology already had a life of its own in some tradition of language, and on the other that the use of this terminology in identifying Jesus involves that kind of amplification of linguistic use which shifts the whole range of use of the terms decisively. If Jesus is *Christos*, is *Kurios*, then Judaism is wound up, Hellenism surpassed and judged, and the central reference of the terms is decisively located.

It is clear that the affirmation that Jesus is Christ, is Lord, could only in a special sense be described as 'primitive'. Although Neufeld refers to Kelly's *Early Christian Creeds*, he does not seem to have noticed Kelly's brilliant dismissal of the whole quest for a 'primitive Christian creed' as based on a misunderstanding. The variety of terms used to refer to the Christian 'teaching' or 'gospel' – *didaskalia* or *euaggelion* themselves, as well as *kerugma, pistis, paradosis, logos, paratheke, didache, martyrion* – indicate a variety of settings in the life of the early Christian communities in which diverse formulae of a credal sort would have been appropriate. There could have been no single 'primitive Christian creed'. To say, as I have just done myself, that the affirmation of Jesus as Christ and Lord is 'central' is not to suggest that it is historically primitive, but rather that it serves to re-focus two entire historical perspectives upon the historical individual whose personal name was 'Jesus'.

This re-focusing of perspectives was not of course confined to the shift in meaning of *Christos* and *Kurios*. I should wish to argue, in accordance with the views of Fuchs and Ebeling, that New Testament Christianity is profitably investigated as a 'language-event', *Sprachereignis*. What then emerges is that (as might have been expected) the historical event of the genesis of Christianity involves not, in general, a new language in the sense of a new vocabulary, but the transformation and recreation of languages already in valid use. With very few exceptions (*agape* and *Petros* are two oddly associated examples of these), New Testament vocabulary does not enlarge in any significant way the vocabulary of extra-biblical Greek. What of course does happen is that this vocabulary is used in new combinations and new applications, involving that kind of amplification of meaning detectably at work in a poem or any other creative use of language. We might take as example the Pauline use of the Hellenistic *soma* to speak of the eucharistic body and the body of the Church in association with the body of the risen Christ.

For the purposes of the present paper, it is of special interest to observe the transformation in the New Testament of terms of general 'religious' application, such as 'sacrifice', 'priest' and 'cult'. In the history of exegesis this transformation has been called a 'spiritualization', in a sense nearly equivalent to 'moralization', and more recently a 'secularization' or 'de-sacralization'. The New

Testament clearly prolongs a prophetic interpretation of Old Testament cult, but it is now fairly widely recognized that this prophetic reinterpretation was not simply a rejection of the cult. What is central to the New Testament reinterpretation of cultic terminology is the identification of an exemplar or paradigm case of worship of God the Father: this is the death and resurrection of Jesus Christ, in the worship of whose personal sacrifice Christians share by participation in his Spirit, *pneuma,* in such a way that the whole movement of their personal lives is itself a worship. This is a 'spiritualization' of cult primarily in the sense of an animation by the Holy Spirit, the *pneuma* of Christ; it is a 'secularization' or 'de-sacralization' in the sense that the whole range of personal life is capable of being assumed into the new dimension of pneumatic life communicated through baptism into the death and resurrection of Jesus.

There can be no question of attempting here a more detailed examination of this transformation; it is sufficient for our present purposes to draw attention to the way in which a whole cultic language is given new life by being deployed with reference to a prime or paradigm case, the event of Jesus Christ, an event, it is discovered by Christians, which can be appropriated and renewed in personal and communal experience. It is just this discovery, what has been called a *Neuheitserlebnis,* an experience of radical novelty, to which I wish to draw attention in reviewing the linguistic transformation of Jewish and Hellenistic traditions of language in the New Testament. Not that the *Neuheitserlebnis* can be divorced from the recorded linguistic shift, any more than the experience which becomes articulate in a poem can be dissociated from the words on the page. But the words on the page are dead if they are not allowed to recreate in one's own linguistic experience the genetic moment of articulate enlargement of insight and experience which they offer and invite. It is to the genetic moment in the *Neuheitserlebnis* of New Testament Christianity that I invite your attention: the spring of water welling up in the community of Christian believers unto eternal life (cf. John 4. 14). That is to say, according to the New Testament testimony itself, the genetic moment in Christian experience is capable of indefinitely extended renewal in space and time in virtue of communication in the Spirit of the risen Christ. Every genetic moment is a mystery. It is dawn, discovery, spring, new birth, coming to the light, awakening, transcendence, liberation, ecstasy, bridal consent, gift, forgiveness, reconciliation, revolution, faith, hope, love. It could be said that Christianity is the consecration of the genetic moment, the living centre from which it reviews and renews the indefinitely various and shifting perspectives of human experience in history. That, at least, is or ought to be its claim: that it is the power to transform and renew all things: 'Behold, I make all things new' (Rev. 21.5).

But, it will be said, even supposing your interpretation of Christianity is just, that at its centre is the genetic moment, the holiness of the new, could not the same claim be made for other traditions, for which, say, the experience of enlightenment is the heart? Either Christianity is merely an instance of a universal type of the humane, whether communicated by religious tradition or not, or your version of Christianity is merely parasitic on some generally available truth about human experience, which historical Christianity as a matter of fact has successfully smothered for centuries of institutionalized timidity, boredom and repression.

I want of course to argue that the Christian experience of the genetic moment is the critical instance, the touchstone of the new. But this is not to say that Christian self-understanding in theology does not allow of exploration of its crucial sense of the genetic moment in terms of other insights into genesis, birth from above and anew. There is at least one aspect of the genetic moment which I should like to explore, within the general interpretative categories of Christian originality and preordained multiple echo.

On the view of Christianity proposed above, Christianity as pneumatic power to transform cultural traditions, evinced in linguistic transformation, there seems to be a disconcerting absence of an identifiable centre, a 'primitive Christian creed', or indeed lofty words of wisdom as a testimony of God. Instead there is only Jesus Christ and him crucified, as a demonstration of Spirit and power. There is nevertheless a secret and hidden wisdom of God which God decreed before the ages for our glorification (cf. 1 Cor. 2: *theou sophian en musterio, ten apokekrummenen*). There is, if you like, a hole at the centre of the genetic moment, a void, which turns out to be plenary, superabundant: a radiant darkness. What I am trying allusively to suggest is that the Christian experience of the genetic moment is at once an experience of the creatively new become manifest in human articulation, and an experience of an ultimate source, the hidden God, *Deus absconditus* who has made his transcendence known in the darkness of a death. If the experience were not *both at once,* it would split apart into an insipid humanism of progress (or a revolutionary arrogance), or an esoteric mystique of world abnegation.

It cannot be said that the Christian tradition has always been very clear about this pregnant junction in the genetic moment. The negative theology of the *Deus absconditus,* for instance, dominated in Eastern and Western traditions by the Pseudo-Dionysius, seems not to have always let the uniqueness of the biblical disclosure show through the neo-Platonist categories used to interpret it. The God who hides himself, *El mistatter*, of Isa. 45. 15, becomes in the Vulgate the *Deus absconditus*, the hidden God. In the Isaian passage, the prophetic writer appears to be reflecting on the distance between present oppression and desolation in exile, and the future glory of the victorious manifestation of Yahweh when Israel will triumph over her oppressors. 'Truly, thou art a God who hidest thyself, O God of Israel, the Saviour.' The presence of God in his people need not be a manifest one; God may hide himself from his people, to show himself eventually through their victory, which is then his own victory and glorious manifestation. God's presence to his people is assured by his covenant with them, but in one way or another the visible token of his presence may be withdrawn – the capture of the ark, the loss of the promised land, the destruction of the Temple, the success of false prophets, the presumption of apostate rulers, the 'abomination of desolation'; and it is then on the word of God's promise alone that faith and hope can stand firm.

For the Isaian passage, then, and, I shall argue, for the Bible as a whole, God's presence is a presence-in-absence; God may hide himself because without ever wholly rejecting his people, he retains his freedom in his gift of himself to his people: because he bestows himself freely, he may freely withdraw himself. Even though his freedom has committed itself in the elective form of covenant, that form must be understood against the background of a limitless freedom which gives the finite form its infinite value. God must hide himself even when he gives himself and even precisely when he gives himself, so that his presence may be recognized as sovereignly free and transcendent gift. In the tokens of his gift we must be able to feel ourselves drawn out beyond them into a reaching out for the surpassing abundance of the giver.

It seems to me that this Isaian reflection on the God who hides himself finds its ultimate validation in the Christian experience of the genetic moment, say, as 'justification by faith'. The crucified Christ, Jesus dead on the Cross in failure and ignominy, his ultimate abandonment ('My God, why have you abandoned me?', Jesus calls out, quoting the psalm) is the paradigm case of the God who hides himself; but, in terms of the passage from 1 Corinthians alluded to a moment ago, the hiddenness of God in the crucified Christ is also the mode in which God shows himself in Spirit and power. God reveals himself in his hiddenness because the hiddenness is the testimony (ambiguous, of course) to the limitless freedom out of which he bestows himself. In another place, speaking out of a sensed identity with Jesus in virtue of his Apostolic function, Paul can say, 'So death is at work in us, but life in you' (2 Cor. 4. 12). In the earlier text Paul speaks of a hidden wisdom of God *en musterio,* the word *musterion* here having its accustomed sense of a hidden purpose and plan; hence Paul speaks of a wisdom '*decreed* before the ages'. It is by an internal and inscrutable purpose of God's free decision, finding its ultimately valid expression in the hiddenness of abandonment and death, that God gives us the new birth celebrated by Christians as a liberation into the freedom of the children of God (cf. Rom 8. 23).

The hiddenness of the God of Christianity is a hiddenness of transcendent freedom, self-bestowal in freedom, *agape*, love. The Christian experience of the genetic moment is the individual and communal discovery of the communicability of this creative freedom issuing from its hidden source. The historical particularity of the death of Jesus is the ordained condition of the transcendent liberation of newness of life in the Lord: Jesus is Christ, is Lord. It is hardly an accident that the noun *agape* (as opposed to the verb *agapao*) is found almost exclusively in biblical Greek. The transcendence of this *agape* is very well brought out in the text from Ephesians where Paul asks that his hearers may 'know (*ginoskein*) the love (*agape*) of Christ which surpasses all knowledge (*gnosis*)' (3. 19). Christian gnosis is the experience of the mystery of love freely bestowed, freely generated; and this central experience is the critical instance of all genesis and enlightenment.

That this central Christian experience has not always found adequate expression in Christian tradition has already been suggested. It is for various reasons convenient to illustrate this from some texts of Renaissance Platonism drawn from Edgar Wind's fine book, *Pagan Mysteries in the Renaissance.* In his final chapter, 'The Concealed God', Wind puts together a text from Nicholas of Cusa with one from Erasmus; both play with the notion of the seed. The first, from Nicholas of Cusa, runs:

> Elementary forces, according to Aristotle, have the smallest extension and the greatest power.... The force inherent in a spark is that of the whole fire.... A small seed has the strength of many grains.... The core of the apparent is in the occult, the outward depends on the inward.

The second text, from Erasmus, runs:

> Thus the most important is always the least conspicuous. A tree flatters the eye with flowers, and foliage, and exhibits the massiveness of its trunk: but the seed from which these have

their strength, what small thing it is, and how hidden!... And in the universe the greatest things are invisible.... And the supreme among these is furthest removed ... God, unintelligible and unthinkable because he is the unique source of all.

It is not without interest to note that the image of the seed, developed in a rather different way, also occurs in the Chāndogya Upanishad, where the sage Aruni, after telling his son Śvetaketu to divide first a fig, then one of the fine seeds, asks what his son sees there. Śvetaketu answers, 'Nothing at all, sir'. Then Aruni says to his son:

> Verily, my dear, that finest essence which you do not perceive – verily, my dear, from that finest essence this great sacred fig-tree thus arises. Believe me, my dear [or, as Zaehner suggestively translates, 'Have faith'], that which is the finest essence – this whole world has that as itself. That is Reality. That is Atman (the Self). That art thou, Śvetaketu.

All these texts seem to be practising a dialectic of the Great and the Small, which inverts the familiar order for religious purposes. Perhaps the two Western texts have a sharper sense of limits, that between the limited and the Unlimited there is a jump, while the Eastern text is more absorbed in the pervasiveness of the Unlimited. Perhaps the Western texts play with the notion of the seed more self-consciously, giving it value as a simile; perhaps the suggestion of the Eastern text is that the virtue of the seed is at one level an actual embodiment of Reality. But leaving aside these doubtful comparisons, we may simply note that in all three cases we are dealing with a parable: the dialectic gets its force from the concrete universality of its starting-point, archetypal though it may be. And in fact the terminus of the dialectic, the moment of insight, is no more than an acknowledgement of the typical character of the universality – not only this seed, but all seeds; not only seeds but the small universally; not only the cosmic small but the small absolutely. The dialectic evokes and exhibits an intuition already latently there; the transcendence pointed to never escapes from the virtualities of the given. Unless, that is, the whole process is embarked on in a context of some other affirmation of transcendence, in our case, the affirmation and the surrender of faith in response to love beyond gnosis.

We return, then, to the question raised earlier, whether the account of the central Christian experience in terms of the genetic moment, in its double aspect of plenitude and emptiness (void), life and death, radiance and darkness, is merely an illegitimate appropriation to Christianity of a universal human experience. I do not doubt that reflection on the genetic moment might be of the same typical universality as reflection on the seed: in fact, the one is not far from being a transposition into subjectivity of the archetypal value of the cosmic instance, the genetic moment as seed of enlightenment. But again the force of the instance depends on the use which is made of it, just as the force of Christian language is the transformation of sense which it effects.

It is, I suggest, a matter of faith that the transcendence disclosed by religious dialectic is no more, within the ascending movement generated by that dialectic itself, than an explication of the virtualities of the given. Further, for Christian faith, a transcendence of freedom and freely bestowing love relativizes the given by claiming for it the unique status of personal *gift*. If this is so, then the universal instance may serve as the point of departure for a two-way process of interpretation: for what is universally human, while remaining universal, becomes particularized as an expression of grace, freely bestowing love. The Christian experience of the genetic moment is seen to be capable of assuming and transforming the universally human; and secondly, the universally human is rediscovered at the heart of the Christian experience. This relativization of the transcendence of the universal by the transcendence of the particular would seem to be an implication of Incarnation as the presence of the Giver in his created and historically bestowed gift.

Perhaps one should add a final note here about the Christian claim to be opened up to a unique (a transformed) transcendence through faith. I do not know how far Professor Zaehner's translation of the text from the Chāndogya Upanishad ('Have faith' instead of Hume's 'Believe me') is justified. But in Gonda's admirable account of Indian religions we find it stated that later Hinduism 'knows of no way of faith apart from the three ways of jnāna, karman and bhakti. Faith does indeed form the presupposition for every intellectual, emotional or ritual relationship to God or salvation; but it is not this relationship itself. It is an "external means", not a "theological virtue" ' (*Die Religionen Indiens,* II, p. 62, referring to Lacombe). This is far too complex a subject to be more than mentioned here; and Gonda himself gives a different picture of śraddha for the Vedic period. It has also to be remembered that the whole discussion is on the level of articulate doctrine; I find it easy to suppose that faith could play a constitutive part in the religious life of many people for whom articulate doctrine has no particular significance; the great majority of Christian believers, especially in the Roman Catholic Church, would be sufficient witness to that.

To conclude, then, the purpose of this paper has been to present a thesis about Christianity as part of a theological self-understanding of Christianity in response to its interrogation by other world religions. The thesis has been that the genetic moment in Christianity, disclosed in its transformation of religious traditions contemporary with its historical origins, may serve as a critical instance for its inward understanding of other religions. The thesis is open to criticism both as an interpretation of Christianity and also as an invitation to followers of other ways or of none to find some way of entry into discussion in the terms proposed. If Christian theologies tend to fall into either a Pauline or a Johannine pattern, the present paper seems to me more Johannine than Pauline; the attempt has been less to survey the history of the world and of salvation from some elevated standpoint of God's eternal, mysterious purpose, but rather to convey, as a 'concentration of multiple meanings' (to use A. C. Graham's phrase about the poetry of the later T'ang), some sense of what it might be to go on being a Christian while remaining open to other sorts of solicitation.

## 4

# The *Concilium* World Congress: Impressions and Reflections

There had been a derailment ahead of us at Dover, so I was late arriving in Brussels. More delay getting a taxi, because I couldn't quite bring myself to use my elbows like everybody else. The hotel room booked for me, I calculated, would cost about £5.50 a night, so unless I stopped eating or found another hotel I should have to return home well before the Congress ended. At last the Congress hall itself: the Palais de Congrès, past the illuminated fountains of the Mont des Arts and a small knot of cameramen, timidly into the Salle Albert 1$^{er}$ – and it really hit one then: the long, high swooping hall, with what must have been a thousand people in it, the brilliant glare of the television lights reflected from the huge black and white poster at the back of the stage, bearing the words in English:

> WORLD
> FUTURE
> CHURCH

Schillebeeckx was speaking in French from the rostrum; his voice resonated effortlessly from the splendid amplification system, though soon one became aware of a counterpoint of high-pitched chirp and chatter from the badly adjusted earphones of theologians unaccustomed to the use of simultaneous-translation equipment; this was to form an accompaniment throughout the Congress. Photographers crawled and flashed unceasingly over the stage; from time to time the television cameras swivelled and turned their black snouts on the audience. I would return to England the next day, I decided; no, no, not this, not this.

More speeches and addresses (Rahner, Suenens): there must have been three hours of them, though fortunately I had missed the first two. Then the audience erupted into the corridor, recognitions and identifications, an invitation to join a select group of some hundred and fifty people drinking whisky and champagne; I nervously clutched my rich blue folder (provided by Sabena Airways and containing Congress documents). Gossip; a new periodical said to be coming out soon to challenge *Concilium*, under the names of H. U. von Balthasar, Ratzinger and Le Guillou. The process of linguistic devaluation gathered way, as everyone began to speak or to listen to a language other than his own.

I could go on endlessly registering these impressions, but let me bring them to an end with an account of my return to England. The Dutch policeman looking at my passport had shouted at me, 'Ah, you have been at the Congress!', laughing uproariously. A still clear dawn at Harwich; London bright, even radiant, as I passed Hyde Park on my way after years of postponement to look at the Victoria and Albert Museum. I cannot describe my refreshment of spirit at finding myself in the presence of such an abundant display of creative human sensibility and vitality, delicate, warm, precisely felt at the craftsman's fingertips; a demonstration of the sense of man's humanity more utterly convincing than the volumes of devalued rhetoric poured out about Man for the six past days. A museum, yes, but a pledge incarnate in stone, ivory, wood, paint, silk, porcelain of the potentiality of the human spirit. A friendly museum, with an excellent, reasonably cheap restaurant and a homely, rather casual quadrangle where one could sit in the soft sun.

The impressions as I have recorded them clearly carry a valuation with them, and imply general views of the nature of theology – or at any rate of how it might most profitably be practised – and of the role of theologians in the Church today. The Congress, it became clear by the first morning, had been conceived of as an exercise in ecclesiastical politics, planned as an Event, to put pressure on Church authorities. There was the matter of the Resolutions. As far as I could make out, none of those invited to the Congress had been warned that the main purpose of the Congress was to discuss and corporately proclaim resolutions which had been prepared in advance by the organizers. As the participants gradually became aware of this design, resistance built up and became vocal; charges of manipulation and even dishonesty were made at the plenary session that evening. At various times some of the chief organizers of the Congress made replies to these charges, replies of extraordinary naivety. There can be no doubt that the affair of the resolutions poisoned the Congress from the start; there was a feeling of resentment at having travelled often considerable distances to a theological congress to find, only after getting there, that casting a vote was supposed to be one's chief contribution. Eventually a vote had to be taken on whether there should be resolutions at all; and this was accepted only on the condition that there should be a qualifying preamble and that the resolutions themselves should be reduced in number and reconstructed by the three speakers appointed for each day. I won't attempt to describe the fantastic muddle and seemingly endless debate over procedure which led to this result. But I had better make it clear at this point that of the twelve 'official' resolutions and the four supplementary resolutions from the floor I voted for all but one official resolution and one supplementary resolution, where I abstained in each case; the latter of these two did not get its required two-thirds majority and so did not become a resolution of the Congress. However, it should be borne in mind that the Congress was not in fact as theologically homogeneous as even the qualifying preamble to the resolutions might suggest. Apart from the fairly consistent minority which voted against all the resolutions, many of those who voted in favour did so with some discomfort.

I shall try to give some account of my own discomfort, without pretending that it was representative. There was a theory behind the design of the organizers, a theory which shows itself fairly inconspicuously in the final resolutions. It is a theory about the practical character of theology, that it has an essential function as a critique of society, including the society of the Church. It isn't necessary to share or even be familiar with the views of the Frankfurt school of sociology in order to assent to this view of theology. But a theory of theology which insists on its character as critical praxis has to be judged at least in part by its own actual praxis; and the praxis of this Congress left me deeply dissatisfied. In part the praxis disclosed an assessment of how to insert Christianity critically into common consciousness – by way of the communications media – which seems to me at the very least naive. One's own experience, one's own sense of how the world is, how human consciousness is deeply shifting and taking new shape, is always limited; but I confess that to my sense the world isn't likely to take very seriously a message communicated in such a medium so glossily packaged. European television viewers might not have known in detail that the *Concilium* organizers were paying over ten pounds a night for their hotel bed and breakfast (each organizer's total expenses for the Congress would have paid for another nun from Kerala), but they probably had a sense that they were being offered something 'important' – so important that the organizing secretary had deliberately chosen expensive hotels for the participants.

Another aspect of the praxis needs to be commented on, if it is to be taken seriously at all. Provision was in fact made for worship at this Christian theological congress: a quarter of an hour at the beginning of each week-day session, and a eucharistic celebration on the Sunday. The week-day worship in fact consisted of what might generously be called a homily, less generously just another paper. The eucharistic session, delayed for an hour by the demands of television, was dominated by a choir of Belgian school-children singing bouncing tunes, assisted by a jazz group and rhythmic hand-clapping (with some diffidence or open hostility) from the largely middle-aged congregation-audience of theologians. Perhaps it looked different on the television screens.

Gregory Baum was very much to the point, it seemed to me, when he drew attention in our working group to the difference in social status between theologians at the Congress. Many of the Continental theologians, especially the Germans, enjoyed all the status of established University connections; but this is hardly true of the majority of Catholic theologians today. It is a little quaint that the critico-practical theory of theology is largely a product of German universities; perhaps this is another version of ideological compensation for reality.

But to speak of 'reality' is to point to what in my sense of things was most problematic about this Congress. One of the most interesting disguises in which the problem showed itself was the repeated appeal, especially in my working group, to leave abstractions and concentrate on the concrete. Now 'concrete' of course is one of the most abstract of words; scholastically, it is a *nomen secundae intentionis*, a way of talking about talking, and one can be fairly certain when complaints are being made about abstractness and appeals for concreteness that something has gone wrong with the whole process of communication. As in this case, the people who make the appeals seem to be confident that they know where the concrete is to be found; one of the examples suggested in our group was clerical celibacy. But one of the difficulties about the concrete, as any reader of Coleridge or Leavis will know, is that it cannot be determined in advance. It needs a patient labour of reflection, suggestion and attentiveness to discover: the concrete can't be pointed to, it has to be constructed. As a matter of fact, the question of clerical celibacy is a particularly good example, as the inadequacies of average discussions show quite painfully. Presumably what is really being expressed in appeals for the concrete is some sense that what is being said doesn't *connect*, that it doesn't issue from and offer a share in some lived and discriminated experience. What makes things even more difficult is that the people who appeal for concreteness frequently don't want genuine concreteness at all, and resist any attempt to search for it, rejecting it angrily and impatiently as an evasion.

In one of the resolutions or 'guide-lines' in their final form there appears a comprehensive (so comprehensive as to be almost empty) enumeration of the factors in 'society' which theology must take into account: 'sciences, arts, literature and religions'. Sweeping though this enumeration may be, I like to take some credit for it, since it does represent some advance over the original restriction to 'human sciences'. The point to be made is that the sort of concreteness achieved and disclosed by a poem or a novel is often disconcerting, shocking – 'scandalous' – in ways which theology needs to be too. It provides a convenient point of reference for discussions about the character of theology as critique of society; since these discussions often display a marked similarity to discussions about commitment in literature or even 'socialist realism'. If I say I am dubious of the value of a theological critique of society which isn't enforced by the discriminated pressure of a felt and lived experience, I doubtless lay myself open to charges of élitism; but I should, I think, be in good company, among those whose connection with their fellowmen needn't always be mediated, and is sometimes restricted, by the schematisms of categorical pronouncement, 'science' in the sense of *Wissenschaft*.

If this will have to do as a rather hesitant reflection on some of the presuppositions about theology active at the Congress, something must finally be said about the sort of pressures which brought the Congress into being at all. Even if one didn't care for the style in which affairs were conducted, should one complain about an assembly of theologians meeting to claim a special place in the life of the Church? Most theologians who have at any time been described as 'progressive' have had to face at least once intervention from ecclesiastical authority in a style far more depressing than anything even the Congress was guilty of – suspicious, ill-informed, clandestine, threatening. Of course this kind of intervention doesn't characterize every relationship between authority and theologians everywhere; but instances of it are common enough to make it impossible to shrug them off as merely exceptional. Isn't there a case to be made for something like a Trades Union of theologians, which might protect their legitimate interests and even issue a collective manifesto?

It seems to me that something of this sort, however distasteful it may be from some points of view, may have to be accepted so long as theologians and ecclesiastical authorities live in worlds so far apart from each other as they now do, worlds of human and Christian experience apart. It is still possible for a bishop to define his ecclesial consciousness by an *a priori* which excludes from it ingredients felt to be part of the ordinary texture of human life by many lay people and theologians; it is perfectly possible for a theologian to put an exaggerated value on such ingredients and make them part of his working definition of the *humanum* (to use Schillebeeckx's term), a *humanum* endorsed in Jesus Christ. While this continues to be the case, presuppositions, perspectives, the whole feel and texture of life, must continue to differ and conflicts must arise; perhaps these conflicts need to be institutionalized and ritualized. I confess that I do not find this prospect pleasing, in part at least because I cannot take theologians (as distinct from their theology) all that seriously. Certainly if theologians are to form associations to promote 'openness' in the Church, they will have to do so on behalf of the Church as a whole and not just on their own behalf. What I should regret would be if such ritualized conflict merely intensified an obsession with authority in the Church which has marked Roman Catholicism for centuries: a mystique of the monarchical principle countered by a mystique of the democratic principle. I do not believe Christianity is about authority.

# 5

# A Theological Critique of Experience

I can't now remember whether this title has been simply wished on me, or whether I proposed it myself a year ago. The echoes of Kant, anyway, are not significant, or significant only as a counter-example. As for 'experience', it may turn out that the slipperiness of the notion, once this is explicitly recognized, may have some advantages. At any rate, these remarks are offered in the tradition of those Christian thinkers and theologians who have been concerned about the way in which theology, reflection on Christian revelation, might find or make a place for itself in the universe of human knowledge, so far as this is organized into appropriate disciplines.

The example of this sort of reflection I have specially in mind is the account given by St Thomas Aquinas, in his commentary on Boethius' *de Trinitate*, of the relationship between the various disciplines – 'sciences' and 'arts' – acknowledged and handed on in his time, and the relationship between all these and *sacra doctrina*, the gospel tradition itself organized as a discipline. The range of Thomas's inquiry is so wide that it can count as a sort of epistemology of culture, and the epistemological integration of culture into theology. I don't want merely to indulge a wistful nostalgia by celebrating the example of Thomas, but would like to inquire into the possibility of doing the same kind of thing in what must be a very different idiom. I shall here merely mention one epistemological principle Thomas employs, if only to hint at a radical alternative to Kant, and so give myself the freedom to move in a way different from either.

Thomas's principle is basically Aristotelian. 'Sciences', knowledge organized as disciplines, are differentiated by their objects. These epistemological objects are most significantly displayed as degrees of intelligibility in the world. Thus physics is concerned with the materiality and motion of the world, mathematics more abstractly with its quantitative character, and finally metaphysics with that character of the perceptible world which it shares with a non-perceptible and purely intelligible world, namely entitative existence. This last step may be described as the sketching of a space for reflection, a space in which the perceptible world as a whole is located, and what is more, a space which is open to the gratuitous self-disclosure of God, who 'contains' this intelligible space and manifests himself in it. The 'way up' of metaphysics provides an epistemological point of entry for the 'way down' of evangelical revelation, and theology consists in the discipline appropriate to the study of ascent and descent on this twofold way.

Those who are familiar with Thomas's style will realize, and those who are not will suspect, that the latter part of this account of Thomas's views is somewhat free. But I hope I may be permitted the liberty in a paper like this, especially as I don't wish to rest any considerable weight on the exposition of Thomas, but only to use it as a device for unsettling or shifting the reader's expectations.

In fact I propose to take a different path, and offer an extremely simple statement of what might define the centre of concern for a theologian today, his permanent point of departure and his point of return, his guiding light and the pearl buried in a field, his treasure and his interior castle, his critical instance and his evangelical pulse, and the origin of his theological co-ordinates – just to vary the metaphors. My thesis is that this centre is the claim, 'Jesus is the Christ'. It is to be noted that the thesis is not merely that the statement, $p$, say, 'Jesus is the Christ', is the centre of theological concern, but that this centre is constituted by the *claim* that $p$ is the centre of theological concern. If the point of this last remark is not immediately obvious, it will, I hope, emerge in due course.

But first I propose to examine the statement itself. A great deal of what follows will be extremely familiar to anyone who has concerned himself with theology at all, and perhaps his only interest will be in assessing the way in which the statement might serve to organize what he already knows. On the other hand, someone less familiar with theology may, I hope, find some interest in an account of the sort of question theologians put themselves. Non-scientific readers of popular science rarely have the opportunity of a conducted tour of a laboratory, and perhaps scientific readers of this paper may like to regard what follows as a sort of theological Baedeker.

The term 'Christ' (*Christos, mašîaḥ*) may be regarded formally as a title, and also as bearing a definite content. As a title, it is one of a set of titles ('Lord', 'Son of Man', 'Word') applied to Jesus in the New Testament, and intensively studied in recent years. Even in the NT, it is clear that its use as title has been largely displaced by its use as proper name (cf. 'Smith'), but not to such an extent that the predicative sense of the term only yields itself to misplaced etymological zeal. In any case, the characteristic 'messianic' sense of the title, as a predicate of an eschatological saviour-figure, is not found in the OT, where the term is attributed to 'anointed' king or priest. The formal or titular sense of the term is invoked in modern theological discussions under the rubric 'The Jesus of history and the Christ of faith'. It is this discussion I have in mind in formulating the thesis-statement 'Jesus is the Christ'.

In this context, the thesis-statement asserts continuity and identity between the historical Jesus and the risen Jesus, between the Christ celebrated liturgically and Jesus who walked in Palestine. That is to say, the thesis-statement implies an intersection of history and eschatology. The difficulty of all study of the NT is that its documents are all composed by writers who in various ways testify to the intersection of history and eschatology in the personal identity of Jesus Christ, so that the whole career of the historical Jesus is seen as consummated in the manifestation of the intersection in the Resurrection. Only extremely laborious sifting of the evidence, now largely out of favour except for the purpose of discriminating the successive layers of tradition and redaction, allows of hypothetical reconstruction of the *ipsissima verba et acta* of Jesus; perhaps the only serious modern exponent of this approach is Joachim Jeremias. The thesis-statement, 'Jesus is the Christ' is claiming that although in fact there is no immediate access to what Jesus said or did, in a sense more radical than is the case with other historical figures, e.g. Socrates, yet Jesus existed historically; that is, the thesis-statement is making an ordinary existential claim as well as a peculiar one. The peculiarity of the claim is found specially in the predicate, since this predicate involves the attribution of characters at the very least 'manifested' after the Resurrection. The thesis-statement runs, 'Jesus *is* the Christ' not, 'Jesus *was* the Christ.' (Query: is the 'is' untensed, 'timeless' – 'Socrates is one of the great figures of European civilisation'; an historical present – 'Socrates is speaking to Alcibiades'; or a real present – 'Socrates is my guide in all moral matters'; or some or all or none of these?)

What I hope has emerged from this summary discussion is that the formal or titular sense of the term 'Christ' in the thesis-statement can be allowed to evoke a fundamental debate involving traditional theological topics, especially when it is realized that eschatological predicates of Jesus soon became metaphysical predicates (e.g. 'Son', 'Word'), as well as 'gnostic' predicates (e.g. 'Wisdom'). The post-Resurrection Christ attracts to himself (Jesus

Christ) the whole spectrum of religious concern in Mediterranean (and later European) civilisation.

If we consider, on the other hand, the content of the predicate 'Christ', it is clear that a whole tradition, the tradition of biblical and post-biblical Israel, is involved. I shall draw attention to just two factors here. In the first place, the Israelite tradition is a tradition about God; and secondly, it is a tradition about a God of 'will' rather than of 'intellect'.

Let us consider the implications of our relationship through the thesis-statement to an Israelite tradition about God. What is obvious is that when we assert the thesis-statement we are simultaneously activating the Israelite God-tradition and any others we have become acquainted with. The claim 'Jesus is the Christ' condenses or focuses any God-experience we may have, i.e. the whole irregular network of God-languages we might or might not be prepared to bring into play. The word 'God' has to be allowed to behave freely in *different* contexts, and to *link* these contexts, both the contexts we are familiar with and any others which we may encounter in future (this is a way of indicating the 'transcendence' of God). The 'universalism' of the post-Resurrection Christ, by attracting the indefinite variety of religious concerns, offers the possibility of indefinite interplay between the biblical tradition of God and unrestrictedly any others. The Israelite tradition continues to be privileged in this interplay, but not in an exclusive, 'henotheistic' way. Yahweh displaces the gods of other nations by critically absorbing them, so that our 'experience of the divine' (the situations in which we should be prepared to talk about 'God') can become more and more charged (we become so aware of the indefinite multiplicity of God-situations that we can only *allude* to a unifying ground of meaning).

We could formulate the theological problem of the relationship between the God-language of revealed tradition and the God-language of philosophy by asking: Are we supposed to try to unify the two ways of talking about God at a peak to which we must climb or at a common ground from which we start? Or less metaphorically: Should we look for a way of unifying the two kinds of language by trying to construct explicit connections between two diversified styles of talking, or by re-awakening our sense of undifferentiated talk, still only implicitly open to diversification?

There is another way of approaching the same problem. Biblical Hebrew contains no equivalent for the word 'nature', in the sense in which 'nature' refers to the distinct character of a thing, or in the sense in which it refers to the all-embracing order of distinctly characterized things. The NT hardly reflects the absorption into

Jewish thinking of Stoic ideas of nature found, say, in Philo. More than any other linguistic fact, this seems to me to throw a light on a fundamental Christian and European debate. Obviously neither ancient philosophy nor 'classical' science could have managed without presupposing 'nature', and modern science and philosophy can't wholly disclaim their origins. What would it be like not to want or be able to ask the question, 'What is the nature of . . .'? So we tend to ask for 'definitions' or 'descriptions' or 'models', in more or less formalized, more or less mathematical-logical ways: explicit statement becomes a goal, where 'structure' has tended to take the place of 'essence'. (The biblical question seems to be 'Why . . .', but we shall come to that in a moment). With regard to our God-problem, the relativization of the nature- or what-question just suggested seems to imply again that we might more usefully look for 'God' as the Meaning of the indefinite variety of meanings in the indefinite variety of ways we talk. That is, if we want to make 'God' into some kind of boundary-concept, we had better do this by allowing for the indefinite variety of boundaries we can draw in our talking, rather than by trying to define as narrowly as possible a boundary of one kind of talking, say, descriptive talking. How does God come to be a word at all? How do we learn to use the word 'God'? Isn't it odd that we expect to use 'God' as subject rather than as predicate, in the singular rather than the plural (compare the Nuer and the early Greeks)? Isn't this because Yahweh has absorbed Elohim?

Secondly, God as 'will' rather than as 'intellect'. We can ask the why-question so as to establish an ordered intelligible connection between means and ends in 'nature', or we can ask it of someone, 'Why did you . . .'. 'I am: that is who I am' is a refusal to provide any ulterior authorization for a purpose. In our thesis-statement, Jesus is the Christ because he is authoritatively sent and sends: 'This is my beloved Son, with whom I am well-pleased; hear him.' The *musterion* is the mystery of God's purpose, the eschatologically ultimate meaning of history. So saying 'Jesus is the Christ' involves learning to use 'God' as a way of answering a why-question, accepting an answer by surrendering to free purpose, God's 'will'. The human historical order (and importantly disorder) of choice turns out to be a better way of drawing boundaries than the 'natural' order.

This becomes instructive in a different way if we remind ourselves that our thesis-statement is made as a *claim*. We make the claim as a response to the purpose of God, to God as purpose. The response in Christian language is called 'faith', which is the way of surrendering to the purpose. But because the claim is a response of surrender to a free purpose, it posits human freedom as a paradigm case; what looks like a single choice turns out to provide the whole context for choice. The will of God – his purpose first, its normative character second – becomes the context within which human choices are assessed in the light of the crucial instance of human decision as a fidelity of communion with God. There is, I think, nothing very strange about treating the claim-character of the response of faith like this; the claim would be one of Searle's illocutionary acts, like questioning, asking, promising. But illocutionary acts imply contexts of meaning, and I am proposing that the context of the claim of faith is as much ethical as it is assertoric. The ethical order enters constitutively into the theological order posited by the claim 'Jesus is the Christ'.

It seems desirable at this point to stand back from the theological thesis proposed in this paper, and ask what general presuppositions about meaning and the order of meaning it involves. I am acutely aware of my incompetence to deal with this topic, not merely because of invincible fuzziness, but because I know in some detail what I ought to be doing and ought to have done to go a little further but what I have in fact been unable to do.

In the course of a discussion printed some years ago in the review *Esprit*, Lévi-Strauss made the following remark to the philosopher Ricoeur:

> In your article you claim that *La pensée sauvage* makes a choice for syntax against semantics; as far as I am concerned there is no such choice. There is no such choice because the phonological revolution that you have invoked on several occasions consists of the discovery that meaning is always the result of a combination of elements which are not themselves significant. Consequently, what you are looking for ... is a *meaning of meaning (un sens du sens)*, a meaning behind meaning; whereas in my perspective meaning is never the primary phenomenon: meaning is always reducible. In other words, behind all meaning there is a non-meaning, while the reverse is not the case. As far as I am concerned, significance (*signification*) is always phenomenal.

It is of no special concern to me whether Lévi-Strauss would still describe his position in the same way; what remains interesting is the opposition he discerns between, on the one hand, a view of meaning for which any instance of articulate meaning arises out of a prior, not necessarily articulate, source of meaning which as source is 'pregnantly' meaningful – a 'meaning of meaning' – and on the other, a view (his own) for which meaning is a product of a structured combination of non-meaningful elements and is sustained by that structure alone. What I should like to use this quotation for is to draw attention to the way in which 'structure' has become a primary explanatory concept. Three observations of decreasing generality may be made here.

(a) 'Structure' seems to have become the paradigm for meaning in general throughout an increasingly wide range of investigations today; at random, 'atomic structure', 'molecular structure' (in biology), 'structure of the brain' (explanation of behaviour, itself structured), the 'structure of scientific revolutions', the 'structure of community'. It seems as though it is no longer possible to characterize the search for explanation, the pursuit of meaning, except in terms of 'structure', as though one were held captive by the language of 'structure'. We may compare Wittgenstein: 'A *picture* held us captive. And we could not get outside it, for it lay in our language and language seemed to repeat it to us inexorably.' The *Bild* which held him captive was precisely picturing something very close to 'structure'. Thus it is fascinating to find David Pears, in his recent book in the Fontana Modern Masters series, describe (inexorably) Wittgenstein's philosophy in both periods as an attempt 'to understand the structure and limits of thought', in what seems to be the hendiadys 'structure and limits' (four times in this paragraph). And yet, if anything is plain in Wittgenstein's later philosophy, it is that limits need not be structured (I attempted some years ago to compare Wittgenstein's account of negation in the *Tractatus* and in the *Investigations*). For 'structures' are in principle capable of being 'mapped', and the later Wittgenstein's 'limits' of language are only ever *provisional* boundaries, capable of indefinite expansion and contraction. To talk *about* something is to provide it with a context of meaning, so I can't say what it is I can't say except by saying it. A prison with rubber walls might of course be even more intolerable than one with rigid walls, but 'prison' would be the wrong metaphor, and stretching can be a member of a group of transformations formalized in mathematics.

(b) It is of course in mathematics that the paradigm of 'structure' finds its clearest expression, especially in the so-called 'new mathematics' (by this I understand primarily *finite mathematics*, as opposed to the mathematics of the countably infinite and of analysis; as far as I can make out, the 'new mathematics' hasn't yet succeeded wholly in absorbing the others, even in topology). Mathematicians themselves can be aware of the problems arising from the nature of formal systems (I should dearly like to follow up these remarks by Lorenzen: 'Gödel proved that in order to prove the consistency of certain axiomatic theories you must have a meta-theory which is in certain respects richer than the object theory. Since then it has become the accepted style not to be critical of the linguistic means on the meta-level. If one talks on the meta-level, one normally says: "I am talking in a meta-language" – though it is all more or less deteriorated English. Now, to the best of my knowledge Gödel's proof is correct, but I have written a textbook on Metamathematics with the hidden purpose of showing that the so-called philosophical consequences which are normally drawn from it have nothing to do with it'). It seems possible in linguistics however for exponents of 'transformational grammars' to embark on elaborate procedures of formalization in which it is difficult to decide which is more extraordinary, the triviality of the results or the naivety of the presuppositions. I shall support this rash attack by only a single instance. In his own essay on 'generative Syntax' in the Penguin *New Horizons in Linguistics,* the editor John Lyons expands a formalization of lexical entries associated with a formalization of syntactic properties as follows:

> These entries may be read as 'the lexical item *sincerity* is an uncountable, abstract noun' and 'the lexical item *boy* is a countable, common, animate, human noun'.

Now I must in a simple-minded way protest that no procedure of formalization on earth is going to persuade me to describe a noun as 'human'. More precisely, if a system of formalization requires me, in order to make sense of one of its rules (not, certainly, of one of the propositions it generates), to lapse into a piece of non-formal muddle ('Ah well, I don't really mean "human" in the ordinary sense' – cf. Lorenzen's remark about 'deteriorated English' above), then there is something painfully and fundamentally wrong about at least *this* procedure of formalization.

(c) As this example shows, 'semantics' in this kind of treatment is specified in dependence on 'syntax', so that Ricoeur's appeal to a priority of semantics to syntax can be made to seem merely a technical alternative, and as such to be technically rejected. But what is odder still is that the formalized transformations which are said to exhibit the passage from 'deep structure' to 'surface structure' appear to be envisaged, by Chomsky at least, as mental operations, psychological processes, and that linguistic competence consists in the ability to perform these operations. Now Chomsky's notion of 'competence', the native speaker's capacity to generate and understand an infinite number of sentences in his own language, seems to be of fundamental importance. It was his recognition of it which led him to the distinction between 'deep structure' and 'surface structure'; what is more than dubious is whether 'competence' needs to be tied to notions of 'structure' at all. As far as I can see, the only reason for talking about 'deep structures' is that there *must be* structures as the basis of meaning, an 'inexorable' must.

What is at issue here, and brings us back to our point of departure, is whether 'structure' is not an undue restriction of notions of 'order' and 'context', which may in fact be given interpretations of a *non-formal* kind, such that 'meaning' is not held to be exclusively supported by 'structure' but to issue from a source of meaning, the 'meaning of meaning'. For Ricoeur, this source of meaning is not the 'myth' but something prior to it both chronologically and in principle. It is the 'symbol', which is 'over-determined' with potential meaning; and it is the function of hermeneutics to recover and renew this primary and primordial meaning by expounding it as a meaning *for* the expositor and his contemporaries.

Now it must be admitted that Ricoeur's notion of 'symbol' is a heavily romantic one, although he is aware of the need for 'structure' (preferably 'context') in order that symbolism should disclose meaning. While he has written a major philosophical interpretation of Freud, he relies unduly on writers like Eliade for his view of symbols as somehow lying about charged with revelatory meaning, awaiting a sympathetic expositor, though he is also aware of the function of (some) literature and art in generating meaning from symbols (cf. his good phrase about *'langage en fête'*).

The point of the foregoing discussion has been to indicate the possibility of a third alternative, for which meaning is not *primarily* either the resultant of a structured combination of non-meaningful elements, or a symbolic concretion in some absolute beginning, but primarily a praxis by which the world to which man belongs becomes the world which belongs to man. My favourite metaphor for this is *gardening*.

This process, which I have called a praxis, by which the world to which man belongs becomes the world which belongs to man, is as much social as individual, historical as natural, mythical as metaphysical. It is the generation of a behavioural environment, the constitution of a context, the integration into a culture. The 'garden' can be set up and set out at an indefinite variety of levels, with an indefinite variety of boundaries, with more or less success. If this process and praxis is called the 'meaning of meaning', the phrase is to be understood not as referring to some permanent store, treasury or bank of meaning on which one may draw as one likes (though this may be a way of referring to a tradition of constituted meanings), but of the actual conceiving and conceptualization of meaning, the exercize of 'competence'. So if we are investigating the possibility of theology, we must say that theology can only make a place or garden or space for itself not in some space or garden already projected or sketched. We must say that theology sketches a space at the origin, at that point at which praxis transfigures the world to which man belongs into the world which belongs to man; at this point at which any and every space-sketching activity originates. It is here then that theology makes its claim, allows the Cross to sketch its embracing space, and awaits transfiguration into the new aion of God.

Furthermore, on this view there can't be any fixed distinction between 'elements' of meaning and their 'structure' or context. In some projections of meaning (some gardens), elements may be set against context as its analysable parts; in others, the elements are meaningless outside the context. 'How many children had Lady Macbeth?' is a silly question, if one is attending to the play. It may be a silly question to ask what is 'represented' by a form in a painting. Some orders of meaning are structured, others not; some overlap, others don't. When we claim that 'Jesus is the Christ', we are claiming that the element 'Jesus' can be picked out as the common element of various orders of meaning; we are saying *here* that various gardens overlap. In particular, we are saying that Jesus belongs to the historical order of meaning, and that he belongs to the higher order of the meaning of meaning. We are claiming that in this higher order he constitutes a fixed and a vanishing point, to which all other orders of meaning have to be referred (perhaps one could say, with all due qualifications, that Jesus 'maps' the origin of meaning on to itself: he is *arche* and *logos*, Son of Man and Son of God).

In conclusion I have tried to suggest a way in which theology as an independent discipline might be unified or given an order of meaning, and I have tried to suggest a way in which it might be related to other disciplines by glancing at some other ways of talking about meaning. It seems finally that my end is in my beginning, in the sense that the thesis-statement 'Jesus is the Christ' only truly succeeds in unifying theology in so far as it succeeds in unifying the meaning of meaning. As in Thomas's account of theology, we need to sketch a space (a meta-space) in which God can reveal himself, a meta-space 'contained' by God and vanishing into him.

# 6

# Metaphor and Ontology in *Sacra Doctrina*

This essay is intended as a contribution to hermeneutic theology, the theology of meaning.[1] Hermeneutic theology can concern itself with any topic within the theological tradition; in this article we shall try to allow a certain conception of hermeneutic theology to arise out of the consideration of a particular conjunction in Christian theological tradition, the interpretation of Pseudo-Dionysius on the divine names by St Thomas Aquinas. For both these writers the divine names were revealed in Scripture; so the conjunction will be viewed in a perspective which refers itself to our own concern today with Scriptures, with its ramifications into matters of exegesis on the one hand and modern awareness of language on the other. Thus four hermeneutical loci mark out the general area of our concern: the Scriptures (making the large assumption here that the Scriptures can be taken as a single locus), Pseudo-Dionysius, St Thomas, and our own times (this latter in the sense of an invisible point of vision). Clearly no claim is made here to be the master, in a scholarly way, of all these fields; and while I have tried to make use of scholarship, this study is not itself offered as a piece of scholarship. Many of the footnotes, and even parts of the text, are best seen as triangulation points from which bearings might be taken; the points chosen are arbitrary but not random. By speaking of hermeneutic theology as theology of 'meaning' the intention is to appeal to the English notion of 'meaning,' which has no adequate equivalents in French or German, and which has been the theme of all sorts of reflection in the English-speaking world. If St Thomas interpreting Pseudo-Dionysius on the divine *names* is at the centre of the discussion, then the primary concern of this arti-

[1] *Hermeneutik* saw its original rise to common consciousness and eventually the commonplace in Germany, with Bultmann, Heidegger, Gadamer, and Ebeling. It is now going through a second phase in France, largely in dialogue with structuralism. As well as Ricoeur's more recent writings, see the collective work, *Exégèse et herméneutique,* ed. X. Léon-Dufour (Paris, 1971).

cle is the hermeneutic theology of meaning itself: the theology of meaning reflecting on itself as it comes to light in a particular historical conjunction.

By *sacra doctrina* we understand that 'science' which St Thomas discusses in the first question of the *Summa Theologiae*. The unity of this science is guaranteed by the uniqueness of its *formalis ratio obiecti*, the *divinitus revelabile* (art. 3): the *subiectum* of this science is God (art. 7). If we ask how the God of *sacra doctrina* is related to the God of philosophy, the answer is always clear: the *same* God is known by different lights, different *media* (art. 1, ad 2). *Sacra doctrina* is a kind of stamp, *impressio*, of divine science, and therefore has access to all that may be known (including God) in a higher or more universal way (art. 3, ad 2); and indeed it has access by revelation to God's knowledge of himself (*ad id quod notum est sibi soli de seipso*), this same God who is otherwise known by philosophers only through the created world (art. 6).

All this is familiar enough. But it may be that in spite of a great deal of scholarly work in this area we are still not quite ready enough to accept the implications of St Thomas's identification – verbally at least – of *sacra doctrina* and *sacra Scriptura*. Let us now resolutely make this identification, in the sense that 'theology' (using the term neutrally) is indeed the rational exploration and declaration of the unified self-disclosure of God in himself and in the world, *mediated by Scripture* (cf. art. 8). There are then three modes of determining the basis of theology: the infallible truth of God himself, *Veritas Prima;* the *articuli fidei;* and the canonical Scriptures. These three are modes of a single revelation. That these modes are distinguished in this way is a reflection of St Thomas's epistemological principles and again raises the question with which we are concerned in this article. *Veritas Prima* is a metaphysical expression, *articuli fidei* (= *principia*) is a logical expression, *canonicae Scripturae* is an empirical-historical expression. The unifying base of theology is determined in three modes, thought of as pretty well equivalent, though there can be no doubt that the metaphysical expression is the primary one (cf. *Summa Theol.* II-II, q.1, a.1). That is to say, even the God of revelation, the God who reveals himself, is conceived of in metaphysical terms – which is not to say that these metaphysical terms still have the same *definite* content as they would have if they were being used purely metaphysically, on the basis of philosophy alone. Because these terms are used to refer to the God of revelation, their content is *indefinite,* or, more exactly (though St Thomas does not and probably would not say so), their content is defined 'contextually', the context being the Scriptures. St Thomas can identify *sacra doctrina* and *sacra Scriptura* because he is guided, both explicitly and also, with a certain sense of the obviousness of it, tacitly, by a 'literal' determination of what God *must* be: the Being who is spoken of in metaphysical terms, terms which are now 'transferred' to the God of revelation, and yet are not 'metaphors'.

It is, of course, from this viewpoint that we must understand article 9 of the question on *sacra doctrina*: 'Utrum sacra Scriptura debeat uti metaphoris.' This article is pervasively Dionysian, as the citations would be enough to show. But an examination of St Thomas's commentary on the *de divinis nominibus* of Pseudo-Dionysius will allow us to see more clearly what basic assumptions St Thomas shared with Pseudo-Dionysius and in what ways he importantly departed from them.[2] For our purposes, the first chapter of *de div. nom.* is the most instructive. Pseudo-Dionysius insists that he draws his account of the divine names exclusively ἐκ τῶν ἱερῶν λογίων of the Scriptures (PG 3.588C; cf. 588A; Pera text nn. 8.4), and St Thomas follows him in this without hesitation:

> De eo quod ab aliquo solo scitur, nullus potest cogitare vel loqui, nisi quantum ab illo manifestatur. Soli autem Deo convenit perfecte cognoscere seipsum secundum id quod est. Nullus igitur potest vere loqui de Deo vel cogitare nisi inquantum a Deo revelatur. Quae quidem revelatio in Scripturis sacris continetur. (Pera, lect. 1, n. 13; see the whole treatment, nn. 6–21)

Now although St Thomas does contrast the *doctrina fidei* he and Pseudo-Dionysius are treating of with any merely natural knowledge (lect. 1, n. 7), he rather surprisingly makes no reference to any natural knowledge of God. St Albert, however, does see this as an objection to Pseudo-Dionysius's assertions (ed. Simon, n. 16), quoting Rom. 1.20, and deals with it by trying to show that philosophical arguments do not lead directly (*directe*) to the knowledge of God; hence the frequency of error about God in philosophy. This would hardly be St Thomas's view; on the contrary, he does allow that the same matters (*eisdem rebus*) are sometimes dealt with by philosophical theology and that theology

---

[2] The text of St Thomas used is that of Ceslaus Pera, who also supplies a revised Greek text and a Latin version corresponding to Sarracenus. A useful comparative tool is the fine edition of St Albert's commentary by Paulus Simon (Münster, 1972). For Pseudo-Dionysius himself, see the numerous writings by R Roques, in particular *L'Univers dionysien* (Paris, 1954), and his introduction to the edition of *La Hiérarchie céleste*, Sources Chrétiennes 58 (Paris, 1958). M de Gandillac's *Oeuvres Complètes du Pseudo-Denys* (Paris, 1943) is extremely useful (his translation of *CH.* in SC. 58 is thoroughly revised).

which belongs to *sacra doctrina*, under different lights (I, q.1, a.1 ad 2).

In fact, St Thomas's view is more radically 'theological' in a modern sense. Even that activity of reason which might seem in a philosophical context to be purely natural is to be understood in the context of *sacra doctrina* as operating within revelation, guided by the truth of sacred Scripture, that light which derives like a ray from first truth (*In de div. nom.* 1, lect. 1, n.15, a Dionysian text frequently quoted by St Thomas). The philosophical activity of reason is at the service of revelation and integrated into *sacra doctrina*. Now while this general statement may be accepted with some hesitations in regard to the argumentative role of the mind, there is likely to be more resistance to it once the perceptive role of the mind is considered, especially when it is directed to the created world as a source of our knowledge of God. What we have to see is the way in which for Pseudo-Dionysius, followed in this apparently by St Thomas, the *Scriptural* names of God seem to include, without any special distinction, names of God which would seem to derive immediately from created nature. There can be no doubt that Dionysius, and St Thomas after him, thought themselves to be expounding a *Scriptural* revelation of God. Thus, however remarkable it may seem to us, the vision in the Temple of Isaiah 6 is offered as an example of the way in which 'ex bonitate Dei intelligibilia circumvelantur per sensibilia, sicut cum Scripturae de Deo et angelis sub similitudine quorundam sensibilium loquuntur' (lect.2, n. 65). It is the Apostolic logia, whether by way of Scripture or also of liturgical tradition, which are held to confer symbolic and revelatory power on the sensible world. The world which is offered to our senses is made transparent by the light of verbal revelation. A list of Scriptural divine names proposed by Dionysius includes the following: good, beautiful, wise, lovable, eternal, existent, mind, intellect, powerful, as well as fire, water, cloud, stone, rock (596A; Pera n. 25). It seems that Pseudo-Dionysius, and, with some important modifications, St Thomas, see the revealed names of God in Scripture as at least sometimes doing no more than pick out a revelatory significance with which items in the created world are already charged; for the two authors there seems to be a single seamless 'veil' between our perception and the transcendent truth of God. In immediate support of this claim we may draw attention to articles 12 and 13 of I, q.12, a question dominated by the idea of the beatific vision as the culmination of all knowledge of God. Certainly by natural reason alone we cannot know of God *quid est* but only *an est*; but what does grace add to this knowledge? Only, so it seems, what can be referred to St

Thomas's standard epistemological structures: fresh *phantasmata*, a stronger *lumen intellectus* (as in the prophets), sometimes special sensible realities like the dove at Jesus's baptism (art.13). We still do not know of God *quid est*, though we have more and better *effects* from which to know of him, and by revelation can make certain new assertions, for example Trinitarian ones, about him (ad 2).[3].

It is surely not enough merely to feel some embarrassment at this account and bury it out of sight and mind. Is this, for instance, a satisfactory way of talking about the revelation of God in Jesus Christ? We must inquire more searchingly into the explicit and tacit ground for such a theological epistemology, in particular the view of language and reality it assumes.

The key-passage here would seem to be St Thomas's *Proemium* to his commentary on the *de divinis nominibus*. According to Thomas, Pseudo-Dionysius makes an 'artificial' fourfold division of what the Scriptures say about God. Firstly, there is the treatment of what bears on the unity of the divine essence and the distinction of persons. Secondly and thirdly, there is what is said of God in virtue of some likeness in created things:

> Quae vero dicuntur de Deo in Scripturis, quarum aliqua similitudo in creaturis invenitur, dupliciter se habent. Nam huiusmodi similitudo in quibusdam quidem attenditur secundum aliquid quod a Deo in creaturis derivatur. Sicut a primo bono sunt omnia bona et a primo vivo sunt omnia viventia et sic de aliis similibus. Et talia pertractat Dionysius in libro *de divinis nominibus*, quem prae manibus habemus.
>
> In quibusdam vero similitudo attenditur secundum aliquid a creaturis in Deum translatum. Sicut Deus dicitur leo, petra, sol vel aliquid huiusmodi; sic enim Deus symbolice vel metaphorice nominatur. Et de huiusmodi tractavit Dionysius in quodam suo libro quem *de symbolica theologia* intitulavit.[4]

---

[3] Cf. the excellent article by G. Ebeling, originally in *Zeitschrift für Theologie und Kirche* 1964, now translated as 'The Hermeneutical Locus of the Doctrine of God in Peter Lombard and Thomas Aquinas,' *Journal for Theology and the Church*, vol. 3 (1967), 70-111.

[4] Things predicated of God in the Bible, of which some kind of likeness is found in creatures, may be taken in two ways.

A likeness of this kind is to be noted when something in creatures is derived from God, as when everything good comes from the Good, everything living from the Living One, and so forth. Such things Dionysius discusses in the *de divinis nominibus*, the book which we have in our hands.

In other cases, the likeness is to be noted when something is transposed from creatures to God, as when God is said to be a lion, a rock, the sun, or something of the kind. In this sense God is said to be named symbolically or metaphorically. And this is what Dionysius tackles in his book entitled *de symbolica theologia*.

But because every likeness of creatures to God is deficient, we have to proceed by way of negations (*remotiones*). 'Non solum Deus non est lapis aut sol, qualia sensu apprehenduntur, sed non est talis vita aut essentia qualis ab intellectu nostro concipi potest.' Hence Dionysius's fourth treatise *de mystica theologia* (Pera, p.1). The key-text in this key-passage for our purposes is 'symbolice vel metaphorice'. We shall have to try to show briefly that the 'vel' conceals a fairly deep division between the Platonisms of Pseudo-Dionysius and St Thomas; and that both Platonisms are fairly remote from any view of metaphor, symbol, language and reality which we could comfortably hold today.[5] It may be noted that this 'vel' is taken for granted by St Thomas from his earliest writings: in the *Commentary on the Sentences*, I, d.34, q.3, a.1, obj.3 (Moos I, p. 796) we have 'huiusmodi metaphorae, vel symbolicae locutiones', where he is speaking of the Scriptures and goes on to refer to Pseudo-Dionysius (the answer to the objection does nothing to modify the language); again I, d.22, q.1, a 2, contra 2 (Moos I, p. 534).

Relying on the copious indices of Chevallier's *Dionysiaca*, it may be said with some confidence that *metaphora* occurs nowhere in the Greek or in any of the Latin versions of Pseudo-Dionysius's works. Why then does it seem obvious to St Thomas that 'symbolice' and 'metaphorice' are equivalent?

\* \* \*

(A note on Latin *metaphora*). The question is complicated by the fact that Eriugena, although he does not use *metaphora* in his version of Pseudo-Dionysius, uses it frequently in his main work, the *de divisione naturae* or *Periphyseon*. For example, we have: 'quemadmodum fere omnia quae de natura conditarum rerum proprie praedicantur de conditore rerum *per metaphoram* significandi gratia dici possunt ... non ut *proprie* significent quid ipsa (i.e. causa omnium) sit sed ut *translative* ... probabiliter cogitandum est suadeant.'[6]

Ultimately any use of *metaphora* must, of course, go back to

---

[5] I take it that my description of Thomas's perspectives as a Platonism is not unduly provocative in view of the works of Geiger, Fabro, and most recently Klaus Kremer, *Die neuplatonische Seinsphilosophie und ihre Wirkung auf Thomas von Aquin* (Leiden, 1966).

[6] Johannis Scotti Eriugenae *Periphyseon*, Liber Primus, ed. I. P. Sheldon-Williams (Dublin, 1968), p. 86, ll. 1-8; *PL* 122, 463C. My italics. Sheldon-Williams translates 'translative' here by 'by analogy'; but on the same page, 1.20 he translates it 'metaphorically.'

Aristotle, primarily *Poetica* 21 and *Rhetorica* III, 2.3.4.10.11, or *Topica* VI, 2. The Moerbeke translation of *Poet.* has *metaphora*, but it can be exactly dated to 1278.[7] The Moerbeke translation of *Rhet.* has not yet been edited, but the MSS are dated at about 1270;[8] no earlier version of *Poet.* is known, while an earlier version of *Rhet.* seems not to have been used in the schools. Quintilian's *Inst. Orat.* was certainly used and in the section *de tropis* (VIII, 6, 4) identifies *translatio* with μεταφορά. The position regarding the translation of *Top.* has recently been clarified by Minio-Paluello.[9] It now seems clear that the Boethian translation available for most of the Middle Ages is not accurately represented by the version printed in Migne, *PL* 94, which represents a revision made by Lefèvre d'Etaples. In Minio-Paluello's edition, μεταφορά is represented by *translatio* or *secundum translationem* (*ed. cit.*, pp. 115 f.). 268 MSS of this version are listed, while only three, two of them fragmentary, are known of another version printed by Minio-Paluello and ascribed by him to an anonymous author of the twelfth century. In this version we have *metafora* and *secundum metaforam* (*ed. cit.*, pp. 256 f.), although both versions have *transferentes, transferunt*, for μεταφέροντες, μεταφέρουσιν (140 a 10-11) in the text cited by St Thomas, 'Omnes enim transferentes secundum aliquam (anonymous version 'quandam') similitudinem transferunt.'[10] In what is almost an exact parallel to St Thomas's use we find in St Albert's little treatise on the Trinitarian names of God, where he is discussing Pseudo-Dionysius,: 'In alio (libro) tangit de his quae secundum translationem, quod ipse *symbolum* vocat, de Deo dicuntur, et de hoc facit symbolicam theologiam'. (*In I Sent.*, d.22, A, *Ad aluid* (5); Borgnet XXV, pp. 567b-8a. Compare *Ad ultimum* (6), p. 569b: 'Duplex est translatio, scilicet secundum rem, et secundum nomen. Translatio secundum rem in divinis nominibus non est nisi in symbolicis.')

---

[7] Ed. A. Franceschini et. L. Minio-Paluello, *Aristoteles Latinus* XXXIII (Bruges-Paris, 1953), pp. 26 f.; p. vii.

[8] *Aristoteles Latinus*. Codices descripsit G. Lacombe et al. (Rome, 1939), pp. 77-8.

[9] *Aristoteles Latinus* V. 1-3 (Leiden, 1969).

[10] *De Veritate*, q. 10, a.7 obj. 10. In the new Leonine edition, vol. XXII, 2 p. 315, the text from *Top.* is referred to one of the MSS. consulted by Minio-Paluello for his edition of the Boethian version. Readers of M. D. Chenu's fascinating chapter on 'The Symbolist Mentality' in *La Théologie au douzième siècle* (Paris, 1957), translated in *Nature, Man and Society* (Chicago, 1968), will realize that a great deal of the above is dependent upon (and revises) the footnote n. 1, p. 186 (French), n. 73, pp. 138-9 (English), where the *de Veritate* reference is wrongly given in both versions, and the Boethian authorship of the *Top.* version is glanced at.

Without claiming any great authority in this matter, I feel bound to conclude that St Thomas could make such free use of his equivalence *symbolum* = *metaphora* in theology because he could rely on a general familiarity among the thirteenth-century Paris masters with the so-called 'Dionysian corpus,' containing a very large number of texts from Eriugena's *De div. nat.* among the scholia attributed to Maximus.[11]

\* \* \*

Whatever may be the position regarding the Latin use of the word *metaphora*, we can be certain that it does not adequately represent the Dionysian idea of symbol. It is true that Pseudo-Dionysius makes a significant distinction between the names proper to symbolic theology and those which belong to the intelligible order, which he treats of in the *de divinis nominibus* (597 A, B; Pera nn. 27, 28). In the former group he refers to the divine manifestations (θείων φασμάτων) in temples and elsewhere, illuminating initiates (μύστας) and prophets so that they name the transcendent good according to its diverse powers and causalities and attribute to it human forms and figures as well as other μύστικά, mysteries. But a little earlier Pseudo-Dionysius discusses the way in which the 'theologians,' the sacred writers, praise God as beyond all names; and precisely by way of a 'symbolic theophany,' ἐν μίᾳ τῶν μυστικῶν τῆς συμβολικῆς θεοφανείας ὁράσεων (596 A; Pera n. 25). The Latin version St Thomas is following here has 'in una mysticarum visionum Dei apparitionis,' which Thomas strikingly amplifies to 'apparitionem divinam *imaginativam*' (Pera. 96). Dionysius's 'symbolic theophany' has become Thomas's 'appearance in the imagination'.

It is extraordinarily difficult to pin down a single definite sense in which Pseudo-Dionysius speaks of symbols. He is not, of course, interested in such a definite sense; his writing is incantatory in style and requires of the reader that he commit himself to the way of *anagoge*, ascent: Dionysius is a mystagogue.[12] However, we may say that his valuation of symbols depends on whether they are being treated of on 'the way up' or on 'the way down': whether, that is to say, they are being treated of apophatically (*via*

---

[11] See H. F. Dondaine, *Le Corpus dionysien de l'Université de Paris au XIIIe siècle* (Rome, 1953); also the chapters 'L'Entrée de la théologie grecque' and 'Orientale lumen' in Chenu, *La Théologie au XIIe siècle*.

[12] On Pseudo-Dionysius's dependence, in language and ideas, on the Neo-Platonic tradition of the mysteries see, e.g., de Gandillac's note to his translation of *CH.*, ed. SC, pp. 71-2.

*negationis*) or kataphatically (*via affirmationis*). But this distinction of modes of theological consideration itself depends on a prior ontological distinction: the procession of things from their source (πρόοδος) or their ascent and return to it (ἄνοδος, ἐπιστροΦή, St Thomas's *conversio;* cf. *CH* 1,1; ed.SC, pp. 70f.).

On the 'way down' symbols are valued positively and participate (deficiently) in the ontological fullness of their source: 'We must not despise them (the sacred symbols) for they are begotten of the divine characters and bear their stamp, manifest images of ineffable and sublime spectacles' (*Ep.* IX; *PG* 3, 1108 C). Again, the symbols used by the ecclesiastical hierarchy, when they celebrate liturgical rites, are valued positively (*CH* 3; ed.SC. p. 72-3). But there can be no doubt that just because the way of ascent to a transcendent mystical union beyond words is the dominant movement of Pseudo-Dionysius's thought, symbols tend to be valued negatively. This occurs in the special form of a recommendation of 'dissimilar similitudes,' which are less likely to mislead the initiate on his way up than those similitudes which partially convey the richness of their source (*CH* 2, 3; ed.SC. p. 77 f.). Certainly Dionysius recognizes that even the most vile and inferior likenesses still resemble their source by participating in it (*CH* 2, 3; ed.SC p. 80).

It is here that a modern reader is most acutely aware of an ambiguity which does not seem to have made itself felt to Pseudo-Dionysius himself, and which is partially solved by St Thomas's equation of symbol and metaphor. On the one hand, Dionysius is quite aware that his symbols are the product of human creation. In one place he even speaks of the 'holy poetic fictions' (ταῖς ποιητικαῖς ἱεροπλαστίαις, *CH* 2, 1; ed.SC p. 74), and in *Ep.* IX he gives as an example of the function of symbols for the 'passionate' part of the soul the way in which some hearers of unveiled theological instruction fashion in themselves some figure (ἀναπλάττουσι τύπον τινά, 1108 B) so as to help themselves to understand the pure theological teaching.

On the other hand, in the lines immediately preceding this last reference, Dionysius says that the 'impassible' part of the soul is destined for 'simple and interior spectacles of deiform images' (θεοειδῶν ἀγαλμάτων). The word *agalma* has a long and interesting history going back at least to Plato;[13] the basic sense is 'image', 'statue,' 'object of religious veneration'. For Dionysius, the celestial hierarchy makes of its followers perfect images, *agalmata,* of

---

[13] *Phaedrus*, 252 D; *Timaeus* 37 C, with F. M. Cornford's commentary, *Plato's Cosmology* (London, 1937), pp. 99 f.

God, stainless and transparent mirrors (*CH* 3, 2; ed.SC p. 88). Pseudo-Dionysius belongs to that whole archaic tradition of thought about symbols and images which finds in them the embodiment of the reality they are meant to express.[14]

It seems likely that for Pseudo-Dionysius symbols belong to the same conceptual world as ikons, which although made by human hands are invested by consecration with the presence of a divine reality.[15] Thus symbols, whether words or rites, are 'fictions', constructed by the sacred writers or ministers, and yet they communicate ontologically *with* the divine reality by participation and communicate this reality *to* the initiate. The gap between 'symbol' in this sense and St Thomas's 'metaphor' is striking. We may perhaps say, simplifying somewhat, that for Pseudo-Dionysius symbols belong to a single continuous hierarchical chain of ontological participation, which includes cosmos, hierographer and hierophant, and initiate. For St Thomas, the symbol (=metaphor) has become partially detached from this chain and is treated by the theologian as a product of the human mind, although sacred writer and theologian still belong to an undivided cosmos of divine creation. Pseudo-Dionysius's practice, of course, is pregnantly symbolic; St Thomas's is almost bare of metaphor.

What, for our purposes at least, distinguishes the whole medieval tradition, from Eriugena to St Thomas (and beyond), is an interest in language, grammar, rhetoric, and logic.[16] The procedures of human articulation have become the object of independent study, and the whole grasp of the world is mediated by an analytical consciousness of the linguistic modes of that grasp. Here we are primarily concerned with the particular form this analytic

---

[14] For a discussion of patristic usage, see interestingly J. Betz, *Die Eucharistie in der Zeit der griechischen Väter*, I/1 (Freiburg, 1955), pp. 217-39. Also F. W. Eltester, *Eikon im Neuen Testament* (Berlin, 1958). A modern attempt to exploit this notion of symbol, K. Rahner, 'The Theology of the Symbol,' *Theological Investigations* IV (London, 1966), pp. 221-52. Cf. the articles on 'Bild' in RAC, RGG, LTK.

[15] St Thomas is acquainted with this use of language. See his remarks in the prologue to the question on oaths, II-II, q. 89, where he speaks of the 'assumption' of something divine for worship, whether this *aliquid divinum* is a sacrament or *ipsum nomen divinum*. But this is not the theologian's use of language.

[16] See the stimulating book by Marcia L. Colish, *The Mirror of Language* (New Haven, 1968). It is a pity that, in spite of some perceptive criticism of modern 'metaphysical' interpretation of analogy, she goes so badly wrong on St Thomas, failing to distinguish the analogical analysis of predication from the recognition of, say, Trinitarian 'analogies' in the soul. Pseudo-Dionysius gets a passing mention, p. 169. More general treatments, still of great value for the non-specialist: H. I. Marrou, *A History of Education in Antiquity* (London, 1956); E. R. Curtius, *European Literature and Latin Middle Ages* (London, 1953).

consciousness took in St Thomas's mind, in particular his account of the divine names.

The passage from the *Commentary on the Sentences* mentioned earlier (*I Sent.* d. 34, q. 3, aa. 1-2) is of considerable interest here. We should bear in mind, while reading these articles, Chenu's extremely perceptive remarks when he discusses 'the mental operation proper to symbolism':

> namely, *translatio*, a transference or elevation from the visible sphere to the invisible through the mediating agency of an image borrowed from sense-perceptible reality. This is what we mean by 'metaphor', except that here the term had a particular orientation; metaphor was obedient to the necessities imposed by transcendent realities, above all in pseudo-Dionysian theology....
>
> Twelfth-century masters made ready use of the term *translatio;* but its inadequacy led them to transliterate its Greek equivalent into *anagoge*, as Latin versions of pseudo-Dionysius had already done. (*Nature, Man and Society*, p. 138)

*Translatio* then can bring together what we should understand by 'metaphor' and by 'ascent to the transcendent'. So when Thomas takes up the *translative* from Lombard's text and questions it, he is firmly within a tradition for which *translatio* meant not only 'transference' within a single order of reality, but also, and indeed primarily, 'transference' from one order or reality – sensible and material – to a higher order of reality – intelligible and immaterial. Hence Thomas's remark (art. 2 ad 3) that names, such as 'cherubim', expressing a limited mode of intelligible perfection, cannot be applied to God even 'metaphorically': *quia metaphora sumenda est ex his quae sunt manifesta secundum sensum.*

But still more interesting from our point of view is Thomas's reply to an objection from the *Topics* (the text quoted above as it appears in *de Verit.*, q. 10, a. 7 obj. 10) and Boethius, where it is argued that no *similitudo vel metaphora* can be taken from the sensible world to be applied to God *translative*. Thomas distinguishes in his reply between two sorts of likeness, *similitudo*: that which obtains by participation in the same form, and *quaedam similitudo proportionalitatis,* as for instance 8: 4 as 6: 3. This latter sort of likeness allows of *transumptio ex corporalibus in divina.* So God can be called 'fire'. As fire makes liquescent things flow by its heat, so God pours out his perfections in all creatures by his goodness ('vel aliquid huiusmodi,' he says, rather offhandedly!).

The language of 'proportionality' comes we know from Euclid.[17] Still from the early period of St Thomas's teaching, we have a parallel distinction of *similitudo*, here referred by Thomas to *Top.* I.[18] The corpus of the article has contrasted the two ways in which names can be predicated of God analogically: one *symbolice*, where the usual 'metaphorical' names are given as examples; the other where no defect is included in the definition of the principal *significatum*. The notion of 'proportion' in metaphor occurs in *Rhet.* (e.g., III, 4; 1407 a 14, τὴν μεταφορὰν τὴν ἐκ τοῦ ἀνάλογον), but its most detailed treatment is found in *Poet.* 21; 1457 b 16-33. As we have seen, St Thomas probably had no direct knowledge of this treatment of analogical or proportional metaphor. But it is deeply interesting that from his earliest writings his account of 'symbolic' or 'metaphorical' names predicated of God should be formulated in terms of a four-term 'proportion' or 'proportionality'. The same account occurs, of course, in I, q. 13, a. 6.

The reader need have no fear; we are not about to embark on yet another examination of the 'doctrine of analogy'. In fact, a subordinate concern of the present article has been to relativize what seems sometimes to have been an obsession on the part of commentators, who have extracted St Thomas's remarks on this topic and used them to pile up enormous metaphysical constructions: towers of Babel, one might suggest, since in general the 'doctrine of analogy' is not placed in what we have tried to present as its proper context, namely, the revelation in Scriptural tradition of divine names, transmitted and interpreted in particular by Pseudo-Dionysius. It is only when this context is appreciated by the modern reader that he can recognize St Thomas's originality within the tradition, and also perceive its limitations.

The originality consists firstly in the formal application of Aristotelian epistemology to the 'symbolic' tradition of divine names. St Thomas's preference for *metaphora* rather than *translatio* would seem to indicate a sharper awareness of the human conditions of talk about God. Thus he begins his treatment *de nominibus Dei* in I, q. 13 with a general account of the genesis of the word: 'Secundum Philosophum, voces sunt signa intellectuum, et intellectus sunt rerum similitudines. Et sic patet quod voces referuntur ad res

---

[17] Cf. B. Montagnes, *La Doctrine de l'analogie de l'être d'après s. Thomas d'Aquin* (Paris, 1963), p. 76, n. 23, 'Note lexicographique sur la distinction *proportio-proportionalitas*.'

[18] *De Verit.* q. 2, a. 11 ad 2. *Top. I,* 17; 108 a 7-16, wrongly referred in the Marietti edition to *Top.* II; I have not been able to consult the new Leonine edition of the early questions of *de Verit.*

significandas, *mediante conceptione intellectus*' (art. 1). We have to note that this crucial shift of perspective – from words as *logia* to words as human products – involves an entire analytic procedure; for what is now analysed is explicitly 'names' as *predicates*. That is to say, we have both a (metaphysical) psychological epistemology and a logical epistemology, the latter benefiting from the tradition of 'grammar' in theology.[19] While Thomas's account of *modi significandi* is not strikingly original, it is interesting to note that, according to Pinborg (p. 42), his view allows greater freedom to the creative activity of the mind. What is certainly true is that St Thomas stands for a demythologization of the word, some of the consequences of which in later times he could hardly have expected. The full consequences of Thomas's recognition of the human creation of the word are still contained for him within an archaic order; for even the human word is still related by *similitudo* to the cosmic world, and thus to the pure perfections deficiently represented in that world.

Here it seems desirable to stand back from St Thomas for a moment and place his views in a wider context. We need perhaps do no more than mention the critique of the exclusive analysis of propositions into subject and predicate by logicians who have been concerned to analyse the propositions of mathematics.[20] More important for our purposes are the implications for an account of metaphor of abandoning the assumption that metaphorical assertions are primarily the application of predicates. If we recall the famous description of Shakespeare's later plays by the critic G. Wilson Knight as 'extended metaphors' we may see how the notion of metaphor-predicate is much too narrow to do justice to metaphorical language. Given our ordinary literary use of 'metaphor', it is only by 'extension' (by 'metaphor') that we can call an entire play a metaphor; but just this extension of 'metaphor' surely draws attention to the important truth that metaphor only functions as such *within* a given human 'world',

[19] Cf. the chapter 'Grammaire et Théologie' in M. D. Chenu, *La Théologie au douzième siècle*, pp. 90-107. The earlier version of this chapter, in *AHDLMA X* (1935-6), carries the discussion on to the thirteenth century. The introductory portions of the basic book by J. Pinborg, *Die Entwicklung der Sprachtheorie im Mittelalter* (Münster, 1967), and of the essay by H. J. Stiker, 'Une théorie linguistique au Moyen Age: l'école modiste,' *RSPT 56* (1972), pp. 585-616, offer summaries of grammatical theories, up to the time of St Thomas, in regard to the treatment of *modi significandi*.

[20] For a modern (favourable) discussion of 'Subject and Predicate,' see the chapter by that title in P. T. Geach, *Reference and Generality*, amended edition (Ithaca, 1968). This might be the place to mention the interesting book by M. Durrant, *The Logical Status of 'God'* (London, 1973), though it deserves more than a mention.

where tacit assumptions as to what counts as 'literal' prevail. The play as a whole can count as a metaphor when it is set over against the ordinary world of our everyday habitation; and the 'local' metaphor of a particular act of speech or writing is a 'play' in detail – a 'play of speech'. Metaphor belongs not to isolated propositions but to entire 'language-games'; in fact, the particular metaphor always involves more than just the given statement with its claim to represent a given state of affairs (*Sachverhalt*).[21] Thirdly, we may consider Sir Edward Evans-Pritchard's reflections in the chapter 'The Problem of Symbols' in his classic account of Nuer religion.[22] The characteristic of Nuer thought about 'God' is that, while their God-term *Kwoth* is predicated of all sorts of things and events, it is rarely that anything is predicated of *kwoth*. Evans-Pritchard analyzes the predication of *kwoth* in terms of a general formula: 'the problem of something being something else'. In connection with our second observation in this paragraph we may note again that metaphorical language *in divinis* cannot always be assumed to consist of predications about God but that we need to take into account the whole language-game of the linguistic community ('tribe') and its 'world', a world which cannot be unambiguously identified apart from the linguistic community which contributes to its manifestation.

Now, of course, St Thomas must insist that it is in fact possible unambiguously to define the world, to speak about it *proprie*, literally; and so to argue that in some cases at least it is possible to speak *proprie* about God. Here again his originality needs to be recognized so that we may at the same time recognize its limitations. Briefly, St Thomas both takes for granted and establishes his own presupposition that the literal sense of language (and we may say the literal sense of the world) can be unambiguously defined in metaphysical terms. Even God can be spoken of *proprie*, not *aequivoce*, because of a similitude of participation between creatures and God which can be in certain cases extracted from the creaturely *modus essendi* by an appropriate negation of the *modus significandi* of our language. The 'certain cases' are those in which

---

[21] The use of Wittgensteinian language of the later ('language-games') and earlier (*Sachverhalt*) periods is deliberate. It is a pity that Marcus B. Hester's *The Meaning of Poetic Metaphor* (The Hague, 1967) has tried to 'amplify' Wittgenstein by introducing a notion of 'seeing as' involving 'mental images.' I cannot refrain from mentioning what seems to be Hester's extraordinary mis-reading (pp. 25-6) of Hopkins's lines 'O the mind, mind has mountains,' where he seems to suppose that Hopkins is relying on a mental image of the *brain!*

[22] *Nuer Religion* (Oxford, 1957). Reviewed by the present writer in *Blackfriars* (December, 1957), pp. 524-8.

materiality or corporeality is not inseparably part of the *modus essendi* or *significandi*.

For St Thomas the world manifests itself as a dualism of spirit and matter, even where the dualism is manifested in substantial unity. Thus it is possible to lay down conditions for 'proper' or 'literal' talk about God in two stages: (1) in general, 'proper' and 'metaphorical' language can be unambiguously distinguished; (2) in particular, proper and metaphorical language *about God* can be distinguished unambiguously on the basis of the dual manifestation of the world. The consequences of this twofold distinction are obvious throughout the writings of St Thomas, not only in his explicit use of the distinction (e.g., I, q. 19, a. 11 on *voluntas signi* and generally to exclude 'anthropomorphisms') but in the way in which a Scriptural or other authoritative text, say in a *sed contra,* is expounded metaphysically in the *corpus articuli,* without any apparent sense of hermeneutic discontinuity. The process is most clearly to be seen in the Scriptural commentaries, which throw a great deal of light on the way in which Thomas saw his own world of interpretation rise without rupture out of the Scriptural world (reminding ourselves of the 'seamless veil' of symbols mediating revelation of God through Scripture and the cosmos). We may compare this lack of sense of rupture to that with which modern readers can comfortably use 'existentialist' language to interpret the Scriptures.

Behind St Thomas there is, of course, a long tradition, especially in regard to the 'anthropomorphisms' of the Bible. Consider, for example, Philo's astonishing exegesis of Gen. 17.1, 'I am thy God', where he insists that this is an abuse, or at least a licence, of language ($\kappa\alpha\tau\alpha\chi\rho\eta\sigma\tau\iota\kappa\hat{\omega}\varsigma, o\dot{\upsilon} \ \kappa\upsilon\rho\iota\omega\varsigma$).[23] The Existent ($\tau\dot{o} \ \ddot{o}\nu$) 'is full of himself and is sufficient for himself.... He cannot change nor alter and needs nothing else at all, so that all things are his but he himself in the proper sense belongs to none' (*De Mut. Nom.* 4, 27-8, tr. Colson and Whitaker, *LCL* V, p. 157). There are however certain 'potencies' ($\delta\upsilon\nu\acute{\alpha}\mu\epsilon\omega\nu$) which can be spoken of in a sense as relative; one such is 'the creative potency called God, because through this the Father who is its begetter and contriver

---

[23] I take this reference from the deeply interesting book by U. Mauser, *Gottesbild und Menschwerdung* (Tübingen, 1971), p. 27. Philo is discussed pp. 23-28. Relying on the impressive and moving account of the divine *pathos* in Abraham Heschel's *The Prophets* (New York, 1962), Mauser sets out to show how the 'anthropomorphism' of God and the 'theomorphism' of man in the Old Testament find their key and consummation in Jesus Christ and are further exhibited in Christian life, especially in the 'suffering Apostle'. H. Corbin, *Creative Imagination in the Sūfism of Ibn 'Abrabi* (London, 1969), finds *pathos* in Islam.

made the universe'.²⁴ Again, the whole point of Maimonides' *Guide for the Perplexed* is to resolve the apparent contradiction between philosophy and religion. 'Human reason has attracted him (the religious man) to abide within its sphere; and he finds it difficult to accept as correct the teaching based on the literal interpretation of the Law, and especially that which he himself or others derived from those homonymous, metaphorical, or hybrid expressions' found in the prophetic books.²⁵ Judaism and Christianity have shared the same tension between a certain metaphysical determination of what is to count as literal, and the metaphorical expressions of the Scriptures.²⁶ This ('Platonist') metaphysical determination of what is to count as literal is not, of course, the only one. An alternative version is analysed with great power by Michel Foucault for the seventeenth and eighteenth centuries in Europe,²⁷ and this version, condensed in the notion of 'facts', has continued to be influential in both explicit and implicit ways; recently it has been revived in the sophisticated form of the mathematical theory of 'models', another avatar of *similitudo*.²⁸

This article has attempted to disentangle some of the implications of St Thomas's 'symbolice *vel* metaphorice', especially in a theological context. The consequences of such an exploration may seem to indicate that he has very little to offer us today except a purely historical interest. The whole tradition of interpretation of Scripture to which he unmistakably belongs is obviously archaic,

---

²⁴ *Ibid.*, p. 159. Cf. *Quod Deus immutabilis sit*, 5, 20-6, 32; 11, 51-14, 69, for a further treatment of anthropomorphisms. Philo himself stands in a tradition. For the Septuagint, see the chapter 'Names of God' in C. H. Dodd, *The Bible and the Greeks* (London, 1954). An interesting example of LXX interpretation in the area 'knowledge of God' is found in Exodus 33.13, quoted by Philo, *de Mut. Nom.* 2, 8. On the names of God in the Psalms, see the excursus (4) to Ps. 24 in H. J. Kraus, *Psalmen* I (BK XV/1) (Neukirchen, 1960), pp. 197 f., with its indication of Canaanite formulae. See also the articles *'ēl*, *'ĕlōhīm* in Jenni-Westermann, *Theologisches Handwörterbuch zum Alten Testament* I (München-Zürich, 1971), and in *Theologisches Wörterbuch zum Alten Testament* I (Stuttgart, 1971). For the tradition prior to Philo, see the magisterial work by M. Hengel, *Judentum und Hellenismus*, 2nd edn. (Tübingen, 1973).

²⁵ *Guide for the Perplexed*, 2nd edn. (London, 1936 (1904), tr. Friedländer), p. 2. See especially Pt. I, chapters 46 f. St Thomas, of course, refers to Maimonides (*Guide*, I, 58) in I, q. 13, a. 2 to criticize his views but in the same tradition.

²⁶ For Islam and the Qur'ān, as well as the standard treatment by Gardet and Anawati, see the useful small book by W. Montgomery Watt, *Islamic Philosophy and Theology* (Edinburgh, 1962).

²⁷ *The Order of Things*, ET (London, 1970).

²⁸ See, e. g., the appendix by Rolf Eberle to Colin Murray Turbayne, *The Myth of Metaphor*, revised edition (Columbia, South Carolina, 1970). Turbayne seems to use the phrase 'extended metaphor' to mean 'model' – an interesting alternative to Wilson Knight's usage taken over in this article.

although his own equivalence of 'symbol' and 'metaphor' suggests in germ the emergence of an acosmic humanism which is still with us. St Thomas contains the humanism within a metaphysical and hierarchical subordination of all being, including the being of interpreting mind, to God.[29] It is here precisely that I should want to claim for St Thomas more than historical interest, in the sense that his approach to the problem of theological interpretation of Scripture has laid down what I take to be an inescapable requirement for theologians of any epoch: that their interpretation must exhibit the ontological primacy of God, God as the ultimately really real. How may we do this today when we seem no longer to be in command of a criterion, metaphysical or other, for unambiguously distinguishing the 'literal' from the 'metaphorical'? Is 'God' a literal or a metaphorical expression? The whole of the present article has tried to lead up to this question in a theological context. It would require something much more substantial than an article to begin to answer it and what follows may be regarded merely as programmatic notes.

To begin with the simpler aspects of our problem, we may say that the context in which 'God' is used will tell us whether the expression is intended literally or metaphorically; the texture of the context can be roughly discriminated. Ordinarily by this rule 'God' – 'ēl, 'ĕlōhīm, *theos* – will have to be called a metaphorical expression in its Biblical context, as compared to its use in philosophical contexts. Of course, this conclusion must make one feel uneasy; in fact, our ordinary reading of the Bible is, I suspect, universally dependent on the assumption that 'God' there is somehow literal. Now that we are more accustomed to reading 'Yahweh' in our Bibles than 'the Lord' ('ādōnay, *Kurios*), we need to feel, for instance, that the identification of 'God' and 'Yahweh' is doing more than claiming the same reference for two names, say, 'Julius' and 'Caesar'. In fact, what this means is that we *cannot* read the Bible without interpreting it ('as literature'), that we *must* have some prior understanding of 'God' in order to make sense of

---

[29] I am sorry not to have been able to discuss in this article the interference of Pseudo-Dionysian and Augustinian Platonisms in St Thomas, especially the historico-temporal and eschatological orientations of the latter. I cannot refrain from referring to Thomas's treatment of the ceremonial precepts of the Old Law, I-II, q. 99, a. 3 ad 3 with q. 101, a. 2, where *similitudo, metaphorica locutio,* and *figura* are simultaneously at play. In beatitude, the expressive role of the body in praising is not 'figurative,' *non consistit in aliqua figura*. Note also the shift to pure allegory from the 'pregnant' symbolism of *imago* in III, q. 83, a. 1 corp., and ad 2. On allegory, see the remarkable book by Angus Fletcher, *Allegory: the Theory of a Symbolic Mode* (Ithaca, 1964), especially the chapter on 'Psychoanalytic Analogues'.

the Bible. But can that prior understanding of 'God' be called *literal*? Our ordinary contexts for 'God' (prayer, ritual, even swearing) are ways of life and behaviour which are discriminated from ways of life and behaviour which are tacitly identified as everyday and which count to make the language which belongs to them 'literal'. The point of the Five Ways was to show how one might *go on* speaking of 'God' in the ordinary world – *et hoc omnes dicunt 'Deum'*. What if or when the Five Ways no longer perform this function? Does one start looking for other 'ways'?

Obviously other 'ways' must be looked for, though hardly in the sense of 'proofs'; even for Aristotle and St Thomas the notion of *demonstratio* is more complex than the usual sense of 'proof' (cf. the *Posterior Analytics* and St Thomas's commentary thereon). The most plausible 'way', it seems, is the exploration of the genesis of meaning, understood as the manifestation of the real. The significance of this 'way', in the present context, is that it is *prior* to any conventional discrimination of 'literal' and 'metaphorical'. It would, I believe, render more adequately our intention when we speak of God or to God to understand 'God' as also prior to any distinction of literal (whether or not analogical) and metaphorical. The later writings of Heidegger[30] are the most important exploration of this 'way' known to me, not least because they can be seen in continuity with the ontological interpretation of the divine names in Catholic tradition, notably by St Thomas.

Finally, this 'way', reaching beyond the distinction of literal and metaphorical, allows Jesus to show himself as the centre of the revelation of God (thus 'Jesus' as the fulfilment of 'Yahweh'). This is not merely a matter of the words of Jesus, his parables, for instance, though we can recognise in them instances of what we have called above, with Wilson Knight, 'extended metaphor' – whole 'plays' rather than predicate-metaphors.[31] Nor again is it only a recognition of the background in apocalyptic without which the figure of Jesus becomes unintelligible in its New Testament setting.[32] Nor, yet again, is it a matter of the actions of Jesus, say his 'parabolic' actions, healing or presiding at the Last Supper; though it is important that we should see the seamless continuity of those actions, in a total behaviour which cannot be divided into 'everyday' actions and 'religious' actions, corresponding to 'literal'

---

[30] Some of the most interesting essays are collected in a remarkably successful translation, *Poetry, Language, Thought*, by Albert Hofstadter (New York, 1971).

[31] See J. Jeremias, *The Parables of Jesus*, revised edition (London, 1963), especially the discussion of the introductory Aramaic 1ᵉ, not 'like' but 'as in the case of', pp. 100 f.

[32] See K. Koch. *The Rediscovery of Apocalyptic* (London, 1972).

and 'metaphorical'. To see Jesus as the centre of the revelation of God is all this and more, something for which a distinction into 'sensible' and 'intelligible' could not possibly do.

We want to see Jesus as someone who walked in Galilee and Jerusalem, who from the originating source of meaning in himself, prior to a literal-metaphorical distinction, was and is the supreme and unique revelation of God, beyond distinctions of meaning. We want to see his whole life, culminating in the Resurrection, as the revelation of ultimate meaning. If by 'meaning' we may provisionally understand the process or praxis by which the world to which man belongs becomes the world which belongs to man, then we may see a man's life as transformation in and of meaning, a 'metaphor' beyond metaphors. In the Resurrection, the world which belongs to man becomes the world which belongs to God; the Resurrection is the ultimate 'metaphor' of the world, its translation and trans-figuration. This seems to make better sense of the Johannine *logos;* for it is important to insist that what is at the end is also in the beginning. Jesus is the 'way'.

These concluding remarks are enough, it may be felt, to suggest what might be involved in surrendering St Thomas's metaphysically based distinction of literal and metaphorical in theology, while trying to retain a version of ontology, here an ontology of meaning. We need perhaps in our own times what St Thomas was in his:

The impossible possible philosophers' man,
The man who has had the time to think enough,
The central man, the human globe, responsive
As a mirror with a voice, the man of glass,
Who in a million diamonds sums us up. (Wallace Stevens,
   *Asides on the oboe*)

I hope it will not seem too unpleasing a paradox to celebrate St Thomas in a metaphor.

# 7

# Theological Methodology

## Principles

*A. Preliminaries*
Various expectations are likely to be aroused by this title. In English it may suggest that general questions are to be discussed concerning the status of religious propositions from a viewpoint which need not be that of Christian faith, or even where it is, would not be chosen with traditional Catholic distinctions, say, of natural and revealed theology in view, but rather discussions concerning the validity of religious statements considered as forming a class alongside the classes of empirical and poetic statements. This article is concerned with the epistemological structure of ecclesial theology, and takes for granted at least the existence of a continuing tradition of systematic theological articulation of the gospel in the Catholic Church.

Clearly theological epistemology consists in a reflection upon theology considered as an autonomous intellectual discipline or 'science'. So long as the scientific character of theology in general, or indeed the specific scientific procedures familiarized by tradition or custom, were not in question, it was possible for a treatise of theological epistemology to take shape and lead an independent existence, even generate its own conventional disputes, without reference to questions of general epistemology, or even to theology itself. It is commonly the case that treatises on methodology at best rationalize inventive intellectual procedures already being practised, or more often simply ossify these procedures in a theoretical structure long after they have ceased to be practized or even relevant. Treatises of this irrelevant kind are still being written in our day by Catholic theologians (which is the only reason for mentioning them), after the closed world of Catholic theology has been notably breached by new creative theological thinking, by intensive investigation of some areas of the history of theology and the pressures of secularization. These latter pressures are intensifying, and should be welcomed insofar as they force Catholic theologians to reconsider the nature of their task of communication with the world, and in particular the structure of theological meaning.

The acceptance of a necessary division of labour, then, must not be taken to prejudge the question as to whether a different approach to theological epistemology may not be more in accordance with a world in which traditional categories are increasingly being revised. Such an approach would not be able to assume in advance the theological distinctions delivered to it by tradition, but would have to adopt a critical role in regard to them. For in the most general terms, the task of theological epistemology, like that of theology itself, is to establish communication between Church and world, in such a way that the internal ecclesial perspectives open out upon and are open to perspectives which emerge immanently in the course of a secular history to which the Church's theology, and revelation itself, provide no immediate key. Theology is an encounter of Church and world in which the meaning of the gospel becomes articulate as an illumination of the world; and the exploration of the structure of this meaning in theological epistemology must itself be the continuing actualization of such an encounter.

No such ambitious claim is made for this article, above all because the new movements in theology make it too difficult to practise that reflexive role of a methodology which consists in making and correlating maps of territories already explored by others. This metaphor is already a simplification, for it transposes into the spatial order a problematic which is temporal and historic; now it is in this latter order, as we shall see, that the theological problem itself today becomes increasingly explicit and that the solutions begin to take shape.

We shall assume, then, in what follows, that there is a 'special' theological epistemology and methodology concerned with the reflexive analysis of theological structures of meaning delivered to us by a continuing tradition of theology practised in the Church, and it is only by implication and on particular topics that we shall take into account problems of meaning and knowledge in general. This special theological epistemology, then, will share with all theology the double *a priori* of ecclesial faith, which will serve as its internal dimension, and in the external dimension proper to all theology it will be concerned to authenticate the claim of theology to intellectual autonomy while assuming without detailed discussion its claim to be 'intellectual' at all, i.e., to propose meaning and truth. That is to say, the basic question as to whether theological statements mean anything *at all* will not be discussed here.

## B. The Internal Dimension of Theological Epistemology

Reception of the Church's continuing tradition of theology is a matter of faith. This is not of course to say that every proposition in every theological system is an object of faith; but faith is a presupposition of insight into the meaning of these diverse theologies, of understanding that they are unified in the object or the realm of their concern; very simply, that they are trying to talk about the same things. This is a point of some importance now that we are more ready to admit the existence of plurality and even profound discontinuities within the single continuing tradition. It is no longer seriously possible to offer an anonymous handbook, however large, and call it simply 'Catholic Theology'; it was not long ago that even Karl Barth, with some justification, seemed to suppose that this was so. Communion, ordinary or extraordinary, in the Church in faith, offers access to a universe of meaning, not open to those who reject this communion. So the Church as a continuing historical institution, and its active spiritual communion of faith together form the double *a priori* of theological meaning. This ecclesiality of faith is of course realized in different degrees, while in all degrees tending by an inner impulse to the union of communion; and the continuing validity of the expression 'Catholic theology' is due to the self-defining activity of the Church from time to time in excluding theological articulations of faith declared not to be Catholic: the *positive* unity of Catholic theology is not itself capable of exhaustive theological articulation but is the one *reality* of God, Christ, the Church. The Catholic theologian accepts this power of the (hierarchically structured) Church community to define itself and its authentic witness, with respect to what it is not, in such a way that the *a priori* of ecclesial faith for a Catholic theologian can be partially exhibited in a series of historical monuments which are moments of the Church's explicit self-definition. The Catholic theologian's world of meaning has fixed points which are themselves meaningful and not just ineffable though these points do not fall into a systematic order among themselves, do not exhaustively display the *a priori* of ecclesial faith, and are ultimate only in the simultaneous alternatives they exclude (i.e., they are open to interpretation within perspectives which are not their own).

Now this faith is not merely the immanent life, in part explicit and in part implicit, of a historic community and a culture in which men creatively bring their own meaning to light. The unifying sense of the whole world of meaning accessible in faith is transcendental disclosure of this meaning to and for men: intrinsically, communication to men of meaning as gift. In the traditional theological terminology, this is the dimension of the theological world of meaning which is called revelation or gospel. The meanings entertained and exchanged in this community inform the community – not only in its language but also in its conduct, its institutions, its rites, its art and music – in such a way that, while remaining human meanings (this will be examined when we look at the external dimension of theology), they are in principle capable of unification not in any human meaning, but only in an ultimate meaning, the Meaning of meaning, God. Further, this ultimate Meaning has declared itself historically as Word made man, Logos and First of many brethren, Son of God and Son of man; and in doing so has associated with this figure in human history other men who would scripturally embody in their witness to him the eschatologically ultimate character of this self-declaration of Meaning. This self-declaration is an $ἀρχή$, an absolute beginning. It is the beginning of the gospel (cf. Mark 1.1; Luke 1.2; John 1.1), which is permanently present in the communion of faith, permanently recoverable as spring and source in the meanings entertained and exchanged in the community. The scriptural deposit of the primitive multiplicity of meanings of the one $ἀρχή$ is continually made present by informing new complexes of human meaning; in its own unity in multiplicity (the 'theologies' of the NT (and OT) writings) it offers a pregnant instance of the nuclear character of the complexes of ecclesial meaning. For every explicit Catholic life is a 'theology', a project and a declaration of the Meaning of Catholic meanings; and theology as 'science' and autonomous discipline can only reflect upon this lived meaning by being itself an instance of lived meaning.

*C. The External Dimension of Theological Epistemology*
The Word which unifies the multiplicity of Christian meanings is offered to us through those meanings not only for our consent (or refusal) but also for our assent (or denial). At one and the same time it invites us, by our consent and assent, to depart from where we are (cf. Gen. 12. 1) to find ourselves in some 'higher' or 'deeper' truth, to ascend the degrees of the 'ontological comparative' (Fink) to find ourselves 'in the Truth', 'in Christ'. Perhaps it is only in the formal system of modern mathematics and logic that truth is reduced to the display of the internal consistency of axioms and postulates; but even here there is the possibility of 'applications', as in the part played in information theory by the 'truth-

table' systematization of the naive Yes-No, assent-dissent, character of human statements. At any rate, both the Yes-No character of statements and their claim to 'significance', to depth of truth, are prominently and actively present in theological statements.

In this section we shall be concerned with the human dimension of theological meaning and its twofold truth, especially insofar as this meaning has been deliberately given structure by the reflexive activity of a theologian's mind. Just because the primitive NT witness to the ἀρχή, itself assumed into the ἀρχή, is language and articulate at all, it is not only 'revelation' but also 'theology', since the gospel, no matter how communicated, is proposed to us as human communication, ordered and unified by a human mind. Even the synoptic gospels, as has been clearly shown in recent years, are not just collections of narratives and *logia,* but each exhibit a unifying constructive intention proper to the evangelist. But even if we had nothing but random collections of sayings and narratives of isolated incidents, there would still be implicit in them a comprehension of the world. In the Pauline texts in particular, it is possible to analyse the constructive and supporting function of concepts available in Hellenistic civilization, and in the Johannine writings one can learn to overhear the resonances of a variety of pursuits of the divine at the end of the first century integrated by John into a concentration of meaning in the Word made flesh. But John is not only a poet of Jesus; as theologian *par excellence* he is at least as insistent as any NT writer on the exclusive and decisive character of his witness in the rejection of false teaching.

The Pauline and Johannine testimonies provide us with two very different styles of theological 'construction', both deriving from and referring to the same ἀρχή (compare John 1.1–18 with Col.1. 15–20, and again Heb.1. 1–4). We may study even in that human meaning which is revelation a human evolution and amplification which continues to be revelation. The rediscovery and appropriation of the *literary* complexity of the NT writings is the absolutely primary prerequisite of any theologizing today if we are to overcome the split between 'exegesis' and 'theology' and avoid certain misguided forms of 'biblical theology' (neither biblical nor responsibly theological) due to the uneven growth of the Catholic mind for many centuries. For the diversification of meaning in creative literature, and its inner integration there into a complex unity of insight and comprehension help us to understand diverse possibilities of organization in the biblical literature. To recognize that saga, gospel, and novel are different literary genres should not mean that we must forget the novel when we study saga or gospel.

It is also through a sense of the insights afforded by creative literature that we can best appreciate the historicity of the NT witness, its character as *Ereignis,* illuminating event. The special significance of literature here is that unlike plastic art and music, it retains not only the invitatory aspect of truth, the appeal to traverse the degrees of the depths of being, but also a continuity with those pragmatic or empirical uses of language which emphasize or isolate its Yes-No aspect. It is this Yes-No or propositional-logical use of language which has dominated Catholic theology for centuries until our own day. Both the dialectic and logical grammar of early scholasticism and the newer 'scientific' logic of Aristotle's *Posterior Analytics* in classical scholasticism helped to construct a theological world in which meaning was articulated as argument and not as insight. The effect of this one-sidedness may still be seen today in textbooks for theological students, ordered in the form of theses to be proved or defended (see, for example, a certain modern French series). Even if syllogistic demonstration is no longer thought to be the normal or the ideal mode in which to manipulate all meaning or manifest all truth, there still seems to be some uneasiness about wholly abandoning a theological style which prized clarity and decisiveness above exploration in depth.

This uneasiness has its real justification. As we have seen, the Church community has repeatedly had to establish its own identity by a process of self-definition involving exclusion. The revealed truth of God has an identity *in* the world. The offer of truth to the Church and by the Church is not only an invitation to ecstatic vision but it also defines the way to that vision. The truth of the Church's witness is still human truth and as such finite; what it excludes is not nothing, for only all-inclusive, infinite Truth could have only nothing to reject. But in this 'ecumenical' age of the Church we have learned to exclude from within, as it were, by taking up into Catholic truth whatever has its rightful place there, by fulfilment rather than anathema. No Catholic theology then can afford to abandon argumentation and the precision which it demands; yet exclusive emphasis on this Yes-No character of truth, and still more, its syllogistic style, would impoverish theology unduly. After all, there seems to be no lack of dispute and controversy in other disciplines, such as history and letters, which do not lay down such artificial standards of rigour; and such disputes are not always about nothing. As has been seen in the theology of the development of dogma, a theory of the amplification of meaning by syllogism alone has the most pernicious effects. In our own times the problems of missionary adaptation and more generally of the communication of the gospel to a new and changing world have made it necessary to take more seriously the complexities involved in the exchange, amplification, translation and reintegration of meaning.

It has appeared in what has been said that the construction of a theological structure of meaning is bound to employ methods which are at least similar to those employed in other disciplines. In the investigation of Scripture, for instance, it must practise the ordinary techniques of historical and literary criticism; explicit logical theory can at least serve as a negative check and an instrument of analysis; the justification of particular propositions may remind us of the procedures by which decisions are arrived at in law, thereby bridging the gap between procedures of verification in theology and in the natural sciences. The question arises whether there is anything uniquely characteristic of theological method in the construction of theology. We may take as our point of departure Collingwood's useful distinction between a proposition as a mere statement and that same proposition as an answer to a question. Certainly this distinction serves to show the interest of the commonest of the scholastic procedures: the use of the *quaestio* as a technique of exploration by interrogation first of conflicting authorities and later of conflicting chains of argument as well. Every theological statement can be put to the question simply by putting it in interrogative form: *utrum*.... As an answer to a question the proposition has a new epistemological status as part of a *structure* of meaning. The questions now arise as to the proper sources of the meaning which is so structured, the nature of the structure, and the perspectives which sustain the structure.

The question of the proper sources of theology as an autonomous discipline has already been touched on under *B*. Here it is only necessary to inquire into those complexes of meaning through which revelation is communicated, in regard to the possibility of ranking them according to some principle. Where theological structure is held to be strictly demonstrative, the complexes are ranked according to their probative force as *loci theologici*. Thus a sort of general theological criteriology can be set up, sometimes pretending to a high degree of refinement, as in the elaboration of theological qualifications. The manifest artificiality of an excessive refinement sought after more for its own sake rather than for the benefit of theology itself should not blind one to the general importance of this discussion (e.g. What exactly is the status of various papal pronouncements on contraception? What difference is made to Mariology as a whole by the definition of the Assumption as a dogma?). Yet as soon as we remember that the original complexes of meaning are not merely isolated items waiting to play their part as arguments in the structure of a demonstrative theology but have their primary value in diversely mediating revelation in a historic process of communication, then we must critically examine the idea of a theological structure of meaning which could tend to distort revelation in this way. In the classical moment of Latin theology it was possible for St Thomas Aquinas, more decisively than any of his contemporaries, to determine the structure of theology as an Aristotelian science, in which the articles of faith, dependent upon the divine vision itself, served as principles for the body of actual or potential theological conclusions which could be drawn from them. It may be observed that St Thomas's actual practice, like Aristotle's own, was fortunately a good deal less rigid than his epistemological theory. The science of theology was seen as another form of the single *sacra doctrina* delivered to us by the (glossed) Scriptures; but this mediation was conceived of as taking place through the summary of the Scriptures in the Creed, such that wherever Scripture dealt with historical particulars not enunciated in the Creed, it had merely illustrative or supplementary value. Once again, fortunately, St Thomas's practice was much more generous and genuinely historical than this theory. But in the last resort it is an archaic theory of meaning and of language which supports both the theory of probative arguments and the theory of theological structure as an Aristotelian science: the theory that meaning is accessible and manipulable only in the form of essentialist concepts. In spite of the considerable sophistication of medieval logical grammar, in spite of St Thomas's own developments of this grammar in an ontological sense in his theory of analogy, the theory of meaning implicit in all scholastic theology is dominantly 'ontic', tied to the specific natures of the cosmic world. Concepts, in St Thomas's epistemological theory, are still 'similitudes' of natures; historical meaning is not genuinely meaning at all, for it is only in the generality of the concept and of 'science' that meaning can be authentically realized.

Thus a critical examination of the presuppositions of the epistemology of scholastic theology leads us to reconsider both its theory of the original complexes of meaning and its theory of the adequate and appropriate structure for that meaning. But before making some suggestions of our own, we must further consider the perspectives which sustain the structure of meaning in a more than logical sense. This is the question of the 'hermeneutic locus' of a theology discussed by Protestant theologians like Fuchs and Ebeling. In simple terms, any theology which is to be more than biblicist, a mere rearrangement of biblical themes, must adopt general perspectives within the horizon of which complexes of meaning acquire mutual significance. In St Thomas's theology, for instance, such a perspective is supplied by the order of creatures to the Creator as *principium et finis,* Origin and End. St Thomas himself mentions another perspective, the whole Christ, which has been taken up in our own day, as seeming to offer a more biblical schema, and there have been many rather naive attempts, since the first shock of Darwinism died away, to adopt the schema of generalized evolution, as by Teilhard de Chardin. It would be a mistake to regard the adoption of a generalized theological perspective as a matter of detached and deliberate choice. The perspective must present itself with the ultimate obviousness which only the sense of an epoch can supply. Certainly this must be so if the theology is to speak to men of its time and to provide a context for continued theological debate. But the fundamental ground for the articulation of the perspective must lie deeper than the individual theologian's own conscious and reflexive mind; he must be guided by a kind of prophetic insight into that order of relevance which is taking shape in history under the sway of Providence. Such a perspective, appropriate to the epoch into which we are moving today, might be provided, we suggest here, by the schema of God as the Meaning of meaning. This is in fact the perspective within which this article has been written.

### D. Concluding Remarks and Prospects

The notion of a theological epistemology, as we have seen, is itself historically conditioned, as indeed is the notion of a general philosophical epistemology. There is a 'family-line' of investigations to which the (primarily 19th-century) notion of epistemology belongs, and whose lineal descendants today form the family of investigations into meaning: Heidegger, Wittgenstein, Merleau-Ponty, Gadamer. This work of philosophical reflection was preceded and is today accompanied by an 'ontic' preoccupation with meaning in such diverse fields as linguistics, existential analysis, behaviour studies, social anthropology or ethnology, and literary criticism, to name only a few. The search for identity in the new nations of the post-colonial era, in a tension between traditional religions and new technology, is a preoccupation with the redefinition of meanings. The personal search for the 'meaning of life' has to be conducted within the transcendental horizon of the question of the meaning or truth of Being and its historicity. If we reject the God 'out there', we must equally reject the God 'in here', and learn to put the God-question as a search for ontological meaning.

These general reflections are intended to support the suggestion that the reformulation of theology taking place in our time demands a corresponding reformulation of theological epistemology. If the schema of God as Meaning of meaning is accepted as a possible perspective for theology, and thus as a possible formula for 'natural' theology, our view of the complexes of theological meaning and their structural reintegration in an autonomous theological 'science' can no longer be governed by an archaic theory of meaning. Theology, while continuing necessarily to practise the onto-theo-logical mode in which its formulations have been uttered historically, must become explicitly aware of its own existence as a kind of meta-theology; the theological epistemology corresponding to this meta-theology would be an explication of the 'meta', the dimension of this meta-theology in the historical process of ontological meaning. We may ask, but only from our 'epistemological' viewpoint, what such a meta-theology would look like, since it seems that there are only anticipations of it today.

It would certainly involve the 'destruction' of all previous theologies and their 'recapitulation' in a history of meaning which is also a history of being. This would even include the revealed biblical 'theologies', although these would continue to retain their privileged place in the history of theological meaning. The considerable body of work which has been done in recent years on the history of theology is an important first step towards this 'destruction', but too little of it has faced up to the real ontological problems involved in this apparently historicist relativization. We have to ask what is the *meaning* of this historic succession of theologies (and of the sterile repetition of unimportant variants), and we have to ask this question not within a presupposed perspective of any one of them but ask it radically as part of *the* theological problem of the meaning of God and man for one another. The substantive ('ontic') answer to this question we already have in Jesus Christ, and can have no other. It is the ('ontological') meaning of this substantive meaning we must continually search for without expecting any final answer. Thus the ἀρχή of this meta-theology would be the λόγος – εἰκών – μυστήριον τοῦ θεοῦ, the Word-Image-Mystery of God, the divine Wisdom, ἁγία σοφία. How could this ontological meaning become articulate? What 'structure' could it have in a single mind? In fact it could only exist as a total human culture, the progressive discovery of a single human identity in Christ as the historic process of the diverse but related processes of self-discovery going on in distinct cultures all over the globe in response to the challenge and threat of a uniform technological mass-culture. There is at least a single discernible adversary, not to be subdued by the mere repetition of traditional truths,

Christian or other. The individual theologian could only make contributions to such a theology-as-culture, and only possess it as his own 'culture' according to his own capacity, and not as a *Summa*.

The cultural 'structure' of such a metatheology is as much or as little a *logical* unity as a song or a smile. It is a comprehension of the depth of meaning or truth in the affirmation of particular truths; it is a standing fast in holiness, a 'Thy will be done'. It passes into music, the inarticulate, into silence. At the same time, precisely because this theology is concerned with the ontological dimension of truth in its cultural structure or organization, it will need to proceed dialectically, by exclusion as well as affirmation, to the inclusive truth of humanity in God. Thus its historic destiny is to 'make known through the Church the manifest wisdom of God' (Eph. 3.10) in that process by which God 'recapitulates all things' (1. 10) in Jesus Christ, the ontological meaning and identity of the multiple history of man.

# 8
## Holy, Holy, Holy

### I

> There was life outside the Church. There was much that the Church did not include. He thought of God, and of the whole blue rotunda of the day. That was something great and free. He thought of the ruins of the Grecian worship, and it seemed, a temple was never perfectly a temple, till it was ruined and mixed up with the winds and the sky and the herbs. (D. H. Lawrence, *The Rainbow,* Phoenix edn., p. 203.)

Will Brangwen has taken his wife Anna to Lincoln Cathedral, which is described with a surcharged sensuous religiosity through Brangwen's eyes. But Anna resists the 'dazed swoon' of the cathedral: she wants freedom, open space, she brings the cutting edge of her separate individuality to bear on Brangwen's passionate intercourse with the cathedral. Brangwen is bitterly angry, hurt, disillusioned; he has lost his absolute, he sees his cathedrals now as 'a world within a world, a sort of sideshow, whereas before they had been as a world to him within a chaos'.

An architectural work, a Greek temple, represents nothing, images nothing; it simply stands there in the valley's rocky cleft. The building encloses the form of the god, contains it and yet allows it to emerge from this containment to stand forth in the sacred precinct through the open colonnade. Through the temple the god makes himself present in the temple. This active intelligible presence of the god itself describes and delimits the precincts as holy. But the temple and its precinct do not shimmer away into the indefinite. The building knits and assembles into a unity all those courses and relationships in which birth and death, misfortune and blessing, victory and shame, perseverance and failure, acquire the form and the direction of human destiny. The valid range of these open relationships is the world of this historical people. Here it recovers and realizes it vocation. (M. Heidegger, 'Der Ursprung des Kunstwerkes', *Holzwege*, p. 31).

The temple is the point of focus in which rock and storm, night and day, space and sea, become manifest; it is a work in which the coming forth and subsiding of things – *physis* – is revealed. In the temple-work, the building, there comes to light the pregnant containing source of all things, the Earth. The work exhibits not by being put in an 'exhibition' but simply by being erected at all, a consecration and a praising in which the holy becomes radiant and the god is invoked to shine forth in an intelligible presence.

Then I saw a new heaven and a new earth; for the first heaven and the first earth had passed away, and the sea was no more. And I saw the holy city, the new Jerusalem, coming down out of heaven from God, prepared as a bride adorned for her husband.... And I saw no temple in the city, for its temple is the Lord God the Almighty and the Lamb (Apoc. 21.1-2, 22).

The whole complex reality of Christian cult may be envisaged as a destruction of the temple. What is involved in this destruction is indicated in the statement attributed to Jesus by 'false witness'; 'I shall destroy this temple made with hands and in three days I shall build another, not made with hands' (Mark 14.58). At least one false element in this testimony is the suggestion that Jesus himself was to destroy the temple; but the Christian reader is invited to discern a deeper misunderstanding. In the Johannine 'sign of the temple', Jesus says: 'Destroy this temple, and in three days I will raise it up'. The evangelist continues, 'But he spoke of the temple of his body' (John 2.19, 21). There is a hidden connection between the destruction of the Jewish temple and the crucifixion. When Jesus dies on the cross, the veil of the temple, between outer and inner sanctuaries, was torn in two from top to bottom (Matt. 27.51). In the Epistle to the Hebrews, at the end of a comparison between the rites of the Mosaic temple and the crucifixion, we are told of the new and living way opened to us 'through the veil, that is, his flesh' (Heb. 10.10), by which we may enter into an inner sanctuary not made with hands but heaven itself before the very face of God (9.24). The way is made open in the crucifixion, and kept open in the living flesh of the risen Christ, who is the Way. Thus the Church, united with the glorified body of the risen Christ, living in the power of the *Pneuma*, is itself the temple of the living

God (1 Cor. 3.17; 1 Cor. 6.16 f.); a spiritual house of living stones, a holy priesthood offering spiritual sacrifices to God through Jesus Christ, the living corner-stone or key-stone (1 Pet. 2.4 f.); a dwelling place of God in the virtue of the Spirit (Eph. 2.20 f.). So too is the individual member of the Christian community, whose 'body' is the temple of the holy Spirit, and who must then with his body glorify God (1 Cor. 6.19–20).

The destruction of the temple is the eschatological fulfilment of the reality of the temple, in the risen Christ and in the members of his body. During the interim until the new heaven and the new earth take the place of the old, this temple-reality of Christian cult is displayed in pregnant signs and images, an adoration in spirit and truth expressed in the tangibility of flesh. In his treatise on the sacraments St Thomas speaks of the *religio Christianae vitae* (3a. 62.5), the religion of the Christian *life.* The signs contain and communicate a sacrificial reality consummated in Christ (*consummatum est,* John 19.30), the Lamb who was slain (Apoc. 5.12), who is our temple.

II

An approach to Dr Robinson's now famous little book[1] by way of the theme of cult and worship seemed not only appropriate for this periodical but also likely to bring us to the heart of the matter. For an attempt like Dr Robinson's to rethink and reformulate the Gospel as an experience of God into which we today, as men of our time, could enter with whole mind and heart and body, must prove itself in the concrete gestures of that experience, in its embodied and incarnate sense. Let me first say (and I am all the more anxious to say it in view of other things I shall have to say) that I wholly endorse Dr Robinson's *right* to attempt a reformulation and wholly sympathize with what he himself, in his reply to the Archbishop of Canterbury's strictures, has called his missionary purpose. And for that reason I appreciate his intentions in publishing his views in popular, paperback form. The real point at issue is whether what he says is true. If it is, his honesty is laudable; if it is not honesty would be no excuse, since all it would offer us is something about Dr Robinson and those who share his views.

It would be comforting if in his chapter 'Worldly Holiness' on Christian worship and prayer Dr Robinson had stated unequivocally whether he held that this worship had an *object.* I am bound to

---

[1] *Honest to God,* John A. T. Robinson, Bishop of Woolwich; SCM Press, 1963.

say that after repeated re-reading I am still not quite certain of his position; but it seems likely in view of his whole approach that he would probably reject the question as 'supranaturalist', since the only object of worship would be a God 'out there'. In this a position which can be tolerated by Christians?

The Heidegger passage cited above is a striking example of an 'objectivity' of the sacral arising from a human *work*. The god is ultimately a form of the 'Earth'; and we may remember Zarathustra's words to the men in the market-place, shortly after he has declared that God – the God 'out there' in a Platonic heaven – is dead: 'You are the sense of the Earth.' The Earth as pregnant source of all things would seem to correspond very closely to Dr Robinson's (and Tillich's) 'depth', especially since it is not merely a cosmic but also an anthropological depth; the very act of positing the human work, the building, is at once an objectification of the depth and an act of praise; the human act is a medium of revelation.[2] Certainly it is a more adequate expression of what may be Dr Robinson's theme than the rather tedious vulgarized Freudianism of 'projection'. For Dr Robinson cannot have it both ways; if the God 'out there' is to be dismissed as a Freudian 'projection', then his 'depth' must be given its Freudian interpretation too: some sort of libido, perhaps, however this is conceived of.

But even supposing we improve on Dr Robinson in this way by indicating a less merely 'psychological' relationship between 'object' and 'depth' (or supposing our psychology goes Jungian rather than Freudian), could Christian theology be satisfied with a God thus objectified for worship? It must be said quite plainly that

---

[2] It may be interesting to plot some family-relationships here. Dr Robinson's chief sources are all Germanic: Bonhoeffer, Tillich, Bultmann. In his prison letters Bonhoeffer writes with enthusiasm of W. F. Otto's *The Homeric Gods;* Otto (W. F., not Rudolf) belonged to Heidegger's circle, and a later collection of essays by him has the significant title, *Die Gestalt und das Sein.* Tillich often quotes Nietzsche with approval; and Heidegger has an important study of Nietzsche's 'Gott ist tot' in *Holzwege,* and more recently has produced a two-volume collection of studies on him. E. Fink, who once studied under Heidegger, has a fine book on *Nietzsches Philosophieren,* as well as a remarkable study, *Spiel als Weltsymbol,* on the Dionysiac reversal of a Platonic 'beyond'. Bultmann's Heidegger has admittedly no more than a family-relationship with the Heidegger of *Sein und Zeit,* and an even more distant connection with the later Heidegger, but family-relationships are what we are looking at here, not interpretation. Heidegger is the major contemporary representative of a movement of German thought since Hegel; see e.g., K. Löwith, *Von Hegel zu Nietzsche. Marx und Kierkegaard,* or J. Hommes, *Zwiespältiges Dasein.* Feuerbach, of whom Dr Robinson makes use, has an important place in this movement. It seems possible that Dr Robinson does not wholly realize how potent a beast he is trying to domesticate and Anglicize.

if the 'depth' or 'ground' is nothing more than Heidegger's *physis* – a *natura naturans*, a cycle of eternal return – then at most we have an illuminating but partial account of the symbiosis of man and nature in history, the 'deep', the authentic form of which would be, in Blake's words: 'Everything that lives is holy.' The Christian God cannot be simply the 'inwardness' of the universe: he is the infinitely separate (separate precisely because *non-finite*) originating source of the universe, such that by being cause of the very being of things, that being which is most inward in all things, he works inwardly in all their operations (*ipse Deus est proprie causa ipsius esse universalis in rebus omnibus, quod inter omnia est magis intimum rebus; sequitur quod Deus in omnibus intime operetur,* Ia. 105.5). That the theophanies of such a God should be mediated by human intercourse with the natural world is entirely acceptable; for such a God could only become object to man either by a human 'work', in a religion untouched by Christian revelation, or by a divine 'work', in the Incarnation.

By a 'work' is understood here any modification of the physical world, a human or divine 'intervention' in that world. Objectivity is not an intrinsic character of anything, not even in the physical world. In order that any reality in the physical world may become an 'object', it must become an object-for-me, or an object-for-us, by being assumed into a world of human purposes and intentions. A 'work' is one such mode of objectification by assumption, where a physical reality is made to embody a human purpose; and at least in the case of an art-work (on Heidegger's view) and often elsewhere, the human purpose may reveal in the work the reality of what is assumed into the work, e.g., we learn about horses by racing them in the Derby. Now because God is not just one thing among others but rather the subsistent cause of everything, he cannot be brought to objectivity simply by being assumed into a human world. He can only become a Thou for us by way of some distinct reality in the physical world which in its turn is capable of being assumed into a human world. Either we build temples in which we make manifest to ourselves the originating source of all things (the source of our own act of making manifest too); or God himself 'enters' our world by so operating in the physical world as to make himself manifest to us: at Sinai, in the prophetic vision (for the prophet himself belongs to the physical world), or ultimately in the Incarnation. God himself builds the temple of Jesus' body. That mode of objectification which depends solely on our own act (God working within us *intime*) only presents God to us as an 'internal' or 'cognate' object, like fighting a battle or winning a victory; we use our own acts as mirrors to see the God behind our backs. In the Incarnation, God 'assumes' the physical world and makes it his own in Jesus *before* we 'assume' it into our human world; the Jesus we greet is not a mirror but a window on to God the Father in the Son: 'He who has seen me has seen the Father' John 14.9). And here too God works within us by the interior *instinctus* of faith (2a-2ae. 2.9 ad 3).

One of the reasons why it is so difficult to be sure about what precisely Dr Robinson is trying to say is the hearty facetiousness with which he rejects the God 'out there'. That this rejection does involve 'questioning the existence of God as a *separate* Being' (p. 130; his italics) is clear. But perhaps all this means is, 'God is not outside us, yet he is profoundly transcendent' (p. 60). It often seems as though for Dr Robinson to call God 'separate' from the world is to say that he is spatially alongside it. He appears not to make any very sharp distinction between 'metaphysical' and 'mythological' (pp. 14–15). He quotes with approval passages from Tillich (pp. 30, 31, 55–6, 57) which on the one hand embarrassingly mis-state traditional Christian theology (when has God ever been talked of by this theology as 'a being beside others', 'an object besides other objects'?), and on the other hand identify God with *natura naturans,* reject the cause-effect separation of God and creatures, and explain that to call God transcendent means that 'within itself, the finite world points beyond itself', that it is 'self-transcendent'. Points *where*?[3] Or does it just point, so that the transcendence of *God* is nothing more than the *world's* manifestation of its own finitude? So that the only real transcendence is the indefiniteness of being-in-general (*esse commune*) and not the wholly actualized transcendence of subsistent being (*esse subsistens*), the infinitely actual source of all beings? We may with Heidegger reject this latter transcendence and maintain only the transcendence of *das Sein* with respect to *das Seiende*; but then let us be honest and reject God too.

Perhaps it is unfair to press Dr Robinson on these points; but he does raise them polemically himself, and he does offer what is apparently an alternative metaphysical view in talking repeatedly about the 'ground' (or 'Ground') of our being. It is curious to reflect that this way of talking goes back to Eckhart, where the *grund* of our being is just that mysterious depth in which God and the soul are 'one'; and that this was one of the points which rightly led to suspicion of his views. The very least that can be said is that

---

[3] It is typical of the Existentialist 'dropping of the object' that verbs which ordinarily take objects, direct or indirect, are continually used absolutely; cf. 'give ourselves to the uttermost', p. 49 – give to whom?

we did not have to wait for Tillich to tell us that God was not 'out there' in a spatially objective sense (we may also remember Augustine in the *Confessions* III, 6: *Tu autem eras interior intimo meo et superior summo meo*). If Dr Robinson's 'ground' is not distinct from that which it 'grounds' then he is a pantheist; if it is distinct, then he is shadow-boxing. The real trouble is that the reader cannot be sure just what Dr Robinson means, and suspects that Dr Robinson isn't sure either.

In a final attempt to clarify his position (pp. 130 f.) Dr Robinson sets out to 'demythologize' the traditional notion of the creator:

> The essential difference between the Biblical and any immanentist world-view lies in the fact that it grounds all reality ultimately in personal freedom – in Love.

This sounds promising: God is Love, personal freedom. We read on, with some slight misgivings:

> For pantheism, the relation of every aspect of reality to its ground is in the last analysis a deterministic one, allowing no real room for freedom or for moral evil.... But the Biblical affirmation is that built into the very structure of our relationship to the ground of our being is an indestructible element of personal freedom.... We are rooted and grounded wholly in Love.

This may be a profound statement that our finite human freedom is only intelligible within God's free purposes. But we remember what has been said earlier on the same page (p. 130) about the 'agape of the universe' and earlier in the book (pp. 48–9) that 'to say that "God is personal" is to say that "reality at its very deepest level is personal", that personality is of *ultimate* significance in the constitution of the universe, that in personal relationships we touch the final meaning of existence as nowhere else'. It is not clear whether our freedom, our love, our personal relationships, are simply the privileged medium in which we can discern God as the personal freedom and love of an other than ourselves, or whether by 'God' is meant just this and nothing else: that *we* are free, loving, and personally related to each other, that *we* communicate with each other in freedom and love. Dr Robinson certainly rejects as 'myth' the idea of the 'personal ground of all our being' as 'an almighty Individual, endowed with a centre of consciousness and will like ourselves and yet wholly "other" ' (pp. 131–2). Is God *other* or isn't he? Is God the 'significance', the 'depth', the 'ground' of our freedom in the sense in which 'significance' is embodied in a sign or in the sense in which 'significance' is embodied in the reality signified by the sign? Is God like 'London' on a signpost or like *London*, the city on the Thames? Does Dr Robinson hold that without the universe there would be no God? The question cannot be shrugged off as meaningless on the ground that (say) if the universe did not exist we would not be able to ask the question. Because the *Christian* affirmation is that what the universe, what Christ, point to, is just this holy God who created us in the freedom of his love, who would be free, would be love, would be *God*, even if we and the whole universe had not been created. I am afraid I cannot accept the responsibility for my lack of clarity about Dr Robinson's meaning. It is painful to see a Bishop of the Church of England shift uneasily in ambiguities like these, and it is comforting to see how promptly and unequivocally the Archbishop of Canterbury has responded in his pamphlet *Image Old and New*.

I have used for the title of this review the *Trisagion* of Isaiah 6 (a text which is sufficient by itself to show up the truly deplorable onesidedness of Dr Robinson's remarks about the Hebrew prophets, pp. 60–1). The introductory texts in section I were intended to focus a concern for the character of our relationship to God as Holy. For this after all is crucial: does Dr Robinson's book really help us to see God more clearly, does he help us to realize more sharply the holiness of God?

This is to take up the question of 'Christianity without religion', as advanced by Bonhoeffer and recommended by Dr Robinson. Dr Robinson does not make matters easier for us by delaying his discussion of what he means by 'religious' until p. 84, and only acknowledging in a footnote on p. 86 that much of the discussion for and against 'religion' is a matter of definition. When Bonhoeffer himself first raises the topic in his *Letters* (paperback edn p. 91) he equates 'religion' with 'inwardness and conscience'. Dr Robinson seems to mean by 'religion' *piety,* conventional piety primarily, though not excluding the possibility of intenser forms of personal piety within the conventional mould: devotionalism and genuine devotion. The passage from Lawrence quoted above magnificently opens up a larger perspective, no less than the 'whole blue rotunda of the day'. It is true and will be true until the Lamb himself becomes our Temple, that human temples, even Christian temples, need to be destroyed so as to share in the death and resurrection of the Temple of the Lord's Body. Simply as liturgical renewal, this means that we must invent, make new 'works', to manifest our participation in the new life of the Lord. For the temples have to be built new, after being destroyed. But just as there must persist through this renewal a continuity with the Temple of the Body and the basic gestures consecrated by that Body, so in the whole of human Christian life the rhythm of death and resurrection must continue to sound. The very grace-life in us is a conformation to the death and resurrection of Christ; it is cult and worship, because that death and resurrection is cult and worship. That this cult has both a 'horizontal' and a 'vertical' dimension is clear from the whole New Testament. In Hebrews, for instance (5.9): 'And once made perfect (*consummatus, teleiotheis,* probably 'consecrated') he became the source of salvation to all who obey him.' Or in what since the sixteenth century has been known as the 'highpriestly prayer' of Jesus (John 17): 'And for their sake I consecrate myself (*hagiazo*: RSV, NEB) that they also may be consecrated in truth' (17.19). Hence the sense of *agape* in I John: 'By this we learned love, that he laid down his life for us; and we ought to lay down our lives for the brethren' (3.16). 'In this is love, not that we have loved God but that he loved us and sent his Son to be an expiation for our sins. Beloved, if God so loved us, we also ought to love one another' (4.10-11). The 'depth' of the Johannine *agape* is in the 'vertical' dimension, the dimension of the love of the Father for the Son and the Son for the Father, made manifest in the death and resurrection of Jesus. Christian *agape* is sacrificial and consecrated love, a 'holy' love because it is, ontologically, a participation in the love which consecrated Jesus to and on the cross; here the *separation* of man from God was 'revealed, and a new and living way made open to us into the holy of holies, heaven itself.

But once again, until the Lamb himself becomes our Temple, there persists in us a tension and a gap between what we are, sacramentally, in our 'ground' or deepest self and what we live out in our particularized life of day to day, between our 'I' in God and the 'I' of our self-conscious experience. Liturgy and the sacraments are an actuation of the archetypes of saving history, a celebration of gestures in the Body which may provoke, sometimes or often no more significant conscious stirring than irritation or boredom. Our prayer when we are by ourselves is a persevering effort to coincide with our deepest selves, not an experience primarily but an orientation in faith. Certainly the range of our human experience must continually expand, with the growth of our personal lives and the pushing back of horizons in human history – 'secular' history, but not for that reason excluded from divine providence. But the mysterious purpose of that providence is the recapitulation of all things in Christ (Eph. 1.10), and its organ is the Church of faith and sacrament, the visible sign of the Temple of Christ on earth. The 'separation' of world and Church is the manifest sign that the plan has not yet reached fulfilment; and even when it does we believe that there will be a definitive 'separation', between the children of God and the light and the children of darkness and the devil (cf. I John). At least in these related senses Christianity is unthinkable without 'religion', because Christianity *is* religion, the worship of the God who is transcendently separate in holiness: a separation which finds its image in our personal lives, in Church and world, heaven and hell – in the cross of Christ.

The 'separateness' of God is not merely a matter of speculation; it is a matter of God's essential holiness and, as Dr Ramsey has very well pointed out, of the possibility of the free gift of a share in God's holiness by grace. We may respect Dr Robinson for his earnest desire to discover the relevance of Christianity in our secular experience, but our final judgment must surely be to confirm his suspicion that he has not been radical enough in his rethinking. He has not been radical enough in his sense of the unconditional demands of God and he has not been radical enough in his sense of the autonomy of human life within the mysterious purpose of God. The real challenges both of God and of man have been resolved into a conventionally progressivist harmony; the strung cord has been slackened instead of being allowed to remain free for a stranger and a stronger sounding. To practise honesty to God we need to remain more resolutely *open:* 'Beloved, we are God's children now; it does not yet appear what we shall be; but we know that when it does we shall be like him, for we shall see him as he is' (I John 3.2).

# 9

# Acts of Christ: Signs of Faith[1]

## Introduction

In a recent article on the catechesis of the sacraments, the writer, a Canadian Dominican, lays down two principles for the presentation of the sacramental mystery; firstly, that 'every sacrament is a saving event'; secondly, 'that this event is brought about by means of a sign-of-faith'.[2] I do not wish now to examine the correctness of such a view, with which I am in general agreement, but merely to ask just what catechumens, and indeed just what catechists, the writer has in mind. When I think of the great body of Catholics both clerical and lay, in England (I cannot of course speak for Ireland), I am afraid my mind simply reels at the thought of persuading them to think about the sacraments in the way described; on the other hand, when I think of a growing minority of Catholics, both clerical and lay, in England, (I shall call them the 'intelligentsia', a word, incidentally, which had its origin in the nineteenth-century Russian revolutionary movement), I realize that unless they are helped to think in some such way about the sacraments they are not likely to remain Catholics very long.

What I am trying to draw attention to here is the real but unhappy split in the whole of modern culture, including theology, between 'intelligentsia' and 'the others'. Certainly this is not the only factor in a divergence of fundamental attitude as far as theo-

---

[1] I should like to acknowledge here a general debt to the writings of E. H. Schillebeeckx, O.P., far greater than can be indicated by explicit citations. *De sacramentele Heilseconomie,* (Antwerp-Bilthoven 1952); *Christus, Sacrament van de Godsontmoeting,* 3rd edn., Bilthoven 1959 (French translation: *Le Christ, sacrament de la rencontre de Dieu,* Paris 1960; English Translation: *Christ, the Sacrament of Encounter with God,* London 1963).

[2] 'Tout sacrament est un événement salvifique; cet événement s'accomplit sous la médiation d'un signe-de-la-foi'. J.-M. R. Tillard, 'Principes pour une catéchèse sacramentaire vraie', *Nouv. Rev. Théol.* 84 (1962), 1044–61. Quotation from p. 1044.

logy is concerned – a fact which has been harshly illuminated in the first sessions of the Second Vatican Council.[3]. But it seems important to realize that just as, say, Picasso, Stravinsky and James Joyce still remain unassimilated, still a preserve for 'intellectuals', more than fifty years after they began their creative work, so too in theology there seems to be a parallel between current movements and the incomprehension and indeed the enthusiasm which they sometimes meet. Perhaps there is one important difference; I am doubtful whether the classic theology, in the form this assumed after centuries of isolation from contemporary life, has or had much pastoral meaning, much power to nourish and sustain Christian life, even among 'the others'. However, it seems likely that the newer theology speaks in the first place only to those in the modern world who are exposed to the pressures of contemporary society and have developed in consequence characteristic styles of self-consciousness as human beings in a shifting and uncertain world, where the one certain fact seems to be that things are changing, that history is on the move.

For the purpose of the present paper it seemed worthwhile to draw explicit attention to this uncomfortable state of affairs, because we shall be concerned here, in however small a way, with an attempt to indicate a new theological perspective, a reorientation of our thinking about God and the world; and I should like to emphasize *both* that this is not merely a piece of free speculation but a serious attempt to deal with real problems, *and* that I am fully aware that for the majority of Catholic people these problems themselves have not yet become real, at least in the sense of not yet having become explicit. Whether the task of *missionary* expansion, either in the old Christendom or in the new, does not of necessity impose the obligation of acquiring an explicit consciousness of these problems, is a question which I cannot afford to pursue here. I hope that both those who are familiar with the line of thought followed and any one who may find it novel will forgive me this prolonged introduction.

## 1. The Perspective of the Mysterion

In recent years a good deal of attention has been given to the Pauline notion of the *Mysterion*, especially as it occurs in the Epis-

---

[3] Cf. E. H. Schillebeeckx, *Vatican II – A Struggle of Minds* (Dublin 1963), 7–16, and his reflections on Evelyn Waugh's article in *The Spectator* of 23 November 1962 in *De Bazuin*, 16 March 1963.

tles of the Captivity.⁴ The study of the Qumran texts has intensified interest in this Pauline notion, since it provides one of the clearest instances of a biblical theme which has undergone parallel developments in the New Testament and in the writings of this presumably Essene sect.⁵ There can be no question here of attempting to cover all this ground again; but on the basis of these studies it may be possible to indicate certain features of this Pauline notion which will allow us to make a formally theological use of it in our present context.

Coppens sums up the generally-accepted view of interpreters of Pauline thought under twelve heads.⁶ Summarizing this account still further, as far as possible in his own words, we may say that in the strong religious sense the term *mysterion* refers to the secret *plan* of universal salvation; the *mysterion* at the level of the divine existence itself. A plan of salvation realized in Christ: the *mysterion* at the concrete level of the divine *history* of salvation. This salvation offered to all mankind by the message of the *Gospel* and by *faith* in it: the *mysterion* at the level of human collaboration in the perfect realization of it. Thus we have three groups of expressions: *mysterion* of God, *mysterion* of Christ, and *mysterion* of the Gospel, of faith, of religion. The Epistles of the Captivity modify the earlier usage in four ways: firstly, the (plural) mysteries of the Christian economy are as it were concentrated in the single mystery of Christ, regarded in his being, his epiphany, the riches which he pours forth and the way he opens up to God; secondly, the mystery is no longer primarily the eventual salvation of the Jews, or the calling of the Gentiles, or the miracle of the parousia, or the glory of final beatification in God, but all these are 'recapitulated' in Christ; thirdly, the mystery is no longer reserved to a restricted category but all Christians are called to share in its revelation; fourthly, the knowledge of the mystery becomes the final goal of Christian experience.

This may seem to be saying a good deal; but we must emphasize certain elements of Coppens's summary and add others to it. For in its formal aspect, concerned less with the content of the *mysterion* than with its divine origin, the *mysterion* is a mystery of God's *will*, τὸ μυστήριον τοῦ θελήματος τοῦ θεοῦ (Eph. 1.9). It is remarkable

---

⁴ See for instance J. Coppens, 'Le 'mystère' dans la théologie paulinienne et ses parallèles qumrâniens', *Litterature et théologie pauliniennes, Recherches Bibliques V* (Bruges-Paris 1960) 142–65.
⁵ P. Benoit, 'Qumran et le Nouveau Testament', *New Test. Stud.* 7 (1960–61), 276–296; id. art. 'Paul: Epitres attribuées à s. Paul', *Dict. Bib. Suppl. VII,* cols. 157–70 (Colossians), cols. 195–211 (Ephesians).
⁶ Art. cit. 142–4.

how frequently, and with what different expressions, St Paul refers to God's will or good pleasure, or purpose, or counsel in Eph. 1:1–14. Again, Christ, the concrete embodiment of this purpose, determined upon before the foundation of the world, recapitulates all things, both in heaven and on earth; Christ is the 'image of the invisible God, the first-born of all creation', in whom 'all things in heaven or on earth were created'; 'he is before all things, and all things are held together in him, and he is the head of the body, the Church' (Col. 1.15–18). Thus Christ has a cosmic role in the *mysterion* of God's eternal purpose, and the Church, his body, is the manifestation in history of this *mysterion* consummated and embodied in the glorified Christ.[7]

It may be helpful to stand back here from this inevitably condensed statement of Pauline themes, themselves extremely dense, and provide a kind of extended commentary on them taken from the second part of Isaiah. Consider for instance the following typical passage (46.8–12)[8]:

> Remember this and consider,
> recall it to mind, you transgressors,
> remember the former things of old;
> for I am God, and there is no other;
> I am God, and there is none like me,
> declaring the end from the beginning
> and from ancient times things not yet done,
> saying, 'My counsel shall stand,
> and I will accomplish my purpose',
> calling a bird of prey from the east,
> the man of my counsel from a far country.
> I have spoken, and I will bring it to pass;
> I have purposed, and I will do it.

The themes of counsel (*'esah*) and purpose, better 'good pleasure', εὐδοκία (*hēphes*), run through all these chapters.[9] The counsel and will of Yahweh span the times, and are efficaciously realized and manifested in history, the history of God's saving interventions, *Heilsgeschichte,* as in the references to Noah (54.9), Abraham

---

[7] Cf. H. Schlier, *Der Brief an die Epheser,* (Düsseldorf 1958); id., essays XII, XX, XXI in *Die Zeit der Kirche,* (Freiburg 1958).

[8] The translations generally follow the Revised Standard Version.

[9] I am much tempted by Dupont-Sommer's suggestion that the name 'Essene' is a Greek rendering of the community of the 'ēsah: *Les écrits esséniens découverts près de la mer morte,* (Paris 1960), 55–6, (E. T.: *The Essene Writings from Qumran,* (Oxford 1961).

(41.8; 51.2), Moses (48.21; the Exodus theme, e.g. 51.9–10), David (55.3), each of them, it should be noted, individual figures through which God's general saving purpose is effected. A culminating intervention is 'anticipated', in both senses of the word:

> From this time forth I make you hear new things,
> hidden things (netsurōt) which you have not known.
> They are created now, not long ago;
> before today you have never heard of them (48.6–7).

The theme of hidden things appears several times: the Servant, for instance, is 'hidden' in the shadow of Yahweh's hand (*hehbī'ānī*, 49.2), 'hidden' in his 'quiver' (*histīrānī*, ibid.), we may say, in his predestining purpose. Yahweh himself is called *Deus absconditus* (*'ēl mistattēr*) in a remarkable passage: 'Truly, thou art a God who hidest thyself' (45.15).[10] The statement should be read as an *O altitudo*, exactly paralleling St Paul's exclamation in Rom. 11.33, where Isa. 40.13 is immediately quoted; it is an expression of awe before God's transcendence as revealed precisely in the wonder of the entry of the Gentiles. Yahweh's ways are unfathomable:

> For my plans are not your plans,
> neither are your ways my ways. Oracle of Yahweh.
> For as the heavens are higher than the earth,
> so are my ways higher than your ways
> and my plans than your plans (55.8–9).

The mysterious divine purpose is revealed as mysterious precisely by way of the manifest historical intervention, the calling of Cyrus, for example. By the very act of showing himself in history God is revealed as transcending history, as *Deus absconditus*. Yahweh's saving action in Israel with its cosmic repercussions is performed

> that men may see and know,
> may consider and understand together,
> that the hand of the Lord has done this,
> the Holy One of Israel has created it (41.20).

Israel is an organ of revelation. She is Yahweh's witness: 'You are my witnesses, says the Lord, that you may know and believe me,

---

[10] Rejecting the emendation of the *Bible de Jérusalem*, which makes the statement part of the *Gentile* acknowledgement of Yahweh's uniqueness: 'With thee, Israel, God is concealed'.

and understand that I am He' (*'ani hū*); 'Here I am', the transcendent one, who speaks personally as an 'I' to his people and *presents* himself to them (43.10 and frequently); this 'people whom I formed for myself that they might declare my praise' (cf. the refrain 'in praise of his glory', Eph. 1.6, 12, 14).

Whether the so-called Servant poems are by the same author as the rest of Deutero-Isaiah or not, it is possible to see in them a prolongation of prophetic reflection in response to the apparent failure of the divine purposes after the first return from exile. The prophet's self-questioning in this critical time reveals to him the figure of a charismatic leader who will in fact be, however unexpectedly, the 'new thing' which Yahweh has devised:

> For that which has not been told them they shall see;
> And that which they have not heard they shall understand.
> Who has believed what we have heard?
> And to whom has the arm of the Lord been revealed?
> (52.15–53.1).

It was the will (*hāphēs*) of the Lord to bruise him, the will (*hēphes*) of the Lord will prosper in his hand (53.10). By becoming *'āsam* for the people he will reveal and effect the saving purpose of Yahweh.

In the final poem of cosmic rejoicing, the fulfilment of Yahweh's purpose is to be a memorial (*sēm*), an everlasting sign (*'ōth 'ōlām*) of the achieved *presence* of the hidden God (55.13); the *word* of the Lord is the expression of a purpose (*hēphes*, 55.10–11).

One last element may be added to fill out the notion of *mysterion* which we are attempting to characterize here with the help of the Old Testament. In an altogether remarkable book[11] Father Louis Ligier studies among many other themes the meaning of the knowledge of God and evil which was forbidden to the first man (I, 173 f.). It is impossible to summarize fairly the detailed riches of his study; and I shall merely quote here his final conclusion:

> How then are we to understand the prohibition of the tree? It teaches us that man can only enjoy the garden and life if, in the submission of faith and obedience, he respects the wisdom which unites from above the order of morality and the order of the promise. Since knowledge has a nomic or ethical aspect, the prohibition means that it is forbidden to evade the obligations defined by the word of God, the commandments. But, because

---

[11] *Péché d'Adam et péché du monde*, I, (Paris 1960); II, (Paris 1961).

of its prophetic signification, the prohibition also proclaims that it is forbidden to anticipate God's gratuitous designs.... Man must accept two limitations before God. A humility of obedience.... A humility of faith before a future whose secret God reserves to himself: a faith open to God's supernatural initiative, a progressive faith which accepts the dispensation of Time (192).

We may I hope be allowed to say that this prophetic knowledge of God's providential dispensation, to which man could have access only by God's free gift, was a knowledge of the *mysterion*. It was only by God's free gift that the First Adam could know of the Second, the last Adam.

The perspective of the *mysterion* which we have tried so inadequately to sketch is in its simplest terms that of a God who makes himself present to us by the free gift of himself, a gift the condition of which is our acceptance of it in obedience and faith: God with us, Immanuel. In the rest of Part One of this paper, we shall try to see how we may exploit this notion theologically: firstly, as a way of defining the object of faith, and secondly, as indicating the relationship between God and time.

One of the great achievements of scholastic theology (I am thinking here primarily of St Thomas) was its elaboration of a metaphysics of knowledge and the exploitation of this metaphysics for theological analysis. The essential feature of this metaphysics of the act of knowing is its recognition of the active role of the mind in constituting its proper object. Knowledge is an objectification of the world by and for the mind. Upon this fundamental act of objectification there depends the further, increasingly subtilized, analysis of formal and material objects and so on. While in the classic philosophy since the middle ages epistemology lost its ontological character, and knowledge was set over against being instead of being regarded as a special kind of being, knowledge was still regarded as consisting primarily in the apprehension of objects. It must be confessed that it is only in comparatively recent times that in various ways we have come to recognize philosophically that our knowledge of each other cannot be adequately interpreted according to the subject-object schema, even when the act of knowing is treated ontologically, as in St Thomas. The fundamental point here is not so much that persons are not objects, for at least in St Thomas's thought nothing is an object till it is made so, by and for the mind; it is rather that persons objectify *themselves*, as it were, or better, that they make themselves *present* to each other. We are not *for* each other by a process of objectification which each party to an encounter carries out privately by himself; we are for each other, present to each other, by a total behaviour of both parties, each having himself *for* the other. It is important that only human beings have faces, properly speaking, because our faces are the chief organs of our mutual presence to each other, the mobile and expressive project of our self-presentation (domestic animals, dogs and horses particularly, have faces of a sort precisely by being assumed into a domestic, human economy). Again, only human beings wear clothes, another style of self-presentation. Or consider the apparently senseless gestures we make when talking to each other over the telephone; divine revelation is sometimes spoken of as though it were a one-way telephone conversation without gestures. It does not seem to me possible for the classic objectifying or abstractive account of knowledge to deal satisfactorily with this obvious and fundamental feature of our knowledge.

If this is conceded, it follows that we should re-examine the exploitation of the classic account of knowledge when it is used for the analysis of faith. The dangers of over-simplification here, particularly in a brief note, are considerable, for it is easy to knock down an Aunt Sally of scholasticism. Banez, for instance, developing St Thomas's distinction between the object of faith *ex parte ipsius rei creditae* and *ex parte credentis (S. theol.*, II-II, 1, 2) into a distinction between the *ratio formalis ex parte rei* and a *ratio formalis sub qua,* can find confirmation for his interpretation of St Thomas's *veritas prima* as a *testificatio Dei revelantis* in the text of 2 Cor. 4.6, 'For it is the God who said, Let light shine out of darkness, who has shone in our hearts to give the light of the knowledge of the glory of God in the face of Christ'. Banez writes:

> As if the apostle were saying, the author of nature himself is the author of grace, who has shone interiorly in our hearts and minds, so that we might be certain (for this is what is meant by 'knowledge', *scientia*) that the glory of God, that is, the divine majesty is in Christ's humanity, which is not improperly called a 'face', with regard to men, since he appeared to us through his humanity. So it is as if the apostle were saying: Our reason for believing that Christ is God, is that we have received God's testimony interiorly, God himself illuminating our minds (In II–II, 1, 1; 6a conclusio).

Rather than dwell upon this attractive text, which may easily lead us into the opposite error of interpreting scholastic theology as a sort of disguised personalism,[12] we may consider the role of *testificatio, testimonium, Deus testis* in this account. Although St Thomas does not explicitly use the notion in his *Summa theologiae* treatment of the object of faith, he does so in the contemporary *de Spe* (art. 1) and of course in the *de Veritate* 14, 8. It has several advantages. It brings out the role of the Church in proposing the faith (*fides quae*) to the individual believer. Thus in the article concerned with the heretic and his failure to accept the infallible and divine rule of the Church's doctrine, we have the fine statement, 'Formale autem obiectum fidei est veritas prima secundum quod manifestatur in Scripturis sacris et doctrinis Ecclesiae'.[13] What is more, it establishes a continuity of ontological identity between this proposition of the object of faith by the Church and by God and Christ. Again, it rests on the Johannine and biblical notion of *martyria,* witness. And yet, if we pursue this notion in St Thomas's commentary on St John, we shall see that its really essential role, that of constituting an object of faith *ex parte rei creditae,* prior as it were to its appropriation as an object *ex parte credentis* by the individual believer, needs to be completed by an account of God's personal self-proposition or self-presentation, through Christ and the Church, to the personal response of the believer.

There is a particularly striking passage in St Thomas's commentary on St John which I hope will allow me to make this point clearly, though it does not contain any of the *testimonium* words. Commenting on John 5.24, 'He who hears my word and believes him who sent me, has eternal life', St Thomas distinguishes between the human word which introduces us to faith, and God himself on whom faith rests (*introducitur, innititur*). St Thomas explains how Christ can say what he does by pointing out that through Christ's human word men are converted to the *Verbum Dei.* 'For since Christ is the *Verbum Dei* it is plain that those who hear Christ hear the *Verbum Dei,* and consequently believe God. Hence 'He who hears my word', that is, hears me, the *Verbum Dei,* "and believes him", that is, the Father, whose *Verbum* I am.'[14] For

[12] I agree with R. Aubert, *Le probléme de l'acte de foi,* 3rd edn., (Louvain 1958), 622 when he criticizes J. Mouroux for this in his otherwise interesting *Je crois en Toi,* 2nd edn., Paris 1954.

[13] *S. theol.* II-II, 5, 3. Cf. M. Seckler, art. 'Glaube' in *Handbuch theologischer Grundbegriffe,* ed. Fries, I, (Munich 1962): 'Die Struktur des mittelalterlichen Glaubens ist sozial: Der einzelne machte sich in Glaube und Taufe zu eigen, was die glaubende Gemeinschaft der Kirche unangezweifelt darstellte' (536). We may note the practice in the later scholastics of inserting the equivalent of a treatise *de Ecclesia* as an appendix to the treatise *de Fide.*

[14] *In Jo.* 5, lect. 4; cf. lect. 6 throughout. *In Jo.* 8, lect. 3: 'Ad hoc ergo quod immediate ipsum divinum Verbum audiremus, carnem assumpsit, cuius organo locutus est nobis'.

the proper understanding of St Thomas's meaning here we must remember that 'Verbum personaliter dicitur in divinis'. The human word of Christ introduces us in faith to him personally, the Word, and through him to the Father. It is only because we want to bring out more explicitly what St Thomas is exploring here that we appeal to a phenomenology of personal encounter; for we want to manifest the connection between the human word and the Word of God. To do this properly we should have to examine the whole notion of the word as *signum conceptionis intellectus*; but it may be sufficient to say here that human language is an articulation of the total behaviour of the human person by which he makes himself present. Thus in Christ we find a self-presentation of the Father in the Son, in the human face, gesture and speech of the Son. The 'witness' in St John's gospel, as well as the witness of the gospel itself, is to the *person of Jesus,* answering the question, 'Who is Jesus?'[15] The difficulty about St Thomas's mode of expression is that *Jesus himself* seems to vanish. It seems to me that an objectifying or abstracting account of knowledge cannot adequately bring out the personal self-presentation of God in Christ which constitutes the *reality* of revelation in which the *word* of revelation has its source and ground: we need to unify Incarnation and Revelation for faith.[16]

It is important to remember here that the *mysterion* is a perspective which can be summed up in the simplicity of God with us, Immanuel: a *mysterion* of God, of Christ, of the Gospel. We may then say that faith is a response, a total response of our whole behaviour and having of ourselves *for,* to the self-presentation of God in Christ, *Deus-in-mysterio* (which includes then *Deus testis*). The face of Christ and the word of Christ in the Church are the project of God's self-presentation to us and for us: 'Philip, he who has seen me, has seen the Father' (John 14.9). Thus the 'objective' proposition of revelation in testimony is contained within the personal reality of God's self-presentation in Christ, such that the whole tangible Christian economy, including our own embodied gestures of faith and summed up in the humanity of Christ, is

[15] So the Catholic exegete H. van den Bussche, *Het vierde evangelie. I. Het boek der tekens* (Tielt-den Haag 1959, 132). We should understand the Johannine Logos not as a *verbum mentis* but as Jesus himself as the definitive self-revelation of God in history: thus the *whole* Prologue is about the incarnate Word, 100–17.

[16] Personal being as being-for is most perfectly realized in the subsistent relations of the Trinity; the Incarnation may then be seen as the transposition into human terms of the *being-for* of the Son. Thus the compatibility of the categories of substance and relation arises at the order of human personality before it becomes problematic in the Trinity. Personal being is intrinsically communication. 'Assumption' corresponds to 'ex-pression'.

informed by the active presence of God revealing (Revelation is *closed* but it has not *ceased*). The unique, total 'object' of faith is *Deus-in-mysterio,* God's face, the smile of his good pleasure; it is the presence of his face to vision that we wait for in hope and faith.

As will be apparent, one advantage of defining faith and its object in terms of God's self-presentation in Christ is that our own response of faith is seen as assumed into an economy, a dispensation of the times, which has its origin in the eternal saving counsel of God's *mysterion,* the *sacramentum voluntatis Dei.* Faith and its object both belong to an historical economy. We may appreciate this better if we consider briefly the relationship between God's eternity and our historical time.[17]

Once again, we shall adopt the procedure of interrogating a classic scholastic position and endeavouring to fill out its implications. We may note by way of preliminary that to call God 'eternal' is strictly to follow the *via remotionis,* to say how God is *not,* that not being subject to change he is not measured by time; that his eternal *now* is to be understood as the unity of something always abiding without change, as opposed to the *now* of time, which is the measure of changing things, distinguishing its before and after by its passage. The negative determination of eternity is thereby seen as characterizing a plenary actuality of being.

In his commentary on Aristotle's *Physics* (IV, lect. 23), St Thomas deals with certain difficulties about the existence and the unity of time. The chief point of interest for our purposes is that the two questions are *distinguished.* As regards the existence of time St Thomas makes it clear that for its full realization it is necessary that it should be actually measured by an apprehending mind, just as change itself, not having, as change, a stable being (*esse fixum*) in the world, can only be grasped as a unified whole by an apprehending mind. Certainly time has an 'ontic' basis, in that the being of the physical world in process of change is dependent upon God and not on the apprehending and measuring mind; but in its proper reality time is 'ontological', assumed into the structuring consciousness of the apprehending mind. As regards the unity of time, St Thomas is quite categorical in his assertion that the single basis of this unity is the uniform, regular circulation of the firmament, and that time is primarily the measure of this primary circulation:[18] day and night are the rhythm of the entire cosmic universe, including man.

---

[17] I very much regret not having been able to make use here of the important book by J. Mouroux, *Le mystère du temps* (Paris 1962).

[18] Cf. *S. theol.* I, 10, 6.

But suppose we are no longer able to grant the existence of such a cosmic clock? I do not see that we can argue to its existence from the metaphysical necessity of the unity of time, for it is possible to establish the unity of time in a different way.

Unlike visual art, music seems never to have been given the benefit of serious philosophical attention:[19] and yet it seems likely to offer an appropriate way of investigating time. For instance, the notion of rhythm, as applied above to the alternation of day and night, is surely in its primary application an anthropological notion: a characteristic of the beating of drums and the stamping of feet, the dance. In his valuable Harvard lectures,[20] Hindemith makes use of St Augustine (especially the sixth book of the *de Musica*) and Boethius to draw attention to the activity of what he calls 'co-construction' required in the perception of music. This co-construction is the active transformation of what is heard into musical meaning by matching it with a known musical image. Perhaps Hindemith's terminology is a little unfortunate here if we take 'image' in too static or visual a sense; but considering the case of someone without previous musical experience he speaks of a primordial musical experience, common both to the novice and to music itself, namely motion: the novice has at least his experience of his own organizing acts of motility which allows him to perceive music as meaningful. We may call this originating motility the existential *a priori* of musical meaning.

To say 'a priori' is deliberately to invoke Kant, one aspect of whose 'Copernican revolution' was his account of time as 'nothing but the form of inner sense, that is of the intuition of ourselves and of our inner state'.[21] In our own times a far more influential revolution has been the re-thinking of Kant by Heidegger.[22] The essential feature of this re-thinking is the emphasis on the ontological foundation of Kant's transcendental method. That is to say, what Kant states in epistemological (and ultimately psychological) terms, Heidegger re-states in terms of the existence characteristic of the human existent, the *Dasein*. Thus the Kantian 'form of inner sense' may be seen as the active 'temporalizing' characteristic of human existence, revealed in the ordering of human existence as before and after in the *now* of a purpose or project. Individual or community time is *historical* time, the active assumption of the world into the orientation of human purpose.

[19] But see the book by the Swiss conductor E. Ansermet, *Les fondements de la musique dans la conscience humaine* (Neuchatel 1961), where he employs Husserl's phenomenology to interpret the musical experience.
[20] P. Hindemith, *The Composer's World* (Cambridge, Mass. 1953), esp. 1–22
[21] *Critique of Pure Reason*, trans. Kemp Smith, 77.
[22] See e.g. M. Heidegger, *Kant und das Problem der Metaphysik* (Bonn 1929).

My suggestion here is that this musical ontology of time, provided that we continue to accept its ontic basis, offers a way of preserving the unity of time as the unified and ordered project of God's providential purpose. Just as God is locally present to all things by containing them within his conserving act, so too he is sempiternally[23] present to them in the same act; present, for instance, by initiating and working within the free historical acts of man. If finally we say that this providential purpose is summed up in the *mysterion* of Christ, then we may say that human history is measured by the economy of saving and sacred history; and that in faith God presents himself sempiternally to and for us in Christ: 'the Alpha and Omega, who is and was and who is to come' (Apoc. 1.8) presents himself to us in the Son of Man, the Living one, who is 'the First and the Last who died and behold he is alive for evermore' (cf. Apoc. 1.17–18).

## 2. The Sacraments as Particular Realizations of the Mysterion

The purpose of an approach to the sacraments which may not unfairly be called *a tergo* has been to indicate a perspective in which they are not simply a special department of dogmatic theology or liturgy, but the paradigms, the typical and pregnant instances, of an entire economy of salvation.

If faith is the response of our total behaviour, our having of ourselves *for*, the *Deus-in-mysterio*, who presents himself *for* us in successive historical interventions culminating in the passion, death and resurrection of his Son and the bestowal of the Spirit of testimony, then all expressions of faith are in their different degrees sacramental, in the broad sense of symbolic embodiments of faith. Our response of faith itself is incorporated into the significant economy of salvation initiated by God in Christ. Clearly a whole range of human activities may be discerned which exhibit our faith more or less manifestly. Through the centuries a whole ritual idiom has taken shape, and taken varying shapes, in terms of which the Christian may spell out his life of faith in his waking and even in his sleeping hours, from the cradle to the grave. In any individual or in any society, there will be not only variations of

---

[23] 'Sempiternal: enduring constantly and continually' (Oxford English Dictionary). As opposed to 'eternal', 'sempiternal' is precisely a name applied to God *ex tempore* (cf. *S. theol.* I, 13, 7); it is intended to bring out that aspect of God's eternity whereby he is present (*praesentialiter adest*) to all time. Cf. *Contra Gent.* I, 66.

idiom but also gaps and lacunae; and there is also the possibility of free invention, professions of faith which enlarge the conventional idiom creatively. In this wide range of human activities, the expressive gestures of faith which we call sacraments in the strict sense have a canonical role, in the most obvious sense of being strictly determined by legislative authority in the Church, and further, as so determined, serving to determine the essential expressions of the faith of the Church. Canon law and rubrics are not, in principle at least, impertinent intrusions upon the expression of our faith (in practice one may sometimes have a rather different impression); for the sacraments are expressions of faith in which the Church realizes her being as *congregatio fidelium* normatively, prescribing ritual actions as bearers and witnesses of a faith continuous with her own origins, acknowledging her Lord as the summary, concrete presence of God's eternal purpose of salvation, and renewing on earth her Lord's own intercession with the Father. As belonging to the present economy of salvation, sacramental expressions of faith will more or less explicitly display symbolically the temporal perspective of the *mysterion*; in the Last Days of the eschatological interim between the Ascension and the Parousia, the faith of the Church is remembrance and expectation, focused upon the Lord of the ages; for upon us the end of all the ages has come (1 Cor. 10.11).

And it is the faith of the Church that when she so realizes herself in a normative gesture of faith, her Lord himself presents himself to her actually and actively, not merely as the initiator of her faith and not merely as hearing her prayer, but as himself the actual fulfilment of the prayer, as himself enacting in the expression of faith the *mysterion* which it symbolically displays. The ritual gestures of the sacraments of the Church are indivisibly the expression of the faith of the Church and the expression, by assumption, of the actual presence of the *mysterion* of Christ. The believing Church in act becomes full of her own mystery and the organ of the Lord's presence. By realizing herself essentially in faith she realizes herself as the Body of the Lord.

It is as we should expect above all in the Eucharist that we may discover in its concrete unity the particularization of the perspective of the *mysterion*. In a gesture the significance of which is obscured by our present rubrics and the printing of the missal, the Lord presents himself to us in his separated Body and Blood. The demonstrative 'this' is the verbal expression of a gesture of self-bestowal in the gift offered to those who share in the fellowship of the table: 'Take, eat, this....' The real, substantial presence in the gift is the pledge of the actual and active presence of the giver;[24]

both gift and giver are at the same time representations of the faith of the Church, embodied in minister and offering. In other sacraments the gift is embodied in the receiver by a like active presence of the giver, embodied as the actual being-for of the receiver to the giver, as an intensification or a vivification of his initial response of faith. Furthermore, as ritually enacted every sacrament is a celebration of 'archetypes', of typical gestures whose ἀρχή and *principium* is the *mysterion* of God's sempiternal presence displayed in the life of Jesus and consummated in the Johannine *hora*, the hour of the passage to the Father. Just as the mystery cults, whose ritual idiom has been assumed into Christian worship, referred themselves not simply to past time but to a primordial time of source and beginnings, so Christian worship refers itself by an anamnesis to the primordial source which is the embodied *mysterion* of the risen Christ, *in illo tempore, in mysterio*.[25]

Those who are familiar with Father Karl Rahner's vigorous and original work, *Kirche und Sakramente*,[26] will have noticed that use has been made here of his notion of a sacrament as a *Selbstvollzug*, a self-realization, of the Church, but that whereas Father Rahner sees the Church primarily as *Ursakrament*, primordial sacrament, here the Church is seen primarily as *congregatio fidelium*. We stand here before two alternative emphases in ecclesiology of which the most prudent view would probably be that neither should be maintained at the expense of the other, even if each has to be maintained by a different tradition. In our present context however Father Rahner's views are of importance inasmuch as they include an interpretation of the Catholic teaching that Jesus instituted the seven sacraments (*Denz* 844).

The great merit of this new approach to an old and vexing problem is that, rather than try to adapt a classic scholastic theology to the great fund of historical information about the development of sacramental practice and theology only assembled after the classic theology had taken definitive shape, Father Rahner starts with his new principle that the Church is the primordial sacrament as the sign of the eschatological real-presence of the victorious purpose

---

[24] On 'actual presence' see J. Betz, *Die Eucharistie in der Zeit der griechischem Väter, I–1, Die Aktualpräsenz der Person und des Heilswerkes Jesu im Abendmahl* (Freiburg 1955); id., art. 'Eucharistie' in *Lex. für Theol. und Kirche* III, (Freiburg 1959), cols, 1142–57; id. art. 'Eucharistie' in *Handbuch theol. Grundbegriffe*, I (Munich 1962), 336–55.

[25] Cf. M. Eliade, *The Myth of the Eternal Return* (London 1955); id., *Patterns in Comparative Religion* (London 1958). Also *Man and Time*, ed. J. Campbell, (London 1958).

[26] Freiburg 1960 (E. tr. *The Church and the Sacraments*, London-Edinburgh 1963).

of God's grace definitively established on earth in Christ. Thus although it is in only two cases, baptism and the Eucharist, that we possess anything like 'words of institution' of what we now generically call sacraments, the Church possessed an *a priori* principle, her own character as primordial sacrament, founded by Christ, which, while only acquiring explicit formulation in our own times, yet allowed her in fact to recognize in her realizations of her own essence what we now call sacraments. Thus to say that Christ instituted the sacraments is to say that Christ instituted the Church as primordial sacrament and, implicitly, those diverse basic acts of the Church which we call the seven sacraments.

It is impossible here to examine these views as closely as they deserve, but some general observations may be made. Firstly, it seems that any criticism of the more conventional interpretation of the institution of the sacraments by Jesus on the basis of historical implausibility tells even more forcibly against the view that Jesus instituted the Church as primordial sacrament. For what we are concerned with here is not the *ontological* foundation of the Church in the mysteries of Christ's death and resurrection, but the institution of the structured community of the Church in accordance with the declared human will of Jesus.[27] Now the primary sources for our knowledge of Jesus's will in this matter include those scriptural texts which are ordinarily appealed to as indications of his will that there should be sacraments: the calling of the apostles, the institution of the Eucharist, together with the command to renew it whereby, according to Trent (*Denz* 938), the apostles were constituted priests of the New Testament, the command to baptize and so on. And it is of course to these texts and related ones (e.g. Eph. 5 for marriage) that Father Rahner makes appeal too. But he appeals to them as capable of yielding their full content only in the light of a basic *a priori*, so basic as not to have achieved explicit formulation until our own day in terms of the church as primordial sacrament. And this brings us to our second observation, that it seems extremely odd that when we already have a *de fide* principle of interpretation of the scriptural texts, namely that Jesus instituted the seven sacraments, we should have recourse to yet another principle, not yet, at any rate, defined authoritatively by the Church, in order to interpret the *de fide* principle and the scriptural texts. Thus, while entirely (and gratefully) granting Father Rahner's case for maintaining that historically Jesus only instituted most of the sacraments *in genere tantum*, it would seem sufficient to say that the *a priori* principle which

[27] Cf. M. Schmaus, *Katholische Dogmatik,* III–1, 5 ed. (Munich 1958), 49–201.

governed the increasing insight of the Church into the nature of the sacraments was precisely the principle that Jesus instituted them: that is to say, that in those pregnant engagements of her faith which we call the sacraments, the Church became increasingly aware that she was both doing and encountering Jesus's human will as the human expression of the *mysterion* of God's eternal saving will, by analogy, then, with those engagements of her faith for which Jesus's command was explicitly given. For (and this is the third observation) any account of the sacraments in their role as organs of grace which depends primarily on the Church ( as primordial sacrament) and not primarily on Christ (as primordial sacrament) seems to misplace the proper emphasis.

Thus on the view suggested here the principle that Jesus instituted the sacraments constitutes indivisibly both an historical and a soteriological principle. It is possible to grant that the historical institution was *in genere tantum* in the sense that the basic declarations of Christ's human will contained implicitly what the Church later unfolded as seven sacraments (though it seems a good deal easier than Father Rahner somewhat polemically maintains to suggest ways in which that significance was unfolded even in apostolic times); but the point insisted on here is that the historical institution was the expression of the saving human will of the Lord of the Church and that the Church in celebrating the sacraments does and meets that will sempiternally concretized in Jesus glorified.

It will be convenient to draw together the themes of this article by way of a quotation from an important book on baptism in St Paul by a modern Catholic exegete. He writes:

> The basic idea of sacramental dying with Christ etc. rests on St Paul's characteristic mode of thought, which unites what belongs to saving history (the Adam-Christ parallel) and what is pneumatic and supra-temporal ($\dot{\varepsilon}\nu\ \chi\rho\iota\sigma\tau\tilde{\omega}$). This bridging of a gap which is both temporal and substantial was only possible for St Paul in the figure of Christ himself, who on the one hand remains for him always the historical Jesus and as such – in the context of saving history – the Messias, and on the other lives on through the times (not supratemporally in the sense of timelessly) as the pneumatic Lord, till he returns again as the Christ of the parousia.[28]

---

[28] R. Schnackenburg. *Das Heilsgeschehen bei der Taufe nach dem Apostel Paulus* (Munich 1950)

God's self-presentation in history culminates in his self-presentation in the glorified Christ, the Lord of the Church. Faith, which is itself an expression of that self-presentation, is also a human response to it. In the sacraments, which are the paradigms and archetypes of this encounter, the embodiment of faith is indivisibly an embodiment of the Lord of the *mysterion,* either both substantially and actively as in the Eucharist, or only actively as in the other sacraments. By our obedience in faith to Christ's command 'Do this' in the sacraments, we behold, as in a mirror, the glory of God on the face of Christ, being transformed into the same image from glory to glory by the Lord Spirit (cf. 1 Cor. 13.12; 2 Cor. 3.18; 4.6).

# 10

# Mary: Sign of Contradiction or Source of Unity?

Contrary to convention in articles of this sort, I shall begin my discussion of three books about our Lady[1] with some personal reminiscences, in the hope that they will not seem too irrelevant. The writer can still very distinctly remember how, after some eight years of determined and even aggressive atheism, on what turned out to be his way into the Catholic Church, he entered an Anglican church and felt there a primitive shock of pure Protestantism on hearing the Hail Mary being recited – 'Romanism!' He remembers too being perfectly content later to accept, as being what the Church taught, all he was told in instruction about our Lady, without any particular personal feeling for or against the doctrines (such a lot of odd things, God, for instance, had to be accepted, why not these too?). And finally he remembers how, as a recently ordained priest, an increasing sense of dissatisfaction with his own position and with the unadventurous, respectable tepidity of official English Catholic attitudes to our Lady finally drove him to explore some of the Continental writers on Mariology, and to learn that something was going on in the Church which could not wholly be dismissed as Italianate extravagance. Since that time, the position in the Church at large, though hardly in England, may seem to have altered significantly; it may turn out that the epochal moment was the steering vote in the second session of the Council, on 29 October last year, to include the schema on our Lady in the schema on the Church.[2] But it is not easy to appreciate the

[1] R. Laurentin *Mary's Place in the Church* (Burns and Oates, 1965); E. L. Mascall and H. S. Box (ed.), *The Blessed Virgin Mary* London, Darton, Longman and Todd (1963); Max Thurian, *Mary, Mother of the Lord, Figure of the Church* (Faith Press, 1963).

[2] The voting was very close. For inclusion: 1114; against: 1074; null: 5. These figures, and a good deal else, are discussed in an absorbing article by Laurentin, 'La Vierge Marie au Concile', *Revue des Sciences Philosophiques et Théologiques* 48 (1964), pp. 32–46. The same issue contains a forty-four page bulletin of writings on Mariology.

significance of this apparent change of direction without attempting some assessment of the specifically English situation, relative as such an attempt must inevitably be.

If the reminiscences just offered are of more than merely private interest they should serve to indicate some of the difficulties involved in any attempt to discuss the place of Mary in English Christianity, Catholic and non-Catholic. I feel fairly confident that the 'Protestant' reaction is typical of by far the greater number of non-Catholic Christians in England, even when this Christianity has become purely nominal. Unfortunately, the consciousness of this non-Catholic reaction has affected English Catholic attitudes too. On the one hand there is still, I think, a deep-rooted and readily intelligible aggressiveness about our Lady as being part of a distinctively Catholic world of faith and devotion, an aggressiveness often of a jingoistic or triumphalistic kind, at least at the level of the parochial sermon and until recently of the popular press. But on the other hand this aggressiveness itself was (or is) a defensive reaction which still finds alternative expression, especially at the 'official' level, in a muting of Marian doctrine, a conscious dissociation of English commonsense and respectability from what could be deprecated as Continental excess. For some at least of the Catholic intelligentsia the 'new theology' – the biblical, liturgical, ecumenical movements – has the added advantage of seeming to guarantee the intellectual respectability of Catholicism by diverting attention from the embarrassments of High or of popular Marianism.

It is even more difficult to assess what primary and fundamental attitudes to our Lady lie beneath these secondary reactions. For an older generation it would still seem right to suppose the existence of an unquestioning warm and personal attachment to our Lady, content to express itself when required in the idiom of chocolate-box devotions for the very good reason that the attachment has hardly any doctrinal form or content. The travel-agency pilgrimages to Lourdes by chartered aeroplane are a good illustration of the ambiguities involved: the authentic and the adventitious in inseparable solution, and the absence of doctrinal content. For a generation now growing to maturity, exposed to all the pressures of a new situation in the Church and the world, it is hard to suppose that this kind of attachment will persist, apart from certain easily recognizable phenomena of adolescence. It will certainly not persist if it is expected to express itself exclusively in the idiom of the old devotionalism. But it would in my view be a great loss if the personal attachment disappeared with the devotions; and it seems clear that if it is to remain active it will have to find that doctrinal form and content (that illumination of intelligence) which it has so largely lacked: it will have to discover an idiom which is continuous with the idiom of contemporary movements in Catholic life and theology. This is emphatically not just a matter of acquiring respectability, of substituting one sort of hymn, say, for another; it is, among other things, a question about the *personal* in 'personal attachment', a re-education in the style of our relationships to God and Jesus Christ, as well as to 'our Lady'.

The foregoing remarks have tried to conduct a brief examination of conscience in response to three books, each of which is, in a very different way, an examination of conscience in regard to Mary. The importance of Canon Laurentin's book – in the Church at large if not in England – is that here we find one of the most distinguished of modern 'Mariologists' (Laurentin himself accepts this designation) seriously questioning the place of the mariological movement in the Church. One after another, as he points out, the 'movements' in the twentieth-century Church – liturgical, ecumenical, biblical – have been officially adopted by the Church, have lost their character of propagandist particularity and have been integrated into the general life of the Church, often thereby losing eccentric features which belonged only to their early propagandist phases. Writing before the vote taken in the second session of the Council, he is clear that the mariological movement too must undergo this integration and offers rules for the guidance of those who will take a part in this common effort to determine the truly ecclesial sense of the mariological movement.

It is perhaps necessary to insist that Laurentin's approach here is enlightening, not only because it is a frank admission of the eccentricities of Marianism in the Church, but also because it indicates a positive role for Marian theology as against those who seem to wish to disavow the movement as a whole, as though it were merely a rank growth in the life of the Church, thankfully to be allowed to wither after the passing of Pius XII. Indeed the heart of his book is a refined analysis (which for that very reason cannot be repeated here) of two tendencies in Marian theology, each of which in a pure form would be a deviation from the true ecclesial sense: 'maximalism' and 'minimalism', the 'christotypic' and 'ecclesiotypic', the 'mystical' and 'critical' approaches. While admitting that none of these characterizations is wholly satisfactory, if only because both tendencies in varying degrees are found in most theologians, he argues forcefully that it is only by resolving these tendencies into a higher unity, by finding the *ligne de crête* between them, that the present crisis in Mariology may be overcome. The principle of this higher unity he finds in the two propositions: Mary is wholly relative to God in Christ; Mary is wholly correlative to the Church.

Now it is easy to give these two propositions one's immediate assent and to use them as a means of discriminating in one's mind between the healthy and the extravagant in the Marian movement. My only reserves here (aware of my temerity in seeming to pretend to a higher standpoint) concern not so much what is enunciated in the propositions as the context which they presuppose. This, I suspect, is due partly to the relative sophistication and advanced development of Marian theology on the Continent compared with the English scene; but partly also to a feeling that while the principle can and does serve to clarify a complicated theological situation, yet this whole situation is itself in need of and is in fact receiving modifications so far-reaching as to involve a complete shift of perspective (an analogous instance would be the disappearance into history of the various theories of the sacrifice of the Mass). The kind of shift I have in mind here would concern the conceptual categories to which one would appeal in order to answer the question: 'Who is Mary?': that is to say, one's understanding of the *personal*. To my mind, Canon Laurentin is *too clear* about the kinds of answers he would get to this question, he knows what the question means. It seems to me however that the sense of the question is itself in question, that something is happening to us, in the Church and in the world, which is changing the sense of the interrogative *who*.

In his preface Laurentin notes the view that the Marian problem today is primarily an ecumenical one, in the sense of being something to be soft-pedalled, and remarks that a critical stock-taking within Catholicism is an essential preliminary to any serious ecumenical initiative. There do in fact seem to be representatives of the view noted by the Canon, even such well-known figures as Dr Küng. The view seems to arise from a mistaken notion of Catholic ecumenism, which is not primarily a tactic of ingratiation but a co-operative search for the plenary ecclesial sense of the whole: Catholic ecumenism is fundamentally an actualization of the virtualities of the Catholic Church itself, in response to the demands of dialogue certainly, but even more from a still deeper recognition that the Church must become what it is. *Werde was du bist,* become what you are, is its never wholly to be fulfilled law in this stage of God's eschatological design.

It is in this sense that I should like to approach the two other books for discussion here, one a collection subtitled 'Essays by Anglicans' and the other by the well-known theologian of the Protestant religious community of Taizé, Max Thurian. The question being asked first, then, is: 'What can we learn from these books?', and I hope it will not seem to discount the obvious learning, sincerity and devotion of the authors of the Anglican book if I say I have not learned a great deal from it. The Catholic reader may learn that there are distinguished Anglicans whose theological views about the Blessed Virgin Mary are almost wholly in accord with the defined teachings of the Catholic Church; that the seventeenth-century Anglican divines, presented in extensive quotations by the Librarian of Pusey House, admirably performed the task (still barely faced by English Catholics) of making their own Catholic teaching about Mary, in a subtle and flexible English prose. He will also learn, from one of the most interesting essays in the book, of the difficulties about Marian doctrine and devotion experienced by an Evangelical (Canon de Satgé) and how in one case they have been met. He may realize more sharply than he did before, from Dom Augustine Morris's essay, the important role which may be played by Anglicanism in bringing Roman Catholicism and Orthodoxy together.

One essay in this collection does however call for rather more detailed treatment, if only because it brings a sharper edge to bear. Wholehearted admirers of Dr Austin Farrer will doubtless admire his essay wholeheartedly; those admirers of his (among whom I count myself) whose admiration is frequently tinged by irritation at what seems to them whimsy, will I think be more irritated than usual. It seems to me a pretty whimsy to suggest that we needn't bother about the *chaire kecharitomene* because it's just word-play ('Good day to you, since God's so good to you'), as though the Annunciation were merely the occasion for an inept but harmless pun, as though word-play were not repeatedly a means in the Bible of communicating the most pregnant revelations. It seems rather more than irritating whimsy to attribute to the Catholic (not necessarily Roman Catholic) theologian before Dr Farrer put him right the view that in the *Ave, gratia plena* he had an 'utterance which virtually informs him that Mary was conceived immaculate'. Of course Dr Farrer is being playful; but what sort of game is he up to? I am uncertain whether he knows the answer himself.

But apart from a good deal of dubious playfulness of this sort, Dr Farrer's essay also conducts an argument: the intention of his essay, he says, is critical rather than theological.[3] Starting from assumptions about a dichotomy between historical fact and interpretation, he summarizes the scriptural evidence for the facts and argumentatively introduces a critic 'uninfluenced by motives

[3] Dr Farrer here expands and re-applies some points made in his contribution to the first volume of the English *Kerygma and Myth* (London, 1953), pp. 212–13.

of faith' who on the basis of this evidence would only allow 'a simple genuine tradition of Mary's virginity, variously overlaid by St Matthew and St Luke with typological decoration'. Of course this is only a grimmer playfulness, the critic is only a pawn in Dr Farrer's subtler game; for he now goes on to point out that it is 'too simple to say that facts are first acknowledged, then interpreted'. All the foregoing, then, has been merely a setting of the stage for Dr Farrer's further concern, the relationship between the two sorts of interpretation, physical and theological, and a determination of theological interpretation as being that which accepts the (interpreted) fact on the basis of the fittingness of that fact to the context of God's ways with Israel, in Christ, in the Church.

The real point of Dr Farrer's concern now emerges: it is a criticism of 'fittingness' as a criterion of fact. For Dr Farrer, it is an acceptable criterion for a Christian believer if it is applied to a professedly historical account; it is unacceptable if what is to be certified is only our conjecture. To the left of Dr Farrer's *via media* there is the modernist, who cannot accept the Virgin Birth because he judges the historical evidence inadmissible; to the right there is the Romanist, who appears to 'accept the traditions about Mary, supported at certain points by an ecclesiastical authority claimed as infallible; but for which no historical testimony in the ordinary sense can be found'. That is to say, there are cases (the Immaculate Conception and the Assumption) where the criterion of fittingness cannot be applied because it lacks appropriate matter. *Decuit, potuit, ergo fecit* won't do.

Dr Farrer now counters attempts to evade the force of his argument. Stripped, as indicated above, of his *Gratia plena,* the Catholic theologian may try to argue to the antecedent event from the given event, the Conception from the Virgin Birth: 'Kettles never boil, unless they have been heated.' 'A man never writes a poem of outstanding merit, unless he has . . .' Dr Farrer continues rhetorically: 'Well, unless he has *what*?', apparently expecting a past participle. Suppose instead that we treat 'has' as a main verb and not as an auxiliary; the answer is obvious, for example, 'native genius'. And this surely is the heart of the (Roman) Catholic position: that our Lady is especially 'bléssed' and was therefore especially 'blessed' – 'natively'.

But Dr Farrer is not done yet. For he is ready for what looks like a variant of our objection, which is that the 'Immaculate Conception and the Assumption are by their nature invisible happenings' and do not need historical testimony anyway. Dr Farrer replies: 'It does not lessen the presumption of inferring what God must have done, that there is not merely no evidence that he did it, but no possibility even, that there should be any.' This does not precisely meet our objection, which is that what is *first* argued to is the personal state and being of the Virgin Mother, and *secondly* to the intervention of God, initiating and fulfilling that personal state and being in the Conception at the beginning, and the Assumption at the end, of the Virgin Mother's life. And *of course* the only function of the argument is to make explicit the intuition of faith by way of which we in the Church have assured contact with the heavenly reality of the gracious Mother, through converse with whom the scriptural words acquire their full weight.[4]

But we need not rely on this late objection to evade Dr Farrer's argument. That argument, as we have seen, is dialectical. It starts with assumptions about fact and testimony which it later criticizes, such that 'fittingness' is provided with a functional definition, as having a definite role to play in the movement from uncriticized to criticized assumption. Certainly, if we *start* from the critical historical examination of the Scriptures, some device for saving the faith will have to be invoked, either Dr Farrer's fittingness or Bultmann's existential authentification. But this is not and never has been the Catholic starting-point. Faith is not mediated by the historical method, though of course faith can and must use the historical method when it is appropriate. Faith is communion with God and the heavenly realities declared by the Church. The testimony of Scripture and Church is intended to introduce us to communion with the realities, here the personal reality of Mary. The role of 'fittingness' is not to hold loosely together the critically distinguished layers of scriptural and ecclesiastical testimony; it is to make explicit by argument a conviction in faith of Mary's unique creaturely holiness. In its turn the conviction has its scriptural 'basis' – better, its *monument* – not in some isolated *testimonium,* but in the whole biblical revelation of Mary, celebrated by the Church in communion with the personal reality of Mary herself. The 'fittingness' argument has its sense and limits just so far as the common conviction of the Church will let it apply: in two cases, so far, and perhaps in no more. It can never provide the intrinsic structure of the object of faith, as Dr Farrer seems to make it do in his account of the place of the Virgin Birth for faith.

Mary in the Gospel: this is what Brother Max Thurian sets out to offer us in a fine and beautiful book.[5] The scope of the study is

[4] Cf. 'The Starting-Point of Marian Doctrine', *Blackfriars* 40 (November, 1959), pp. 450–66.

[5] For a general survey of recent Continental writing, see J. Galot, s.J., 'Marie et certains protestants contemporains', *Nouvelle Revue Théologique* 85 (May, 1964), pp. 478–95.

limited in advance to exclude the dogmas of the Immaculate Conception and the Assumption; Thurian hopes that his Catholic brethren will not be offended by this. It seemed to this Catholic reader when he found, right at the end of the book, the bare statement of these dogmas, in quotations from the Bull and the Apostolic Constitution respectively, that they set their seal to and found their meaning in what had gone before. (Thurian, it may be noted, needs over 80 pages to deal with the Gospel of St John, which is an interesting commentary on Dr Farrer's remark: 'St John's Gospel adds little that is positive to Mariology.'). It is clear that he has learned much from recent Catholic exegesis (Laurentin on Luke 1–2, Braun, Feuillet), and it is a pleasure for me to say how much I feel I have learned from him. It is clear too from his quotations from Luther, Zwingli and even Calvin, how much our preconceptions about the Marian views of the great Reformers are in need of revision. On the other hand the Catholic reader will note with regret, here as in one or two places in the Anglican book, how strong non-Catholic resistance is to the invocation of our Lady and the saints. For all my Protestant background I find it inexplicable how genuine conviction as to the reality of our communion in Christ with the saints, and a genuine devotion to our Lady, can coexist with an inhibition which would prevent us from asking for her and their assistance. For a Catholic it is just as natural and obvious (no matter what the theological mechanics) as asking for the assistance of those other of our companions who have not yet died into glory. It does seem that the Catholic awareness of the presence of the saints in their personal reality is more simple and vivid than that of many of our fellow Christians.

It is clearly impossible to summarize a book which is essentially cumulative in its structure and movement, a condensation of scriptural signification on the nucleus provided by the title of the book, 'Mary, Mother of the Lord, Figure of the Church'. When one has finished reading the book the title has acquired a wealth of scriptural meaning rather like the recapitulated themes of a movement in sonata-form. One question, however, becomes more and more insistent as we read on: 'What does the author mean by *figure* (or symbol or image or type or archetype or even 'first realization', *réalisation première*)?' It is certain that the author does not ask himself this question in the book; from the first page to the last 'figure' or its equivalents are used as though they were self-explanatory. And it is by no means easy to construe his usage so as to answer the question for him.

We are here faced directly with the issue which has been alluded to repeatedly in the course of this survey and which seems to me a fundamental issue in Mariology: the sense of *who* in the question, 'Who is Mary?'. A satisfactory solution of this issue would, for instance, resolve the difference between the 'christotypic' and 'ecclesiotypic' tendencies in Catholic Mariology. We may think of similar discussions about 'corporate personality' in Christology-ecclesiology, and be warned by them that solutions in terms of 'Semitic modes of thought' are inadequate. Whatever stimulus to our own thinking alien modes of thought may be, they do not absolve us from the responsibility of thinking true and thinking whole ourselves.

Approaching this problem by way of Thurian's book, we may ask a connected question. What for Thurian is the connection between Mary in her scriptural monument and Mary *now,* in her present reality? The answer is not clear. Mary *was* undoubtedly an historical personage, her life undoubtedly *was* of the saving significance which Thurian finds in her scriptural monument (credibility has no need to be filled out with 'fittingness' here); but it is not clear whether that saving significance which she possessed as a personage in saving history is *now* actual in her person as a heavenly reality. That is to say, one possible interpretation of Thurian's use of 'figure' (or more generally, of any use of 'figure' or its equivalents, *Urbild* or the *imagine-tipo* of the Italian Press's version of Abbot Butler's Council project) is to say that while Mary *was* historically the Mother of God and *did* in the past perform actions of saving significance, that significance is *now* embodied as an actuality only in the Church which can read off that significance as 'figure' in the Bible. This cannot satisfy the demands of Catholic faith, and it may not be Thurian's position either. A comparison with 'succession' and 'sacramental reactualization' may help here. Some part at least of Peter's saving significance is possessed by his successors, so that to this extent Peter is the 'figure' of the reigning Pope in the sense indicated; and again the Paschal mystery could be called the 'figure' or type of the sacraments which reactualize it. But Mary has no sacramental or quasi-sacramental successors or antitypes to re-present her *within* the Church. We must say not only that the Church now, as a whole, in heaven and on earth, is Mary's re-presentation, as embodying the saving significance which the Church in its self-interpretation can read off Mary in the Bible; we must also say that Mary now, as a heavenly reality, actually possesses that saving significance in her own person. 'Figure', then, must not only mean *historically* 'first realization', but also *ontologically* 'first realization', that is, primary or primordial realization.

This is not something utterly unique and without parallel, in that within the scope of God's eternal design, the historical life of any person sanctified for God's purposes displays a significance which is not only available for imitation but is concretely actualized in the achieved sanctity in heaven of the saint for whose intercession we ask. The saint *has become* what he is in God's plan and *is* what he has become. And of course this is supremely and normatively true of Christ himself; 'normatively' because the saving significance of Christ's life, death and resurrection is the source and statute of the life of the Church as a whole. But it is also specially and normatively true of Mary, because the saving significance of her life (and surely death?) and assumption is the ontologically first realization consummated in her person of the saving significance of Christ communicated to the Church as a whole. She *is* what she has become; and what she is the Church has *not yet* become. It is precisely in this sense that she is extra-sacramental; she is the personal realization of what the Church is sacramentally.

Mary is then the real, and not merely the ideal, figure of the Church: the personal, here and now actual bearer of the communicated significance of the real and actual Christ. The communication of the significance was not sacramental but historical; it was by playing her role vis-à-vis the historical Christ that she acquired her own significance. If we say that this significance is *actual* in her now, it seems that we must also say *active,* that she actively exercises the saving significance she possesses actually. She is then the actual and active figure of the Church, so that she still exercises in glory the role she played as a personage in saving history; in her, person and personage are one. Her role was and is doubly maternal: Mother of God and mother of the disciples of Christ; mother in the service of the life of her incarnate Son, and mother in the service of the communicated resurrection-life of the incarnate Son glorified. This role she plays as a *person,* so that it can never adequately be analysed by abstract concepts like 'mediation'. Her maternity is not an Idea but an expression of her personal reality, a concrete and incarnate significance. Our question about the sense of the interrogative *who* and our question about the meaning of *figure* have both led us to the same result: Mary is a person who by playing a certain role in God's predestining purpose has acquired an actual and active *significance* which enters constitutively into our redemptive situation, which can be read off the Bible, and which is correlatively though only sacramentally embodied in the Church. Grace is not faceless.

The maternal presence of Mary is the simple and permanent experience of every Catholic; he finds it in the sponsal presence of Christ's Spirit and he finds it in the reality (*res*) of the Church's sacramental self-expression. The pastoral task of Marian piety today is to help the faithful (ourselves included) to know for what it is this presence which they have already found: Mary's presence as the personal reality of the presence of the Church.[6] This is not a matter of new devotions but a training of the eye to see what is normative in the Church as the communion of the faithful assembled in the Spirit of Christ, a communion about the responsive centre upon whom the Spirit descended at the Annunciation and at Pentecost. If we hold, as we must, that when God created Man male and female and united them in one flesh with the command to multiply, he had his eye upon the great mystery of Christ and the Church, we will not find it strange that in that same design God chose Mary to play an enduring personal role. Our own sexually differentiated humanity is the divinely ordained presupposition of the redemptive consummation of the world.[7] Familiarized with perspectives like these we may be able more easily to say with St Cyril of Alexandria, 'Mary, that is to say, the holy Church'.[8]

---

[6] Surely it is time to revise the Rosary so as to include the Proto-evangelium (Gen, iii, 15) at the beginning and the descent of the heavenly Jerusalem at the end, and in the middle at least the marriage feast at Cana and probably also the baptism of Jesus and the Transfiguration. If we retained just fifteen mysteries this would mean abandoning the 'little way of the Cross'; and of course any change, as things stand, would mean losing the indulgences.

[7] For an Orthodox approach to these questions (a rather typically Parisian émigré one), see P. Evdokimov, *La Femme et le salut du monde* (Tournai-Paris, 1958).

[8] This text is commented on in the classic work by A. Müller, *Ecclesia-Maria*, 2nd edn. (Freiburg Schweiz, 1955), pp. 153–7.

# 11

## Philosophy in the Seminary

This article[1] is concerned with the practice of philosophy in religious institutions such as seminaries or the study-houses of religious orders. But it is clear that the possibility of such a limitation – the practice of philosophy in some particular setting – is itself problematic. Philosophizing would seem to claim that it is independent or can become independent of the setting of its practice in all relevant respects. Speaking as a theologian (as I intend to do throughout this article) and claiming therefore complete freedom to appeal to revelation in Scripture and the Church, I must maintain that there is one setting, one *Sitz im Leben,* of which philosophizing can never become independent: the concrete economy of sin and salvation which embraces humanity and the whole of creation with it. But to admit this is not yet to commit oneself to the view that the theological *Sitz im Leben* of philosophizing is philosophically *relevant,* i.e. that philosophical discourse is dependent for its shape and content on the theological existence of philosophers. If it is possible for any intellectual activity to release itself from the constraints of the concrete conditions of its exercise (we can think in spite of a feverish cold though not when we are delirious) then there would seem to be no obvious reason why philosophizing, the intellectual activity *par excellence,* should not precisely define itself as just that discourse which actively releases itself from the particularity of all and any concrete conditions of its exercise, including theological ones, by simple

[1] A paper given to the Priests' Philosophical Group in December 1964. Some bibliographical references may be appropriate. R. Aubert, 'Le Concile du Vatican et la connaissance naturelle de Dieu', *LumVie* (1954), 21–52; H. U. von Balthasar, *Karl Barth* (Köln, 1962²); H. Bouillard, *Karl Barth* (Paris, 1958), esp. vol. III; G. Ebeling, 'Der hermeneutische Ort der Gotteslehre bei Petrus Lombardus and Thomas von Aquin'. *ZtTheolKir,* 61 (1964), 283–327; K. Jaspers, *Der philosophische Glaube angesichts der Offenbarung* (München, 1962); O. Pöggeler, *Der Denkweg Martin Heideggers* (Pfüllingen, 1963); K. Rahner. *Hörer des Wortes* (München, 1963²).

(though perhaps costing) pretermission or by reflexive objectivization.

It will be apparent that whatever truth there may be in such a conception of philosophical activity, it depends for its immediate plausibility on a Platonic model: the ascent by dialectic from the sphere of the material and the conditioned. If intellectual activity, as 'spiritual' or 'ideal', is only conditioned *extrinsically*, by 'body' or 'matter', then 'release' or 'liberation' is always intrinsically possible as issuing from the very nature of intellectual exercise. It is curious to note that the model continues to exert its dominance even in Marxism, which has a special role for the 'intellectual', who as such has declassed himself; he can thus, by practising the critique of his own class-conditioned ideology, liberate himself from it and identify himself with the true dynamic of history. But suppose that intellectual activity may be conditioned *intrinsically*, say by its finitude, with all that this may imply; or suppose that the Platonic model is misleading in its intellectualistic identification of transcendence, so that not liberation from but engagement with the concrete conditions of philosophical exercise is what provides philosophical activity with its fundamental orientation? These appear to be genuine alternatives, in the sense that they are at least open to discussion. The artificially contrived Cartesian stoves for philosophical contemplation erected in seminaries (and in universities) may need to be dismantled; or again the recognition that philosophy is a way of life may enforce an assessment of criteria by which to judge of the appropriateness of the *Sitz im Leben* of philosophy; not that setting which it has evolved for itself in the course of European history but that which, in the light of revelation, it *ought* to have if it is to exercise itself profitably.

It will I hope help to locate the problem under consideration here if we examine the admittedly quaint conditions of philosophizing in a Catholic religious institution. The most patent, and apparently the most flagrant, scandal of this situation is that the activity which above all activities claims, as 'rational', total human autonomy, the power and the right to survey all other activities (whether as Being, Existence, Idea or Meaning makes no difference for the moment), is here subjected to authority in the form of directives issued by a body whose claim to allegiance is not founded on reason and which selects and prescribes for study, and seemingly even intellectual acceptance, just one among the many historically particular systems of philosophy. This is surely an intolerable violation of the mind; it is surely to vitiate seminary philosophy before it has even begun, to make a nonsense of the whole concept.

Before any answer is attempted to this critique, it would be as well to disarm one's hypothetical opponent by admitting that it is very largely true, in practice if not perhaps in ultimate principle. I cannot think of a single clerical philosopher of real distinction since the Middle Ages (and whether it is appropriate to speak of any medieval thinker as a 'philosopher' is of course problematic). What philosophical activity of any interest at all that does emerge from seminaries and religious institutions is always a response to an original departure from non-seminary philosophical tradition by a non-seminarian philosopher. But at least this very admission suggests the kind of concession one would require from one's opponent – or better, debating-partner. For extra-seminarian philosophical originality is also to be construed in terms of a philosophical tradition. Whatever radical autonomy may be claimed for philosophical reason, it is still exercised within an historical tradition which may be all the more dominant for being unacknowledged. What remains true is that while the tradition of seminary philosophy is explicitly and artificially tied to an historically localized philosophical view, on the ground that this view somehow escapes, in essentials, historical conditioning and has a kind of extra-philosophical absoluteness, the tradition of non-seminarian philosophy is subject in its freedom to evolve only to historical conditions themselves – a planned and a free economy respectively. Non-seminary philosophy immanently tends to become 'contemporary', 'actual', because it is (or becomes 'academic' if it is not) itself one of the factors which constitutes contemporaneity: seminary philosophy must always tag on uneasily behind, never quite able to catch up, uncertain whether it ought to adopt a posture of lofty sophistication or one of progressivistic radicalism; all this because it lacks the very conditions of originality, a kind of permanent wall-flower at the dance of life.

It is difficult to see how there can be any justification for this state of affairs. Yet it is not impossible to show that it reflects, sometimes in a very distorted way, a genuine, ontological opposition between Church and world, not to be reconciled merely by progressivist denials of the necessitating force of the opposition (I do not of course deny that a good deal might be done in constructive particular), but ultimately only in an eschatological transfiguration of the world.

As Catholic Christians we must say in faith that our existence, and indeed the existence of all creation and history, is dependent, positively or negatively (for or against), on the 'eternally actual deed of salvation in Christ' (cf. Schillebeeckx):

He is the image of the invisible God, the first-born of all creation; for in him all things were created, in heaven or on earth.... All things were created through him and for him. He is before all things, and in him all things hold together. He is the head of the body, the Church; he is the beginning, the first-born from the dead, that in everything he might be pre-eminent (Col.1. 15–17).

If we are to take the ontological sense of this hymnic passage, we must first examine it as literature. Christ is proclaimed the transcendent Wisdom of God, in terminology derived from the sapiential literature of the Old Testament[2]. 'In him are hid all the treasures of wisdom and knowledge' (Col. 2. 3), and so he is set over against the false *sophia* and *gnosis* of the Colossian heresy, its '*philosophia* and empty deceit according to human tradition' (2. 8). A similar critique of errant human wisdom is made in 1 Corinthians: 'Has not God made foolish the wisdom of the world?' God's transcendent wisdom has allowed for the strayings of human wisdom by revealing his wisdom in Christ the Wisdom of God (1. 20–25: 2 6–16). In Romans 1. 18f. the culpability of this errant human wisdom is emphasized in a statement which has long been taken in the Church as the biblical charter of natural theology:

For what can be known about God is plain to them, because God has manifested it to them. Ever since the creation of the world (*apo ktiseos kosmou*) his invisible nature, namely his eternal power and deity, has been perceived by the mind's insight in the things that have been made.

And yet, St Paul has said, the truth has been suppressed; men claiming to be wise have exchanged the glory of the immortal God for images. Thus St Paul echoes the OT polemic against images, especially as found in Wis 13s., where the possibility of a knowledge of the true God from created things is enlarged upon (an 'analogical' knowledge, *analogos*, 13.5, the biblical charter of *analogia entis*!). A slightly more optimistic view of the achievement of human wisdom is taken in St Paul's Areopagus speech (Acts 17. 22–31), but even there, after recommending the rejection of idols, he speaks of the times of ignorance, *agnoia,* prior to the proclamation of the living God, hitherto worshipped as 'unknown'.

---

[2] E.g. Prov 8. 22–31; Ecclus 24; Wisd. 7. 22–8: 1. Cf.John 1. 1–18; Heb. 1. 1–3. See J. Dupont *Gnosis* (Louvain-Paris 1960²).

It is of the utmost importance to remember that the constitution *de Fide Catholica* of Vatican I is claiming to expound texts like these when it declared that God could be known with certainty by the natural light of human reason from the created world (Denz. 1785). Thus Bishop Gasser, in his *relatio* on behalf of the *Deputatio fidei*, makes use of the text from Tertullian: 'Nos (sc. contra Marcionem) definimus Deum primo natura cognoscendum, dehinc doctrina recognoscendum, natura ex operibus, doctrina ex praedicationibus' (*adv. Marcionem* 1, 18; note that Tertullian is insisting on the unity of God, Creator and Redeemer, against Marcion's Gnostic separation of the two), and declares that Tertullian is certainly in agreement with Scripture on this point, referring to Wisd. 1. Rom. 1. Acts 14 and 17, and also with the Fathers (Coll. Lac. VII, 129; cf. Franzelin, *De Deo Uno*). The Vatican Council is not somehow endorsing a philosophical proposition in which reason asserts its own powers; or, at any rate, its sanction consists in an interpretation of Scripture and Tradition in respect of those of their utterances which contain revealed teaching about the powers of reason. Human reason itself, its scope and limits, is contained within the scope of divine revelation, which offers us, here and elsewhere, matter for a theological anthropology and this should not be surprising, since man as a whole is embraced within a revelation of God which reaches its summit in the God-Man.

However paradoxical it may seem, the teaching which we as Catholic Christians must accept in faith, is that human reason, in the highest philosophical flight of which it is capable, the knowledge of God, is guaranteed by revelation. It is revelation which allows us in faith to circumscribe the scope of reason. Reason is not transparent to itself, nor does it even become transparent to itself under the light of revelation; for what it can learn from revelation about itself remains an extrinsic determination of its proper powers. Revealed truth about reason remains the object of faith, and does not become by faith the connatural vision available to reason itself. Not even reason illuminated by faith can perceive by reflection upon itself those truths about itself to which it assents in faith. The *kind* of certainty which reason may achieve about matters other than itself is intrinsically limited by its incapacity to achieve that same kind of certainty about itself. Reason reflecting upon itself in faith is confronted with its own mystery within the mystery of God. It may be that I only *believe* that I can know God certainly by reason.

It may however be argued that although *in fact* the scope of reason is part of what God has chosen to reveal to us, *in principle* reason can acquire a reflexive certitude about its own powers. Thus the revelation of reason would be exactly analogous to God's revelation of his own existence: a revelation not *absolute necessaria* but only to be referred to God's goodness in view of the present condition of the human race (Denz. 1786). Again, reason can assure itself in the manner indicated by Aristotle for justifying the principle of contradiction (*Met. Γ* (iv), 4) by pointing out the absurdity of the use of reason against reason: communication presupposes rationality. It may further be argued that to make reason dependent on revelation is precisely to fall into the fideism condemned by Vatican I.

All these three arguments, two defensive and one counter-offensive, seem to me to rely on what I might call the unilateral priority of nature to existence. It is no part of my present intention (and this I must make absolutely plain) to deny that there is a certain priority of nature to existence; all I am trying to suggest is that there is *also* a certain priority of existence to nature: that in fact nature and existence are a reciprocating pair, and that this theological commonplace has acquired a new importance with the growth of philosophies of 'existence' and 'meaning'.

Thus the fideist error consists in asserting that reason is dependent upon revelation in the order of *nature,* that is, in inverting the *objective* order *primo natura, dehinc doctrina.* There is no objection whatever to holding that in the order of *existence* the scope of reason is known first by revelation and only then in its 'nature', that is, in the objective order of priorities. This is in fact precisely what the first argument has relied on, to show that rationality is only historically (or existentially) dependent upon revelation. The power of reason reflexively to be able in principle to certify its own scope may be admitted if reason is confined to reason as nature (though even here the intrinsic finitude of human reason necessarily restricts the *kind* of certification possible); but for reason as existence and history this is not so. That is to say, *if* we are concerned with the priority of nature to existence, firstly as regards the objective scope of reason and secondly in its power to certify itself reflexively, *then* it must be asserted that reason is 'in principle', that is in 'nature', capable of God by its own power and (finitely) self-certifying: but if we are concerned with concrete existential reason in enacted history, then not only is the possible scope of reason undefined but its reflexivity is incomplete. What the Aristotelian procedure for justifying the reduplicative or reiterative certainty of rationality does not sufficiently allow for is a rational activity which is wholly 'dialectical' that is to say, one which does not stand in a relation of dependence on 'substance' or 'nature', but stands over against nature as existence and history – a rational activity which achieves philosophical pregnancy not only in 'existentialist' procedures from Hegel onwards but also in the linguistic analysis of meaning; both are 'styles of reason' not certifying itself in a 'closed' but creating itself in an 'open' context.

Since Vatican I until recent years Catholic theology has taken an increasingly unfavourable attitude to the alternative priority of existence to nature proposed here; a good instance is the addition of *demonstrari* in the anti-Modernist oath to the formula of Vatican I, an addition which was proposed at the Council and rejected by the *Deputatio fidei*. For a theological tradition increasingly on the defensive and dominated by the priority of nature to existence this was inevitable. Now that theology itself has become more 'existential', it is at least open to question whether it is not necessary to take the alternative priority of existence to nature more seriously. What it demands of a philosophical practitioner in a religious institution is a certain flexibility of mind, a readiness to turn intellectual somersaults from one reciprocal to the other. It does not seem to me that Catholic theology can ever simply abandon an orientation to 'substance' and 'nature'; and so long as the seminarian philosopher accepts his subordination to theology, he is bound to accept this external discipline while at the same time exposing himself to and sharing in a history of existence and its philosophical articulation. The really fundamental error would be to suppose, even unreflectingly, that the position in which he finds himself then – the 'meta –' or 'trans-position' in which he simultaneously grasps the reciprocal priority of 'nature' and 'existence' – that this position was autonomously self-determining, that it was not itself determined or determinable, and that it somehow escaped from the comprehension of the living God.

Such a self-interpretation of the trans-position would manifestly be illusory. This paper itself is meant to be a piece of theology, submitting itself to revelation in the Church; it claims that the trans-position is to be determined theologically, and that it discloses itself philosophically as a *Grenzsituation*, a situation in the limit. If the text from Colossians is taken seriously, then it is clear that all creation and re-creation find their fullness in the embodied Wisdom of God, and hence all and any human wisdom too. But it should also be possible to show in a more precise way, in terms of a theological epistemology, that the trans-position is the existential theological *a priori* of philosophical exercise. For if it is possible to define the utterances of revelation in such a way that the scope of human reason becomes an object of explicit faith, then the scope of human reason can also become an object of implicit faith; and that it should *not* become an object of either explicit or implicit human faith is suppression of the truth. This statement requires careful unpacking, to which we now proceed.

In the first place, it is not of course being suggested that faith is a prior condition of the exercise of reason. It would obviously be absurd to pretend that reason only became active after the assent of faith, since faith itself demands even that minimum of reason which consists in the capacity to hear and to hear discriminatingly, to take part in a communication. But the scope of this capacity to hear and the horizon of the power to communicate are not capable of unambiguous internal definition, though they can exhibit themselves in particular instances seen to exemplify universal validity. *The* logic of a language is either capable only of being shown (cf. Wittgenstein's *Tractatus*), or it is not even capable of that, since only one logic of an indefinite number of alternatives is capable of being displayed (cf. his *Investigations*). What one might even *mean* by 'certain knowledge of the existence of God through reason' can only be grasped in particular exercises of human reason, for example the Five Ways. The definition of the possibility of 'certain knowledge' is formally theological, inviting an assent of faith which constitutes the immanent existential *a priori* of reason corresponding to its transcendental formulation in the theological definition. The explicit or implicit assent of faith to the proposition explicitly or implicitly charges reason with its own rationality, a rationality which is inserted in a 'natural' order of man, creatures and God – to this we may add being and substance. Faith gives reason to itself, though not, as was said before, in reflexive self-intuition[3].

But in what could such an implicit faith of reason in itself consist? It might consist in a con-sent of reason to its own finitude, an acknowledgment of itself as intrinsically determinate 'nature', an acceptance of its own limited but authentic certitude. This would differ from mere scepticism or agnosticism in being fundamentally open to enlightenment; not the taking-up of a position pretending to detachment from and superiority to reason on the ground that it could never achieve certitude, but engagement in reason and its activities in nature in and through a recognition that logic is an activity of the Logos and that communication is an expression of communion in being. This moment of free play between reason as nature and reason as existence, *ratio ut natura* and *ratio ratioci-*

---

[3] Catholic Christianity implies an ontology. It is for this general reason that I find unacceptable two recent Catholic reinterpretations of transsubstantiation, by Fr Charles Davis, in *Sophia* 3 (1964, Australia), 12–24, and by Fr Herbert McCabe O.P., in *The Clergy Review* 49 (1964), 749–59. Existential communication in speech and gesture is dependent upon and interpretative of communion in being, not just of human life lived.

*nans,* is the existential crisis of the trans-position, the moment at which reason both as nature and as existence is accepted in a consent of faith, or reason as existence is chosen *against* reason as nature. Seminary philosophy has sometimes seemed to choose reason as nature *against* reason as existence and condemned itself to the sterility of an historical absolutism; secular philosophy more often than not has chosen reason as existence against reason as nature (even when it has claimed to be vindicating the rights of reason against superstition) and has thereby entered into and helped to constitute secular history.

Thirdly, this consent, acknowledgement, and recognition of reason having faith in itself is reason in act and exercise, reason as existence. The very consent of reason to its own insertion in an order of nature is the realization of reason as existence. Thus the exercise of reason, in its metaphysically first act, is constitutive of history and exposed to the historical process. It is also subject to the Lord of history under the aspect of *gratia sanans* (together with in the concrete *gratia elevans*) so far as it does in fact consent to itself, or, by a failure to consent expressed in a choice of itself as existence against nature, under the aspect of condemnation to error. For reason thus to recognize itself as nature is to recognize itself as *created* nature, not simply as *physis* but as part of an order of creation dependent upon a creator[4].

It may help to particularize the foregoing remarks by distinguishing four types of 'natural theology' constituted by the activity of reason (hence reason as existence). Two types are due to explicitly Christian practitioners. Of these the first is found unsystematically in the Bible and, say, Gerard Manley Hopkins. It consists above all in the vision of created nature as a gracious revelation of the living God, God's *self*-revelation through nature. In the Old Testament its formula is found above all in the identification of El/Elohim, the general Self-revelation of the divine, with Yahweh, the unique personal founder of the covenant relationship with Israel: 'The Lord, he is God; Yahweh, he is the (*ha*) Elohim' (1 Kings 18.39). Nature in this type of natural theology is considered as belonging to *sacra doctrina;* this is natural theology as the dogmatic theology of nature.

[4] I am not of course suggesting that the philosophical distinction of nature and existence coincides with the theological distinction of nature and 'economy' (grace and sin). But the philosophical distinction which I am employing as a theologian is open to particularization in theological terms, if for no other reason than that it is in itself vague and ambiguous and only acquires any kind of sharpness in a theological context. The distinction would seem to have relevance for the theology of marriage and of death.

The second type of natural theology practised by Christians is the sort commonly found in our seminaries. It consists in an artificial abstraction of those parts of *sacra doctrina* which deal with nature, treated now not as occurring on the way down from the living, self-communicating God, but as providing the starting-point of the way up. This type of natural theology has its own genuine value: it is the fulfilment in act of the Vatican I definition of the scope of reason. But it is fulfilled in act only in the total existence of Christians who have temporarily bracketed off their Christianity. It can never allow itself seriously and existentially to doubt the validity of its own procedures – seriously to doubt the existence of God.

Two other types of natural theology are practised by those not explicitly Christians. The first is of the kind recognized by St Paul in his Areopagus speech: it is the natural theology of the 'pagan of good will'. This natural theology, if not often systematic, effortlessly arrives at the affirmation of a divinity in and behind nature and society, the Semitic El or its equivalents – *le Dieu cosmique.* It must be seen theologically as a *praeparatio evangelica,* an existence of reason which looks to its purification and explicitation in *sacra doctrina.* 'What therefore you worship as unknown, this I proclaim to you' (Acts 17.23).

The last type of natural theology is only theology in a Pickwickian sense. This is clearly recognized for instance by Professor Flew in his introduction to *New Essays in Philosophical Theology,* when he discusses the appropriateness of the general title for essays most of which are concerned to deny the existence of God. Seminary natural theology (type two) sometimes pretends that it is of the same type as this fourth type of natural theology. I must be allowed to describe this pretence as nonsensical, using this word not only as a term of abuse, but also to indicate the muddle which arises from confusing two different existential modes of reason (if not three, since type three is sometimes involved as well). Yet it is in this area, explored by the fourth type of natural theology, that the real *Gottesfrage* of our times is to be found, so that we are faced with the peculiar situation that seminary philosophy is existentially and inevitably cut off from the serious questioning of our contemporaries – unless of course we are prepared to go through a Kierkegaardian and not merely scholastic or even Cartesian doubt in our seminaries. This would be presumption rather than heroic faith.

This reference to the practical problems of the study of philosophy in religious institutions will serve conveniently to introduce the conclusion of this paper. If its theoretical findings are at all acceptable, it seems clear that we would be mistaken in any attempt to assert in our seminaries an autonomous philosophy in genuine symbiosis with philosophy pursued elsewhere. We shall always have much to learn from secular philosophy but nothing to contribute except a theological witness. This is by no means an unimportant role but it is not a philosophical one. As regards our students, the one thing we can fairly expect from all of them is Catholic faith, whatever reserves we may have to make about their philosophical intelligence; not many seminary students are born philosophers. Would it not be as well to accept this state of affairs honestly, and introduce them to philosophy as part of the whole process of making the Gospel explicit, a Gospel which is revelation in reality as well as word, which declares the truth about nature, human as well as cosmic, truth moral as well as speculative, a Gospel which is the manifestation of the mystery of Being, rather than to try to impress upon them the structures of a reason abstracted from existence? At least our reasoning existence would then be as serious as that of our secular contemporaries.

## 12

## The Significance for Ecclesiology of the Declaration on non-Christian Religions and the Decree on Missions of Vatican II

**1 Introductory**

It seems especially appropriate to discuss the topics of non-Christian religions and the missions in a Spanish Dominican house, where the memory and the traditions of Raymond Martin, Las Casas and Vitoria are still cherished. The case of Raymond Martin is particularly instructive, for here we see in the first years of the Order a serious and scientific interest in the study of Oriental languages, Arabic and Hebrew, for an apostolic and missionary purpose. Even if it is now thought unlikely that St Thomas composed the *Summa contra Gentiles* for the mission to Islam, yet the two activities of serious missionary reflexion and of the theological effort in a University context of *fides quaerens intellectum* are necessarily bound together in the authentic life of the Church and of the Order of St Dominic. My only regret is that my competence to deal with so important a subject is so limited; I know there are many Dominicans who are much more competent to deal with it than I am. I am not an expert on non-Christian religions and I am certainly no missiologist; but perhaps there are certain advantages in not being a specialist in either or both of the fields of comparative religion and missiology.

The subject of our discussions is the significance for the teaching of ecclesiology of the Council documents of Vatican II. That is to say, we are primarily concerned with general ecclesiology and not with special topics to be treated of in special courses of lectures. As I shall try to suggest in this paper, this means not only that we may leave to specialists the study of the special subject of missiology. It also means that within a general course of ecclesiology we shall not be meeting the demands of the Church simply by inserting into our general course of ecclesiology a brief course of lectures on non-

Christian religions or on the missions. We never solve our difficulties in the teaching of theology (and philosophy) in our studia simply by adding on new courses. We all know that students and professors are already carrying too heavy a burden. We are not like the editors of an encyclopedia who simply add on a new article to cover some subject which has come into existence since the last edition – automation, say, or Vatican II. The fundamental question we have to ask ourselves is the question of the modes of unity of knowledge. In St Thomas's division of the sciences, as in the commentary on Boethius *de Trinitate,* qq. 5 and 6, a whole civilization is articulated into an epistemological structure which claims to render an ontological structure. Our present *ratio studiorum,* even in its revised form, although it derives rather remotely from St Thomas's division and perhaps precisely because it does, represents little more than an external adaptation of this scheme which bears little relation to contemporary civilization and appears to have little sense of the need to unify this civilization ontologically. Of course this is an enormous problem to which – need I say it – I have no solution; but the present article is meant at least to contribute to the analysis of the general problem by examining it in the particular context of ecclesiology and, more narrowly, of the place of the theological study of non-Christian religions and missiology within ecclesiology. It seems to me that examination of the particular problems forces us to recognize that we must expect to undertake a far-reaching reorientation of our whole system of studies, in the attempt to define perspectives which will allow us to exhibit an ontology of culture.

## 2 The General Problem of a Tractatus de Ecclesia

The first problem which I must face in this paper is the common problem of everyone who has to concern himself with the teaching of *de Ecclesia*: that there is no generally accepted theological treatise of ecclesiology in the sense in which there is a tractatus *de Incarnatione* or *de Sacramentis*. There is no such treatise in St Thomas, though as Fr Congar has shown, there are many materials for such a treatise. Officially of course there is a part of Apologetics called *de Ecclesia,* for which many more or less adequate textbooks exist; but no one supposes that this *de Ecclesia* in Apologetics is sufficient for theological purposes. Once again it does not seem to me that we can meet the need for a dogmatic *de Ecclesia* simply by inserting such a treatise between, say, *de Incarnatione* and *de Sacramentis*. It does not seem to me that the relation of the theology of the Church to the rest of theology is simply that of a part to the other parts of a single whole. Here I should like to offer some suggestions in order to outline a working hypothesis with which to approach my special subject.

If ecclesiology is not simply a part of the whole of theology, what relation to theology does it in fact have? I suggest that ecclesiology should be conceived of as the ontological *a priori* of theology. By this I mean of course an *a priori* of *theological* ontology: the *a priori* belongs intrinsically to that of which it is the presupposition and precondition, and it is not being suggested that the ecclesiological *a priori* is some sort of non-theological presupposition of theology. I am prepared to allow for a certain historical relativism in my suggestion. We have often enough been reminded, by Pope Paul as well as others, that the study of ecclesiology is the principal concern of theology in our time. It may be that in some future epoch another topic will take the place of ecclesiology in our theological concerns, and it may then seem extravagant to give ecclesiology this *a priori* character in relation to theology in general. But we can only speak for our own time; and for our own time it seems to me that my suggestion provides a more adequate place for ecclesiology than the idea that it is (or should be) merely the subject of a single tractate among others. It would also provide some explanation of why there is no tractatus *de Ecclesia* in St Thomas or the other medievals. For an *a priori* is *implicit* in the total structure of comprehension (*Verständnis*) which depends on it. It is in St Thomas's *Summa Theologiae* as a *whole* that we may expect to find his ecclesiology, as that dimension of his theology which in his time it was unnecessary (in providential terms) to make explicit. In our time it is our task to make that ecclesiological dimension of all theology explicit. This requires (a) that we should introduce our study of theology by an examination, *via inventionis*, of the ecclesiological *a priori;* (b) that we should repeatedly exhibit this *a priori* as the dimension of all our theological study (including exegesis, supposing that this continues to be a separate part of the studies, and above all canon law, in its historical dimension as studied by Le Bras and his school in Paris and by Kuttner and Tierney in America); (c) that we should conclude our theological study by a synoptic review of theology as a whole, *via disciplinae*, as seen in terms of the ecclesiological *a priori*. (a) and (c) would then provide two explicit treatments of *de Ecclesia*, at the beginning and the end of theological studies. I shall add here that the synoptic and systematic treatment of *de Ecclesia* at the end of theological studies is far from obvious to me, and that I am speaking here very much *via inventionis,* in terms of an *approach* to ecclesiology. Such an approach would take the place of the old *de Ecclesia* in Apologetics, as it would also take the place of the old *de Revelatione* as well, though some aspects of the latter might be treated together with 'natural theology' under the general title of the *Gottesfrage.* In this sense we may indicate what is meant by the ecclesiological *a priori* by speaking of *ecclesia ut sacramentum salutis et revelationis;* or in Pauline term of the *mysterion tou theou* as realized in *ekklesia* and *pistis-gnosis;* or in Johannine terms of a *koinonia tes zoes kai aletheias.*

One last point should be noted about this ecclesiological *a priori.* By speaking of it as *ontological* I intend to exclude the notion that this *a priori* is merely epistemological in character, in a Kantian sense, as supplying the general noetic condition of a science entertained in an individual mind. The *a priori* we are concerned with here is more like a Heideggerian *Existential,* something to do with our very Being-in-community, and hence as supplying the foundation for a comprehending (*Verstehen*) which arises out of our historical existence (*geschichtliches Dasein*). In this sense 'ontological' has a wider sense than if it were used to describe the metaphysics of St Thomas (who does not himself of course use the word 'ontology' at all). The partial justification for this approach to a working hypothesis for general ecclesiology will I hope emerge from the particular problems of non-Christian religions and missions to which we now turn.

## 3 Non-Christian Religions

The most striking feature perhaps about the declaration of Vatican II on non-Christian religions is that it was made at all. It is unfortunate that this really fundamental aspect has been obscured by the controversy about that paragraph of the document which deals with the Jews. Both in this document and in *Lumen Gentium* a positive attitude is adopted to other religions practised today (Hinduism, Buddhism, Islam, Judaism are mentioned by name) and discussion with a view to mutual understanding is encouraged.

As has already been suggested, it does not seem that the mere addition of a new course of lectures on comparative religion would be a sufficient response to this directive of the Council, if for no other reason than that comparative religion, or the study of religions from a phenomenological point of view, is not of itself theology. On the other hand, a theology of non-Christian religions in abstraction from any particular non-Christian religions is likely to become artificial: some concrete experience of these religions must be provided. We need to exercise theological insight in some area of concrete encounter of religions, without at the same time demanding too much particularized knowledge of non-Christian religions from students and professors alike. I should like to point out here that the Bible itself is the supreme example of an encounter of Christianity and other religions. My suggestion is that within general ecclesiology, or within the course of exegetical study of certain books of the Bible, special attention be given to this historical shaping of Christianity as a Yes and No to contemporary religious traditions. The exaggerations of the *religionsgeschichtliche Schule* are well known; but these exaggerations are themselves instructive and in any case should not deter us from making use of these studies. Perhaps an example worked out in some detail may help to make my suggestion clearer.

In an illuminating passage from the introduction to an English translation of Chinese poetry of the late T'ang period, the author and translator, A. C. Graham, points out that the English reader has so far only had access to a certain kind of Chinese poetry, that kind which lacks the shadow and mystery of Sung landscape painting and Taoist philosophy. The poetry of the late T'ang, from the latter part of the 8th century, shows the emergence of a new sensibility, like that of Japanese poetry in the 9th century, English in the late 16th century, and French in the 19th century; what is common to all these periods in which a new sensibility emerges is what the author calls the 'concentration of multiple meanings'. My suggestion is that we may consider the end of the first Christian century as such a period of emergent sensibility in which the religious literature of the time, including above all the Gospel of St John, shows a concentration of multiple meanings. It is to my mind utterly impossible to ignore the likenesses between St John's Gospel and the non-Christian literature of this period, especially the Hermetic literature, or the gnosticism of the Odes of Solomon or the newly-discovered *Evangelium Veritatis*, or what might be called the mystical apocalypticism of the Qumran writings. These likenesses can be exploited in terms of 'influence' or 'borrowings', as in Bultmann's brilliant if erratic *Johannesevangelium*. The suggestion being made here is that the idea of a cultural shift, the change of sensibility in an epoch in the history of civilization, such that in various ways there takes place a 'concentration of multiple meanings', is a better way of comprehending the likenesses and unlikenesses between St John and his contemporaries. It is perhaps worth pointing out that there are now available modern Catholic commentaries on St John, most recently the first part of Schnackenburg's commentary, which may help the theologian to find his way in this complicated field of scholarship.

There are two points in particular to which I should like to draw attention. Firstly, the approach I have been describing demands a *literary* discrimination of the diversities and complexities of meaning, in immediate contact with texts; and in this connexion it should be remembered that in our European civilisation it is perhaps primarily through creative literature that human life has been interpreted, and that in consequence there is a real need for literature to take some clearly recognized place in our studies. Secondly, the literary appreciation in its turn requires a sense of the historicity of culture, by way of a realisation of the genesis of meaning in history. In the study of a biblical text, this literary and historic appreciation is directly illuminated by revelation. Similar studies could be made of the captivity epistles (here Schlier's *Epheserbrief* is extremely valuable) and also of the Old Testament, as well as, say, Irenaeus in his struggle with later Gnosticism. If some such grounding has been provided, it then becomes more plausible to suppose that a brief course of lectures on the major modern non-Christian religions might be of some real profit to the student.

However, all this could only be a beginning, an approach to the *theological* understanding of non-Christian religions. Here I must refer to the very striking writings of Heinz Robert Schlette, stimulated by some remarkable articles by Karl Rahner. The point is roughly speaking that the universal saving purpose of God in Jesus Christ from all eternity must be embodied historically not only in individuals isolated, as it were, from the concrete society, with its religious traditions, in which they have lived. This saving purpose must be embodied in these social religious traditions themselves, in spite of all the distortions to which they are subject on account of human ignorance and sin. This is not the place to discuss the conclusions of these authors; the point is that their approach, by way of an ontology of *Heilsgeschichte,* seems to me of the utmost importance. Salvation is offered to men in terms of meanings which have their genesis and growth in history; the particularized approach to the historical genesis and growth of meaning within Revelation itself as studied in biblical texts could offer an illuminating theological datum for the general theological view which sees foreshadowings – frequently distorted foreshadowings – of the fullness of Revelation in Jesus Christ. 'Anonymous Christianity' is never wholly anonymous; it must have some kind of expression, inevitably within a given traditional idiom: grace must have a human face. It is important to realize that the history we are considering here is comprehended ontologically: it is a history of Being, of the meaning of Being, a *Seinsgeschichte*. An important treatment of this theme by a Catholic writer seems to be Adolf Darlap's contribution to the first volume of *Mysterium Salutis*: *Grundriss heilsgeschichtlicher Dogmatik*, edited by Feiner and Lohrer (1965).

It seems then that the theological consideration of non-Christian religions involves us in a general way in questions of the hermeneutic of Being, of the interpenetration and distinction of secular history and the history of salvation, of the role of language as the way of life of a community, and of the history of culture as the bearer of ontological meaning. It seems too that an approach of this kind throws new light on familiar theological questions such as those of nature and grace, *extra ecclesiam nulla salus*, and the universality of salvation in Christ. For it does not seem that a non-historical metaphysics or a non-metaphysical history is either of them capable of providing an adequate framework for answers to these old theological questions.

There are indeed more specialized questions which arise from the theology of non-Christian religions, such as that of the 'Christian value of a non-Christian religion' like Buddhism, studied by de Lubac and Cornelis; but these questions, fascinating as they are, are best left to specialists, though it should be emphasized that the fascination should be personally experienced if a satisfactory theology of non-Christian religions is to take shape. Unless a theologian has felt for himself the real profundity of the Rig Veda or the Bhagavad Gita, of the Qu'ran or the Persian Sufis, the attractive forces of the Avalokitesvara of Mahayana Buddhism, the piety of Jewish Hasidism or the dynamism of African traditional religion, he is not likely to take very seriously the possibility of Christian truth and holiness outside the visible communion of the Church. But the chief value of the theological study of non-Christian religions for general ecclesiology is that it forces the theologian to adopt new social-historical categories for the Church itself. We have all doubtless experienced discomfort in trying to find adequate *social* categories for the Church, the sense that neither the medieval interpretation of the *corpus mysticum* as a *corporatio* or the later interpretation in terms of a *societas perfecta* allowed sufficiently for the historical dimension of the Church. To say that the Church is the People of God introduces this historical dimension but only in biblical terms (I am not enthusiastic about Rahner's use of *das Volk Gottes* in a sense which seems to derive from German Romanticism): it does not allow us to think of it in concepts which manifest this historical community to ourselves and the world. The notion of culture, in the ontological sense indicated above, does something to help us here, by allowing us some insight into the human meaning of the historical solidarity of the Church. In this sense the 'culture' of the Church is the context or world of meaning within which the Church community discovers and creates its identity. This notion of culture incidentally throws some light on the concept of theology itself, which is to be thought of as a process in this ecclesial culture, evolving in more or less differentiated ways in those who share in the culture, rather than a 'science' entertained by single minds.

One last point needs to be made here, by way of transition to the significance of the theology of missions for general ecclesiology. It is noticeable in the Vatican declaration on non-Christian religions, as well as in many theological writings on the same subject, that these religions are considered as more or less static unities, and approached very largely in a literary way through their scriptures. We must I think explicitly realize that this kind of literary approach is restricted, and that a more adequate approach to these religions would have to take into account the concrete life of the people who live by these religions. If I may be allowed to mention it here, I have myself had the good fortune to experience at first hand Buddhism in Ceylon and Judaism in a Jewish school in England; and I have also been able to discuss Judaism in Israel with Fr Fontaine of St Isaie in Jerusalem, and African and Indian religions with members of the School of Social Anthropology in Oxford. I can at least say with confidence on the basis of these experiences and discussions, as well as of reading, that a much wider gap exists between reflexion and practice in non-Christian religions than is the case even in Catholicism. This is not merely a warning against supposing that a religion is known merely through its scriptures, if any, or even a wish that somehow in our studies a place can be found for firsthand experience as well as for reading; it is once again a recommendation that we should learn to look at religions as historical cultures – this is of course essential in the case of non-literate, 'primitive' religions. For while these latter religions are precisely characterized by the lack of any real historical dimension (the 'beginnings' are thought of as simply some few generations before) all religions today, including Catholic Christianity, are engaged in a struggle for self-identity in a world which is being secularized by modern technology and the mass-culture which accompanies it. We are now all inhabitants of one world, taking part in a single historical process, as *Gaudium et Spes* notes. The implications of this truth are best discussed in considering the theology of missions.

**Missions**

Both *Lumen Gentium* and *Ad Gentes* remind us that the Church on earth is essentially missionary: 'Ecclesia peregrinans natura sua missionaria est' (*Ad Gentes*, c. 1, n. 2); and while every professor of ecclesiology would of course immediately affirm this, it is, I think, open to some doubt how much significance this affirmation really has in the actual teaching of ecclesiology. It is to be noted that the decree requires all professors of theology, not only those concerned with the training of future missionaries in the narrow sense, constantly to bring out the missionary dimension of what they are teaching (ib. c. 6, n. 39).

It is not my business here to comment on the long and rich decree on the missionary activity of the Church, but only to suggest its methodological significance for our teaching of ecclesiology. With this in mind, I should like to draw attention to two points in particular: (a) the truly generous recognition of a genuine pluralism within the ecumenical unity of the Church; and (b) the concern for what, in general terms, may be called the *political* destiny of the different human groups in our single technologically unified world. These two points are not of course unrelated.

(a) Pluralism is not a theological condition with which Dominicans are equipped to deal by their studies. This simply seems to me a fact which we have to face and take action about. It is of course true that we hear a good deal in our philosophy about the analogy of Being, but this makes rare re-appearances in our theology. If we really took the analogy of Being seriously we should by now have very much enlarged its scope by taking into account the vastly expanded field of studies in semantics and linguistics and the philosophy of language, we should have tried to come to terms more seriously with the philosophy of history or rather of historicity (*Geschichtlichkeit*), and we should have recognized and come to terms with those forms of human communication (in literature, music, art, and the cinema) in which human meanings are most creatively embodied. And while we cannot and need not stop thinking theologically as Europeans, we must stop thinking as though 13th century Europe ('Europe' itself is a Renaissance concept) was the only really important moment in the thought of all mankind. We have to be ready and able to take part in a genuine dialogue with utterly different civilizations. Rome, we may believe, will continue to be the centre of Christianity, but Europe seems to be unlikely to be the centre of Christendom: Christendom has a plurality of centres linked in communion. Once we recognize the absurdity of teaching cosmology, psychology etc. out of textbooks in seminaries in Africa and the West Indies, it will not be long before we interrogate ourselves on our own practice at home. Once we take seriously the planting and growth of autochthonous churches throughout the ecumenical Church, we must ask ourselves what as European Christians we really wish to contribute to a creative dialogue with these younger churches, what our European Christianity really is; it is certainly not just scholasticism. If we really recognize the missionary nature of the Church and its pluralism, we shall have to ask: 'What is Europe?', and ask this question really seriously in our studies (not just after our studies or by the side of our studies). Some attempts at this kind of dialogue have been made with greater or less success, as for instance by Fr Tempels, with his account of Bantu philosophy. My anthropological friends confirm my suspicion that this attempt is romantic and takes too little account of local differences; does it not in any case suffer because the dialogue is seen as one between a decadent version of scholastic philosophy and what is articulated as a Bantu philosophy? We may quote from an extremely penetrating study of 'Christian presence amid African religion' by an Anglican missionary, *The Primal Vision:*

> If an honest meeting between Christianity and the African world-view may be creative on the frontiers of the Church, it may be even more creative within the body of the Church itself. For *de facto* it is precisely at that point of the encounter and contrast and choice that the Church will get its own authentic insights into the Word. It is at the danger point, the point of interchange and temptation, that a true African theology will be born, not out of syncretism but out of understanding (p. 42).

I only add to this that the European contribution to this non-European theology in the making will only be significant if the European theology itself accepts the demand that it should re-create its own identity.

(b) This brings me to the second point, the Church's concern for the *political* destiny of human groups. There is a marked change of emphasis between more recent documents of the Church, including Pope John XXIII's encyclicals, and earlier statements, in the recognition of and sympathy with the historical development of peoples. The fact itself, of course, is something new, in the sense that the world we live in, after the dissolution of the colonial empires, displays a pullulation of new nationalisms each seeking to discover and create its own identity. It is not always easy for Europeans, even European Catholics, to understand this wind of change in the world. If the study of ecclesiology in our studia is to avoid the sterility of theologizing in a vacuum, it must continually pursue this understanding of a world breaking out in revolutionary novelty. Politics, in this sense, is the effort freely to accept and create a communal destiny. Any Christian missionary who simply stands aside from this interior debate in the new nations and tries to restrict himself to pure 'religion' is doing no service to the Church. This is not to say that the Church must herself become an independent political force, seeking its own advantage: its real presence among the peoples must be one of service (*Ad Gentes,* c. 2, n. 12). The Church has her intrinsic part to play in the eschatological manifestation of the Son of *Man.*

The bearing of all this for our own studies seems luminously clear: that we too in our studia should make the recreation of our own European Christian identity our fundamental concern; and the first step in this direction is the simple and honest recognition that it no longer exists. That is to say, the European Christian identity of twenty years ago means very little to those who were born about that time – and I am thinking of my own students here. The whole of our tradition is being challenged, healthily, I believe; because out of this questioning a new identity, in continuity with the old one, will emerge. I might add here that to the younger students and their contemporaries in the Universities, in England, at any rate, Vatican II as a whole means very little; after all, Vatican II represents the victory of the generation of the 1940s, after what painful struggles they only know, and those who were born in the 1940s have very little conception of what has really been achieved.

I am afraid that much of what has been said in this article may seem vague and merely edifying exhortation; and yet I feel sure that a proper sense of the true horizons of our studies is essential if we are to embark on their reorganization. This is why I should like to appeal most earnestly that the new *Ratio Studiorum* will give only the most general directives, and allow the studia to work out by themselves ways of defining and resolving the problems of our times, meeting from time to time to compare results at conferences like the present one; in this way we may hope to progress towards the truth according to our traditions in a spirit of inquiry.

## 13

## The Significant Life of a Dominican House of Studies[1]

It has not been easy to decide on a suitable title for this address. The phrase 'significant life' has been chosen in preference to 'role', 'function', or even – wilder flights, these – 'inner life' or 'soul'. The point has been to indicate a perspective (rather than to frame a policy) for our common life of study at Blackfriars, and to propose it for inspection and reflection (not for instant discussion). I am conscious that many of my hearers this evening have had to listen to me before, sometimes for many years, and it is hardly likely that they will hear anything new from me today; and yet there would seem to be some value in publicly rehearsing, with some ceremoniousness, views which are intended to elicit positive attitudes of assent or dissent, to contribute to a common if differentiated consciousness. With this in mind, I have upon careful consideration determined to speak with as much honesty as I am capable of; the time has really passed, if it ever existed, for triumphalism of any form, conservative or progressive. What is offered is a 'Here I stand', like Luther's; but it is not necessarily, not yet, anyway, an 'I can do no other', provided someone shows me how. Those of my hearers who are not Dominicans have at least done us the honour of sharing our erratic pilgrimage, and I must suppose that they too will not be without concern for an attempt to sketch out its horizons, if hardly to plot its future course.

I shall begin with a statement, or rather a resolute affirmation, of the utterly obvious: the significant life of a house of studies is to be assessed by its concern for study. No one who is familiar with the recent history of this house is likely to doubt the need for the assertion of anything so obvious. It is not indeed my purpose to offer this statement in a limiting or exclusive sense as though study

---

[1] An inaugural address as Pro-Regent of Studies given at the opening of the academic year at Blackfriars, Oxford, October 1966.

and nothing else, and study irrespective of any further discriminatory analysis of what might be involved in such study, were alone to serve as a criterion of the significant life of this or any other house of studies. The point of resolutely affirming the obvious is to insist on an order of priorities, such that whatever else this house may achieve either as a community or through individuals in it, the significant life of the house would not be intensified or enlarged unless these achievements issued from or contributed to a shared life of study.

Even with the preliminary qualifications issued a moment ago – qualifications which will shortly be examined in more detail – the absoluteness of this affirmation is likely to arouse disquiet. I hope I may be allowed to say that one contributory cause of any such disquiet would be the general ambiguities and uncertainties which have been allowed to cloud the essential Dominican vocation. I regard this vocation as a service of the Word, involving a reverence for the life of intelligence in the economy of our redemption in Christ, an intelligence which is compassionate without sentimentality, creative without eccentricity, sensitive without preciosity, contemporary without servility to fashion, and wholly absorbed by and transparent to the Gospel in the mystery of the Church. By study, then, I understand the disciplined cultivation of such an intelligence, and it is for the life of study understood in this sense that I am making the assertion of unconditional priority.

To make an assertion of priority is at least implicitly to reject alternative systems of priorities; and it may help to make more concrete what is involved in the system of priorities now being recommended if some of the alternatives are briefly inspected. It appears to me that the most important of these can be formulated in the injunction, 'In the destructive element immerse'. In one or another of a variety of senses this imperative has been a dominant theme of Western civilization since at least the Romantic movement (Blake is a key figure here): the replacement of the Other world by the Under world, whether this underworld is conceived of as individual or social unconscious, what the individual or society refuses to admit to the light of common day, and now felt to be more real than the world of public acknowledgement. By a strange reversal, the dwellers in the sun are consumed by a nostalgia for the cave. It is surely unnecessary to document this preoccupation with illustrative texts: the theme is obvious enough. For our purposes it is sufficient to note that the most interesting variants of the theme are genetic or evolutionary: concerned, that is to say, with the passage from darkness to light, such that the passage is conceived of as redemption or salvation. The destructive element is also the source of fertility, the pregnant chaos of energies awaiting transcendence and liberation. It is hardly surprising that two variants of the theme, the Marxist and the Jungian, have exerted a special fascination on English Dominicans in the last thirty years, the Jungian variant more persistently and on the whole more professionally. But even where the preoccupation with the publicly unacknowledged has not acquired ideological consistency it continues to be active in a distrust of the common order and a concern for what it seems inevitable to exclude, a distrust and a concern which would count itself spurious if it did not share compassionately in the sickness of the afflicted or the constraint of the captive. 'In the destructive element immerse.' That form of common public order which has been codified as a regular Dominican way of life seems for this concern (which I share) expressly designed to inhibit access to the real sources of life, to smother the processes of transcendence.

Now no assertion of the absolute priority of the life of study, even in a house of studies, would deserve the least attention if it were deaf to this appeal *de profundis*. The redemptive process as integration of the personality or as historical liberation sufficiently resembles the redemption in the passion, death and resurrection of Christ to allow us, at least provisionally, to articulate our concern as Christians in the language and in the style of release of energies from sociological or psychological constraint; in fact any concern claiming to be Christian which simply rejected these contemporary styles would no longer be Christian. Nor again is it particularly to my purpose here to argue that the Christian doctrine of sin and grace could not accept without serious qualification accounts of redemption in terms of the release of energies which are only by their dissociation or alienation morbid. My point is that the significant life of this house of studies must consist *primarily* in the articulate interpretation of the concern in the service of the Word. The *primary* concern of a house of studies must be a *contemplative* engagement in the world.

'Contemplative engagement' or 'engaged contemplation' may still be a faintly unfamiliar combination of terms; engagement may still be felt to exclude that sort of withdrawal from the world felt to be proper to the contemplative life. Once again, it should be sufficient here to say that the engaged contemplation envisaged and recommended is not a *theoria* opposed to *praxis,* but a (Pauline) *gnosis* into the *mysterion* of Christ as this is disclosed in the history of mankind; not a withdrawal into the cell of self-knowledge but an entrance into the Christian meaning of time by way of the Christian meaning of our times. The common and shared activity for which priority is being claimed continues to be contemplative in that it is primarily a concern with meanings: the significant life of the house should be a life which contributes to the evangelical clarification of our historical epoch. We have, in contemplative engagement, to search for a focus of meaning, that Meaning of meaning to which we already have access in faith, God in Christ.

What this involves for our intellectual life is that we should continually raise the question of ultimate meaning, while confidently living in the presence of the ultimate answer: in the beginning was the Yea. The Gospel is promise and judgment at once; as judgment 'the word of God is living and active, sharper than any two-edged sword, piercing to the division of soul and spirit, of joints and marrow, and discriminating the thoughts and intentions of the heart' (Heb. 4.12). No merely human word or perspective can be exempt from the *krisis* of the Word of God, its continuous critique of pure reason. But it is only in the promise of the Word of life that we can endure the relativity of every human perspective and continue resolutely to put the ultimate question: 'What does it all mean?' This is not only an abstractly intellectual matter but something to do with the seriousness with which we take ourselves and the way we lead our lives.

There are two familiar styles of Dominican life which I shall refer to as the Angelo syndrome and the Peter Pan syndrome. J. M. Barrie being better known in England than Shakespeare, I should explain that the Angelo I have in mind is the Duke's deputy in *Measure for Measure*,

> a man whose blood
> Is very snow-broth; one who never feels
> The wanton stings and motions of the sense,
> But doth rebate and blunt his natural edge
> With profits of the mind, study and fast.

The precariousness of this Angelism is central to the play; we soon see the austere figure promising Isabella her brother's life in return for her surrender to his craving. I am not suggesting that Angelo is a portrait of any Dominican, living or dead, not merely because our Angelic figures are less prone to solicitation but also because they are less prone to study and penance. But an Angelo-image often seems discernible behind some of the exhortations to seriousness in the Dominican tradition. The Peter Pan syndrome is even more familiar among English Dominicans. Its more attractive features are a readiness to accept and produce the novel and the unexpected, a distaste for the merely conventional, an openness to the underworld, and a refusal to confuse seriousness with solemnity. The less attractive features, perhaps inseparable from the more attractive ones, tend to a cult of squalid and irresponsible Bohemianism, pretending to seriousness in virtue merely of habitual departure from the common order. A habitual regard for the common order may easily harden into an inert and timid formalism, but this alone is hardly sufficient ground for habitually disregarding it. One simple criterion, though by no means the only one, which will allow us to discriminate between the more and the less attractive features of our Peter-Pannishness is to enquire of ourselves just how costing is the word or gesture or action we are on the brink of. It is easy and cheap to cock a snook at the English hierarchy, for instance, while quite possibly maintaining the high line of Vatican II on the bishops; it may even be necessary to do just this from time to time just to keep sane; but the Christianity of an in-group intelligentsia is just as much a distortion of the Gospel as a Christianity of the clerical establishment. The whole of I Corinthians, with its discrimination between wisdoms and enthusiasms, is appropriate here; I am sure that as I write and read the words of this paper I must remind myself that 'the kingdom of God does not consist in talk but in power' (4.20).

Yet it is precisely in our talk, our service of the Word, that we are called to exhibit the transcendence of God; our language *has to be* the form of our life. 'For God is my witness, to whom I render religious service (*latreuo*) in preaching the gospel of his Son...' (Rom. 1.9). St Paul's use of the language of religious cult in which to formulate his self-consciousness as apostle has been carefully studied and seems to me of capital interest for anyone concerned for the Dominican religious vocation in a secularist age. The use of the language of cult to articulate the apostolic self-consciousness is itself one instance of the generally Pauline, and indeed New Testament, re-interpretation of religiousness as a worship in spirit and truth; so for example St Paul bows his knees in thanksgiving and petition to the Father of *agape* (Eph. 3.14 f.). This is by no means a worship in the head or a metaphorical dodge but a trans-figuring of the body, an anticipated resurrection witnessed to in an evangelism of style of life as well as of word. At the same time it seems to me an inescapable truth that the Christian witness to the world within a sacramental economy which awaits its own withering away in the general renewal of all things must accept, together with its responsibility for institutional signs of eschatological renewal, a real and definite limitation and even impoverishment of human creativity. The token of this exchange and mutual dependence of Church and world is the Cross: 'So death is at work in us, but life in you' (2 Cor. 4.12). 'For we are glad when we are weak and you are strong' (2 Cor. 13.9). Clericalism is the kenosis by which we take on the form of the servant. As clerics we need the laity, as Christians we need non-Christians; the non-Christian, the autonomously human in ourselves has to submit to the cross of the institutional sign of Christ's redemptive work, and in this sense fill out by representation and in reality here and now what is lacking in Christ's afflictions for the sake of the Church of which we have become ministers, making the word of God fully known, the mystery hidden from past ages but now made manifest (cf. Col. 1.24–26). It seems to me of the utmost importance not to confuse this 'economic' need for dialogue and mutuality with the autonomously human in the world, with a congenital weakness, moral and psychological in character, which cannot endure the institutional sign of the cross of Christ, the yoke of the servant. There is a yearning for secularist achievement which is no more than a symptom of vital debility.

Fundamental to this revaluation of the religious in Christian faith and love is the sense of its eschatological conclusiveness in a world still open to continuous (and discontinuous) change and evolution. The revaluation of sacrifice as human death and resurrection is an ultimate, but an ultimate which needs constantly to be refigured in human historical change, to be shown there for the ultimate, consummation *and* crisis, that it is. This is a *task*; for a house of studies a task of contemplative engagement. The common task of this house of studies is so contemplatively to sketch a horizon that the world in which we are engaged may disclose its significance in the archetypal mystery of God. We find our own significance by disclosing (by seeking to disclose) the significance of the world.

It is absolutely manifest that this task, involving as it does a sustained sense of the seriousness of God's destiny for man in Christ, ineluctably demands a personal and communal discipline: not an extrinsic discipline but one intrinsic to the task itself. It is clear that this discipline has historically been formulated as a monastic or quasi-monastic code of prayer and silence, acquiring its intelligibility from the task with a view to which it was formulated and observed. It is clear that this code is being found increasingly unintelligible, cripplingly restrictive, and unadapted to the given task. Here the realm of clarity ends. For on the one hand the nature of the task itself has become increasingly obscured (consider, for instance, those Dutch Dominican novices who sought and obtained permission to study agriculture instead of theology so as to work in under-developed countries); and on the other, and partly as a consequence, the progressive erosion of the monastic code has led to a deterioration of commitment to the task which quite frequently shows itself as moral flaccidity and nihilism. Speaking as one for whom the code used to provide a tolerable and convenient context for what, subjectively felt, didn't seem a wholly insignificant life, but speaking also as one who freely recognizes that an increasing number of his fellow-Dominicans find that code intolerable, inconvenient and trivial, I ask with some passion (if I may) just what is being conceived of as a way of life which will continue to carry the seriousness of genuine and enduring commitment. For it is simply naive to suppose that mere private spontaneity or endless discussion will do. Into whatever form of communal religious endeavour we are emerging, whatever long revolution of underworlds is labouring for birth in us in that *Seinsgeschichte* in which we share, I do believe that the Dominican service of the sacrificial word of God has its continuing intrinsic significance in that revolution, and that this service and task demand its sacrificial discipline. Not unreasonably in our day, we look for our hagiography not in the lives of the martyrs but of those others, non-violent freedom marchers it may be, who have dedicated themselves to the emancipation of an underworld. At least one of the themes of primitive monasticism was an endeavour to represent the martyr in the idiom of engagement with the devil in the desert. I am not clear what new idiom of dedication is being suggested by the new hagiography, though I do recognize that some of the emergent forms of community life, the common service of the table, for instance, embody a discipline of mutual charity, which I at least find quite as demanding as the service of the capuce (also, quaintly enough, an item in a discipline of charity directed to the construction of a common order by way of the construction of a common sign).

It is not however my business here to do more than raise the question of what in general would be the appropriate structure of discipline in view of the Dominican service of the Word. It is clear to me that the question cannot be answered by the absolute imposition of authority from above, but only by a dialogue between *all* the members of the Dominican community on the one hand (as a common 'laity' or Dominican people of God) and those members on the other hand (the distinction therefore not being exclusive) who have the authority to witness to tradition, to send out in mission, and in the last resort to guarantee witness and mission by sanction. My business here is to insist that study as engaged contemplation intrinsically requires study as personal and communal discipline. Such a discipline would seem to be the very structure of the engagement. A beautiful simplicity has never seemed to me one of the Dominican excellencies, any more than the role of the charismatic Fool. And yet evangelical simplicity has to be allowed to warm and sustain sophistication, and fantasy and charism must not be driven underground. Every academic institution, simply by promoting a discipline of study, tends to be a killer of the dream. It may be that the academic institution by itself cannot hope to overcome its own built-in imbalance, though the provision of opportunities for some personally creative work in essays and seminars may help. But every academic institution needs its wider human context, in such a house as this primarily the local community. If one cannot expect of academic discipline that it contribute to every need of the whole man, one can at least demand of it that it does not smother growth and transcendence and so breed nihilism and apathy, remembering always that an essential need of the whole man is some fixed point of reference and some commonly accepted public order.

The significant life of a Dominican house of studies then consists primarily in the discernment and construction of significance, of meanings, in the face of the Meaning of meanings to which – to whom – it is consecrated. Without a common awareness of the presence of ultimate Meaning amongst us the search for meaning itself becomes meaningless; yet the common awareness itself can only rise through a common search. 'You would not seek me unless you had already found me.' *Nisi credideritis, non intelligetis.* Perhaps that Meaning has always to be found in contradiction; it is certainly how it has to be sought today, in Europe, in Oxford, at Blackfriars. Writing in India the introduction to his *Christian Ashram* Bede Griffiths says:

> It is this experience of Christ as the ground of all being which must be the inspiration of a Christian monasticism. For this means that in Christ we not only discover the centre or ground of our being, but we also find a meeting point with all other men and with the whole world of nature. There is a discipline of silence and solitude which is necessary for the discovery of this inner centre of our being. But this separation should not divide a monk from the world but on the contrary enable him to meet the world at the deepest level of its being. 'A monk is one who separates himself from all men in order that he may be united with all men', was one of the sayings of the monastic fathers (p. 25).

Griffiths goes on immediately to speak of the problem of poverty in India; and one may feel that contemplation as he describes it is possible only in a subsistence economy where the 'world of nature' has not yet been assumed into history by the accelerator of technological advance. We, on the contrary, live in a world of history; and our problem is to find a centre of being in becoming (let the nonsense stand): our contemplation has to be in some sense Dionysiac rather than Apollonian, an identification with, by free surrender in faith to, the mysterion of God's destiny for mankind. I do believe (and here I stand) that without some such contemplative dimension and the discipline it involves there can be no significant life in this house of studies or indeed in any Dominican house.

One last word, so as to end if not exactly with a whimper at least not with an inappropriate bang. The lectors and students we have are the lectors and students we are. We may be witting or unwitting actors in a dramatic universe but we bear our treasure in earthen vessels. This is even the point of the drama: 'We bear our treasure in earthen vessels to show that the transcendent power belongs to God and not to us' (2 Cor. 4.7).

# 14

## Priesthood and Ministry[1]

### I

Whatever may have been the case at other epochs of the history of the Church, it is clear that today treatments of confined topics of theology which can afford to take for granted theology and Christianity as a whole are no longer possible. This is true in a special way of the topic which concerns us here, the theology of the priesthood and the ministry, since we have to examine an essential element in the structure or form of Christianity itself, and since we are making this examination not as detached observers but as people who are considering the fundamental sense of our own lives.

Consequently it seems suitable to make explicit two presuppositions of what is to be said later. Firstly, Christianity is real. That is to say, it is real not only with the kind of reality which will allow it to be included among other realities in accordance with a scale of reality already set up apart from Christianity itself. Christianity is real in the sense that its reality modifies the scale of reality itself. Whether we say that Christianity is a new reality in a world considered as being without it (say, as being prior to it, or posterior to it, hostile or neutral to it), or whether we say that Christianity has always been and still is 'anonymously' present in the world (as, say, prefigured in a total history of humanity within the eternal design of God), we must, in terms of Christianity itself, claim that Christianity is at the very least a dimension of reality which needs explicitly to be taken into account if the ontological scale which we use to assess it and indeed anything else is to function as a true criterion of the real. If in some of its aspects, Christianity is a social phenomenon, it cannot be assessed adequately in terms of sociology; if it is a 'spiritual' phenomenon, it cannot be assessed adequately in terms of the *Geisteswissenschaften,* the humanities; if it is a

[1] This article is based on a paper given at the Clerical Students Conference at Spode House at the end of August 1969.

religion, it cannot be assessed adequately in terms of comparative religion.

If then Christianity is a novel reality or a novel dimension of the real which modifies our total apprehension of reality, it should be possible to specify in what its characteristic modification of apprehended reality consists. Rather than undertake the complex theological and epistemological analysis which this would involve if it were to be done seriously, I shall merely say here that the novelty of Christianity emerges in experience as an opposition to the 'world', an opposition which is in part the opposition of contraries and in part the opposition of perfect and imperfect: in the exhortation, 'Have courage, I have overcome (*nenikeka*) the world' (John 16.33), both kinds of opposition are united dynamically, as the dynamic transcendence of Christianity in the victory of Christ over the world. It is this experience of dynamic transcendence, shared victory in Christ, which is the expression of the ontological novelty of Christianity: 'This is the victory that overcomes (*he nike he nikesasa*) the world, our faith' (1 John 5.4). The dynamic transcendence of the world is achieved once for all, *ephapax*, in the paschal mystery of Christ which ontologically transfigures the world, and is shared in and appropriated by Christians in faith; and it is figured (socially, culturally, religiously) in the phenomenon of the Church. The Church is, we say, the figure or 'sacrament' of the dynamic transcendence of Christianity. In this paper, we are concerned both with the dynamic transcendence of Christianity 'in itself', in particular in one of its historical interpretations (notably the Epistle to the Hebrews), as sacrifice and priesthood; and also with one of the elements by which this dynamic transcendence has been sacramentally figured, also including a 'priesthood', the apostolic ministry of the sacrament of Order. This characteristic figure is neither identical with what it figures, nor is it the only figure, even in terms of 'priesthood', of what it figures, since baptism too constitutes a 'priestly' title. In what follows, we shall discuss the 'real' priesthood, that is, the dynamic transcendence of the victory of Christ and its appropriation in faith by Christians, in its interpretation as 'priesthood'; and we shall discuss 'sacramental' priesthood, that is, figure of this victory, and in particular the ministerial form of the latter. It may be helpful to anticipate here, and note that the ministerial priesthood is primarily episcopal and only subordinately presbyteral; so that member of English society whom we call the 'Catholic priest' (Roman collar, black suit, with or without black hat) is a sociological variant of a presbyteral grade of an apostolic ministry figuring a dynamic transcendence of Christ and Christians, which itself has historically been interpreted as priesthood; so that he is not connected with the Christ of the Epistle to the Hebrews in any simple way.

The second presupposition which it seems appropriate to make explicit in advance is concerned with the nature of self-understanding. Self-understanding is intrinsically diversified. The personal 'I' of each one of us is a principle and a possibility of dynamic transcendence (which is what makes it possible for us to enter by faith into the dynamic transcendence of the eschatological victory of Christ); but none of us is purely this. The transcendence is exercised in a history of personal experience of the self with others, contemporaries, predecessors and successors, related in a variety of ways, biological, social, spiritual; every personal achievement of identity is a modification of the history of the whole. At any given moment prior to death a personal identity is achieved as a partial integration of a past, conscious and unconscious, into the roles and relationships given and assumed, which provide the ground and matter for future integrations. The role and relationships accepted in ordination to the ministry imply a permanent identification with the figure of God's saving purpose in Christ in the Church: an identification which has the form of a 'consecration'. It is perhaps instructive that one of the senses which can be taken by the word *mysterium* in liturgical texts is precisely *ministerium* (cf. Blaise, *Dictionnaire Latin-Francais des auteurs chrétiens*, s.v. 'mysterium', n.9): the acceptance of this ministry is the acceptance of oneself as ritually figuring a mystery, consequently as affording inexhaustible possibilities for future integrations. Here 'role' becomes 'type'. Incorporation into the typical ministerial role of the Church's figure is acceptance for one's personal growth of a typical constituent of identity; and just as one's interpretation in a personal idiom of this type is indefinitely variable, so too the history of the Church provides and allows for an indefinite variety of styles of interpretation of the ministerial role (diocesan and religious clergy, to take an obvious example). The first task of theology is to identify not so much what is common but what is typical in this variety. It may be noted here that precisely because the ministerial role in the Church is typical it figures an essential element in the real victory of Christ and is therefore imitable even by those who do not possess and do not wish to possess the role, i.e. the laity: the ministry is imitable as transcendent type and not as role. All Christians are 'apostles' but only some are incorporated by consecration into the apostolic ministry (cf. H. U. von Balthasar, 'Office in the Church', *Church and World*, New York, 1967, pp. 44–111).

## II

The dynamic transcendence of Christ, the 'Christ-Event', receives a variety of determinations in the New Testament. Characteristically this Event is unique and unrepeatable in Christ; it is also communicated, reactualized in Christians. Christ and his victory are One and Many. The author of the Epistle to the Hebrews interprets the Christ-Event and its communication in terms of priesthood and cult. If he does not himself speak of the *communicated* Christ-Event as a priesthood, elsewhere in the New Testament (1 Peter 2.5, 9; Rev. 1.6; 5.10; 20.6, in dependence on Exodus 19.6 and Isa. 61.6) the generalization of priesthood is made explicit. But just as in 1 Peter the priesthood offers *spiritual* sacrifices, just as in John 4.23, 24 a worship 'in spirit and truth' is announced, so in Hebrews Christ is the priestly mediator of the New Covenant foretold by Jeremiah, a covenant in the mind and heart (Heb. 8.9–12; 10.16 citing Jer. 31). The blood of Christ alone 'who offered himself as the perfect sacrifice to God through the eternal Spirit, can purify our inner self (*suneidesin*, 'conscience') from dead actions so that we do our service to the living God' (Heb. 9.14). The elaborate and unfamiliar machinery of Old Testament cult on the one hand, and the author's effort to transpose this into a cosmic dimension in the case of Christ's priesthood on the other, tend to obscure for the modern reader of Hebrews the spirituality of Christ's priesthood and sacrifice and its effects which it is the main purpose of the epistle to insist on. Certainly the 'spirituality' is not one which is divorced from the 'matter' of Christ's blood or his human sympathy (cf. 4.15; 5.1); but it reaches to that inwardness of sin exposed by the judging word of God which is like a two-edged sword, 'piercing to the divisions of soul and spirit and discerning the thoughts and intentions of the heart' (4.12). The heavenly throne to which Christ the high priest penetrates does not separate him from us but brings him into more intimate connection with us: his blood is the new and living way opened for us into the heavenly sanctuary (10.19–20).

The theological idiom of the author of the Epistle to the Hebrews provides us with what was called above an 'interpretation' of the dynamic transcendence of the Christ-Event. To speak of interpretation is to recognize the possibility of alternative interpretations; it is not to suggest that alternative interpretations are open to us today as a matter of free choice. The priestly and cultic interpretation of Christ in Hebrews is one of those inspired and canonical interpretations of Christ which, together with, say, the

Johannine and Pauline interpretations, help to constitute the very reality of Christ himself in his communicable meaning. The Epistle to the Hebrews, inspired as we believe by the Spirit of Christ, is an intrinsic element in the mystery of Christ, such that *no* communication of Christ to Christians is possible which may not be interpreted in priestly and cultic terms: so St Thomas can speak in a fine phrase of the *religio Christianae vitae*. Thus not only the Christian's external acts of cult but his whole life in the Spirit is religion, cult, sacrifice: participation in the priesthood of Christ. Congar is surely right to say that the 'universal priesthood' of Christians is not *primarily* a title to a part in the Christian liturgy ('Structure du sacerdoce chrétien', *Sainte Eglise,* Paris 1963, pp. 239-274; 'The two forms of the Bread of Life', *Priest and Layman,* London, 1967, pp. 103-138). The Christian liturgy is an aspect of the ecclesial figure of the mystery of Christ, participation in it is itself granted liturgically, in the ecclesial figure of Christian baptism, so that the Father may be worshipped in spirit and truth even by those who do not bear the ecclesial figure of Christ. That there must be some 'figure' of this worship in spirit, though not an ecclesial one, is not being denied; all that is being said, briefly, is that wherever there is the grace of Christ, there is his priesthood.

It should now be clear that no direct application of Hebrews may be made to what is usually called the Catholic priesthood. What we may say is that the Catholic priest, in virtue of his ministerial priesthood, serves as an emblem of the 'real' priesthood he shares with every worshipper of the Father in the Spirit, and as a type of the sacramental figure of this worship in the liturgical worship of baptized Christians. But this emblematic or typical function is derived from a ministerial role in the Church which is not to be defined in purely sacerdotal, cultic terms.

### III

One of the major doctrinal achievements of Vatican II has been its full treatment of the apostolic ministry in the Church. For our purposes the two most important documents are chapter III of the *Constitutio dogmatica de Ecclesia* (*Lumen Gentium*) and the *Decretum de Presbyterorum ministerio et vita* (*Presbyterorum Ordinis*; the original title of what was to be only a series of propositions was 'De ministerio et vita sacerdotali'. The English translations seem to be unwilling to follow the Latin text, and translate both 'sacerdos' and 'presbyter' by 'priest').

As the title of chapter III of *Lumen Gentium* ('De Constitutione

Hierarchica Ecclesiae et in specie de Episcopatu') makes clear, the term 'hierarchy' is used in Vatican II as it was used in the Council of Trent (Denzinger-Schönmetzer 1768, 1776) to refer to all the grades of the ministry and not, as has regrettably been the custom in recent years, merely to bishops. It is to be hoped that in future we shall hear less of activities of 'the English hierarchy' which have in no way involved the co-operation of the clergy apart from the bishops. The first sentence of the chapter tells us in what this hierarchical structure consists: 'For the pasturing and constant growth of the People of God, Christ the Lord instituted in his Church various ministries, which work for the good of the whole Body' (LG 18). The notion of *ministerium,* explicitly connected with *diakonia* (LG 24), is central to the treatment of 'office' in Vatican II. As the text continues: 'For ministers endowed with sacred power are at the service of their brethren.' It should be noted that the ministry is not only 'pastoral' (*pascendum*) in a restricted sense but includes the promotion of the increase of the People of God (*semperque augendum*). In accordance with the explicit recognition in *Lumen Gentium* of the role of images in reflection on the Church (cf. LG 6, *'figuris'*, *'imaginibus'*, including those of 'flock' and 'shepherd', *pastor*), we should allow our sense of the pastoral ministry to be reanimated by the biblical imagery behind the formalized expression.

The foundation of this ministry in the Church is *mission*; as the Son was sent by the Father, so the Apostles were sent by Jesus Christ in the construction of the Church; it is by his will that the bishops, as successors of the Apostles, should continue this pastoral ministry to the end of time (LG 18). Recalling and restating the teaching of *Lumen Gentium, Presbyterorum Ordinis* has a fine passage in which the unity in diversity of the apostolic mission and ministry is clearly brought out:

> So it was that Christ sent the Apostles just as he himself had been sent by the Father. Through these same Apostles, he made their successors, the Bishops, sharers in his consecration and mission. Their ministerial office (*munus ministerii*) has been handed down to presbyters in a lower degree (*subordinato gradu*), so that established in the Order of the presbyterate, they might be co-operators (the traditional term in the ordination prayers of the sacramentaries) of the episcopal Order in the proper fulfilment of the apostolic mission entrusted to them by Christ. (PO 2)

Ministry in the Church is the expressive figure of the single mission and ministry of Christ and the Apostles. There can be no genuine understanding of what is commonly called the 'Catholic priesthood' unless this is seen as the permanent presence and exercise, in a limited degree, of the Apostolic office and ministry. There are extremely complex historical questions concerning the definition, differentiation and transmission of the Apostolic office in the first two centuries of the Church; if the letters of Ignatius of Antioch show us a recognizably Catholic order, it is far from clear how this emerged even from the state of affairs discernible in the Pastoral Epistles, and every attempt at reconstruction has to admit honestly the existence of considerable gaps in the evidence (cf. P. Benoit, 'Les origines apostoliques de l'Episcopat selon le Nouveau Testament', *L'Evêque dans l'Eglise du Christ*, 1963; P. Grelot, 'La vocation ministérielle au service du peuple de Dieu', *Aux Origines de l'Eglise*, Recherches Bibliques VI, 1965, pp. 159–173; see also various books by J. Colson). But these complexities should not obscure the fundamental Catholic truth of the permanence of the Apostolic office in the Church, however this office was at first differentiated. The episcopal function may well have been shared in a given community by the entire presbyterium, so that the individuals we should now call bishops may have had regional rather than local responsibilites like Timothy. But this should rather be seen as an aspect of the episcopate which has been restored to Catholic consciousness in the teaching of Vatican II on episcopal collegiality: once again, it is the continuance in the Church of an Apostolic office, a re-presentation of the Apostles, however differentiated, which is the essential.

The later history of the Church has also shown fluctuations in the differentiation of this single ministry, but we may say that essentially two contrasting ideologies have succeeded each other. And to understand the nature of this contrast, we should notice that two different kinds of analysis of the apostolic ministry are simultaneously at work in discussions of this kind. In the first place, there is a distinction of the *content* of the powers handed down in the ministry; secondly, there is the question of the *grading* of these powers.

Now according to a long and honourable tradition going back to St Jerome, bishops and priests were seen as equal in sacramental priesthood (regarded as primarily a power to consecrate the eucharistic bread and wine), and differing only in 'jurisdiction'. This view has been maintained as part of a more general theory of a two-fold division of 'powers' in the Church, priestly and pastoral, an analysis strongly influenced by canon law. If the council of Trent maintained the superiority of bishops to presbyters (DS

1768), it did so in a not wholly unambiguous way (including, for instance, the power to confer the sacrament of confirmation as a power possessed by bishops alone); and it has in fact been widely maintained that episcopal consecration was not part of the sacrament of Order. Rather than attempt here to examine the complex ecclesiological problems involved, it may be helpful to recognize the strong unconscious hold of attitudes like these even in consciously progressive Catholic lay writers today. It has for instance been argued that a Catholic community should choose one of its members to perform the sacramental rites, in particular to consecrate the eucharistic bread and wine, while the community itself should see to its own running and its understanding and spread the Gospel by democratic discussion. This is a view of the ministry which reduces the minister to the status of a tame witch-doctor or medicine-man; from a different point of view, it has a curious resemblance, in its democratic idiom, to the imperial or royal claims to dominate the ecclesiastical hierarchy in earlier periods of the history of the Church.

In other words, in the complex of views at which we have just been glancing, a single 'power' of the apostolic ministry is isolated – the *sacerdotium* – and this is defined in a narrowly sacramental, or rather ritual, sense. Once the power has been defined in this sense, it seems that the grading can proceed only in terms of another 'power', the pastoral power of jurisdiction. Scholasticism provided this view with an ontology of the sacramental character and the sacraments in general; canon law with a legal theory not uninfluenced by papal centralization; popular superstition (clerical and lay) gave it a mythology of 'anointed hands', and secular authority served as a dialectical opposite in such a way that a claim to universal ecclesiastical *regnum* was based on *sacerdotium*.

*This whole complex ideology has been set aside by Vatican II.* Whereas in the former ideology, the grading was in terms of different contents or powers, now the content of the powers of the apostolic ministry is *in all cases* analysed in terms of participation in the threefold office of Christ as Teacher, Priest and King; and the grading of the ministry is seen in terms of *degrees* of participation in the fullness of the ministry granted to the episcopal Order.

On this latter point Vatican II is quite explicit. With a solemn 'Docet Sancta Synodus', *Lumen Gentium* declares that the plenitude of the sacrament of Order is conferred by episcopal consecration, in which ancient tradition has seen the supreme priesthood and the fullness of the sacred ministry ('summum sacerdotium, sacri ministerii summa', 21, with references to ordination prayers in the sacramentaries). It is Christ himself that the bishops make present in the midst of the faithful. They play the part of Christ himself as Teacher, Pastor and High Priest (*Pontificis*), and act in his person (*in Eius persona agant,* ibid.). But this ministry is exercised in the Church at different levels (*diversis ordinibus,* 28). Presbyters too, although lacking the supreme office of the high-priesthood (*apicem pontificatus,* a phrase taken from St Cyprian), are joined with the bishops in the sacerdotal dignity, and are consecrated into the image of Christ, the supreme and eternal priest (*sacerdotis*), for the preaching of the Gospel, the shepherding of the flock, and the celebration of divine worship (ibid.). Within the three degrees of the apostolic ministry, bishops and priests share a *sacerdotium,* unlike deacons.

We meet here an ambiguity, partly terminological, partly an index of something deeper, concerning this *sacerdotium,* said to be exercised in preaching and shepherding as well as the celebration of worship; and we shall return to this threefold activity in a moment. But first let us notice that the grading of the ministry is seen, in accordance with pre-conciliar studies, notably by Botte, in the terms of the liturgical prayers of ordination; presbyters are the '*providi co-operatores*' of the Episcopal Order (cf. e.g. B. Botte et al. *The Sacrament of Holy Orders,* London, 1962. cf. A. Béraudy, 'Les effets de l'ordre dans les préfaces d'ordination du Sacramentaire léonien', *La Tradition Sacerdotale,* Le Puy, 1959). It may be remembered that in the important Apostolic Constitution of Pius XII in 1947, it was laid down that the essential form of ordination to the presbyterate consisted in the formula containing the phrase *secundi meriti munus,* as against the form for the episcopal consecration, *Comple in Sacerdote tuo ministerii tui summam.* In neither form, it should be noted, is there any explicit mention of sacrificial, cultic powers. Presbyters exercise in a second, lower degree, the fullness of the ministry exercised by the bishops. In a way, presbyters render the bishops present in every assembly of the faithful (PO 5).

If this account may be allowed to suffice for the grading of that 'one and the same priesthood and ministry of Christ' shared by presbyters and bishops (PO 7), we must now examine briefly the *content* of this ministry. As has already been suggested, the ministry is consistently seen by Vatican II as a representation of and participation in the three offices of Christ as Teacher, Priest and King, this triple function being expressed in a number of equivalent ways. The systematic analysis of the offices of Christ in this threefold form seems to have been due in the first place to the theologians of the Protestant Reformation, though of course it has a long history in scholasticism and the Fathers (cf. Schmaus, art.

'Amter Christi' in *Lexikon für Theologie and Kirche,* I). In the years before the Council this threefold analysis was strongly recommended by Congar for ecclesiological purposes, in conscious opposition to the analysis in terms of two powers mentioned above. What it is important for us to see is that the totality of the ministry, analysed in this threefold sense, is possessed by bishops and priests in different degree. *The 'Catholic priest' is not defined primarily in cultic terms.*

A historical example may help to bring out the significance of this point. In an essay written in 1954, 'Le sacerdoce des prêtres ouvriers', Chenu felt bound to defend the priestly character of the worker-priests, on the ground that the preaching of the Gospel to the unbeliever was an essential element in the priesthood, since the regime of the sacraments is essentially a regime of faith *(sacramenta fidei)* and demands as its precondition the active presence of the Gospel *(L'Evangile dans le temps,* Paris, 1964). Catechetical, didactic, sacramental activity is only possible where the Gospel is already present, so that in a world in which whole sectors of society are ignorant of the Gospel it is no longer possible for priests to forget their evangelical role. In a footnote added in 1964, Chenu remarks that his essay caused considerable controversy at the time, although the essay itself now seemed to him to belong clearly to the past. We may wonder how generally the evangelical role of the priest is in fact recognized even today.

At any rate Vatican II is insistent on this point. In chapter II of *Presbyterorum Ordinis,* which is structured on the familiar threefold pattern, it is even said: 'Since no one can be saved who has not first believed, presbyters, as cooperators of the bishops, have as their primary duty the proclamation of the Gospel of God to all' (4). Later in the same paragraph, after the missionary ministry of the Word has been recalled, the essential connexion between Word and sacrament is reaffirmed; at the celebration of Mass, for instance, 'the proclamation of the death and resurrection of the Lord, the response of the people who hear, and the very offering by which Christ ratified the New Covenant in his blood, are inseparably united' (ibid.). The sacramental Word is in one sense the fullness of the Gospel as a power unto salvation, and the dissociation of Word and sacrament, even in the modern form noted above, is a surrender to superstition.

But the apparent ambiguity mentioned above, where the three functions of the ministry, evangelical, pastoral and cultic, are all attached to the *sacerdotium,* still remains. I have not noticed in the relevant documents of Vatican II an explicit treatment of the *interpenetration* of these three functions, and it is only when a terminological oddness of this sort occurs that a question arises about their relationship. However useful the threefold analysis may be, it seems to me that this distinction of the ministry into three functions is at most highly convenient. Fundamentally the ministry is the ecclesial figure of the ministry of Christ and the Apostles, and the threefold analysis should help to remind us of the complex unity of this mission and ministry: the evangelical ministry is pastoral and sacerdotal, the pastoral ministry evangelical and sacerdotal, the sacerdotal ministry evangelical and pastoral. The sacrificial and cultic terminology which St Paul used to speak of his evangelical ministry has often been noticed, and has been carefully studied by A. M. Denis ('La fonction apostolique et la liturgie nouvelle en esprit', *Revue des Sciences Philosophiques et Théologiques,* 1958, pp. 401–436; 617–656); consider, for instance, Rom. 15.16: God has given Paul the grace 'to be a minister (*leitourgon*) of Jesus Christ to the Gentiles in the priestly service (*hierourgounta*) of the Gospel of God, so that the offering (*prosphora*) of the Gentiles may be acceptable, sanctified by the Holy Spirit'. But the cult too may be evangelical: 'For as often as you eat this bread and drink this cup, you proclaim (*kataggellete*) the Lord's death until he comes' (1 Cor. 11.26). The proclamation is not a separate activity alongside the cult, but is exercised in it. Or consider the pastoral reminder to the 'newborn babes' (1 Pet. 2.2) of the generative power of the Gospel: 'You have been born anew through the living and abiding word of God' (1.23). It is not merely that the 'Catholic priest' is an evangelical as well as a pastoral and cultic minister; it is rather that he is all three simultaneously and inseparably, in a complex and unified representation of Jesus Christ. 'The pilgrim Church is missionary of its very nature (*natura sua*), since it takes its origin from the mission of the Son and the mission of the Holy Spirit according to the purpose of God the Father' (Decree on the missionary activity of the Church, *Ad Gentes* 2). From this point of view, the priestly (episcopal and presbyteral) ministry is not simply a figure of the high-priestly interpretation of the dynamic transcendence of the mystery of Christ; this ministry is a figure of the total mystery of Christ the Victor.

Perhaps this helps to bring out the full sense of the repeated statements in Vatican II that bishop and presbyter, in virtue of their ordination, act *in persona Christi* or *in nomine Christi* or *in persona Christi Capitis.* There is a rather formalistic use of the Head and Body language to speak of Christ and the Church even in such a document as Pius XII's *Mystici Corporis.* Without attempting to sort out the complex history of the notion of the 'mystical body of Christ' (this too was a part of the ideological complex discussed above), it can simply be said here that the Christ of faith, the Head of the Church, is identically the historical Jesus or he is only a figure of myth, a Gnostic redeemer. The priestly representation of Christ is a representation of Jesus of Nazareth and not only of the risen Lord. If the priest, bishop or presbyter, is to be a figure of Christ the Head in this world, he must be so plausibly and credibly, as the historical Jesus himself was.

## IV

Would it be unfair to say that if bishop and presbyter were really a representation of Jesus Christ, Jesus of Nazareth, Christ the Lord, there would be no reason for us anxiously to be questioning ourselves about the place of the priest in the modern world? At any rate Pasolini in his film *The Gospel according to St Matthew* has seen, and has made us see, something in Jesus of Nazareth which was there to be seen if we hadn't seen it before; and pop groups, and the society they sing for, seem to need an experience of transcendence, or else they wouldn't turn to LSD or pursue a Hilton Hotel swami to Bangor. Why don't we help them find the transcendence of Christ the Lord? Can it be because we ourselves don't know how to find Jesus Christ whom we are supposed to represent? Could it be that we might be able to discover him again for ourselves if only we could hear the inarticulate appeal for the Gospel which is there to be heard if we listen for it?

We are living, it has been said, at the end of the Constantinian era, for which the central task of Christianity has been to sacralize the institutions of society: typically in the anointing of the king, more familiarly in the ratification of the Establishment. We have hardly begun as Christians to live in the era which has been displacing it – let us call it the Romantic era (cf. J. L. Talmon, *Romanticism and Revolt: Europe* 1815–1848, London, 1967). It seems to me that the central task of Christianity in this new era is the sacralization of the central theme of this era: revolt. Can one seriously envisage a Christianity in the historical form of a sacralization, or better consecration, of revolt, of revolution, or is one, in a sickeningly familiar way, merely playing at 'radicalism'?

It would of course be possible to speak, less provocatively, of a consecration of growth or of historical change. But it seems an inescapable truth, if we listen to the appeal for the Gospel in our time, that growth and significant historical change can only proceed by negation of the whole order of society in which we find ourselves. The growing points of our society are not found in its order but in the rebellion against this order. The world has to be overcome: the 'world' as the systematization of the good life of affluence and the masked or open exploitation and suppression of whole sectors of society, even in the West; the 'world', which as affluent or impoverished blights the growth of the spirit in transcendence.

The sacralization or consecration of revolt: not merely its endorsement. The efficacious symbol of the consecration of revolt can only be the death and resurrection of Jesus Christ. Here there arise for the Christian and the priest those painful problems of violence which are, minimally, his problems to endure if not to resolve. The Christian and the priest have to sanctify revolt and growth from within, by 'a priestly service of the Gospel of God, so that the offering of the peoples may be acceptable, sanctified by the Holy Spirit'. Make love, not war.

It seems that the priest may have a special role in this Christian sanctification of the *populorum progressio*. The rising and assembly of the peoples is the eternal secret of God and his transcendent purpose. The apostolic ministry has a special responsibility to announce the transcendence of God in the midst of his historical manifestation; but one can only announce the transcendence authentically (let us face it) if it is a matter of one's own experience in faith. Perhaps it is only by losing one's soul to the world for God's sake that one may gain both the world and one's own soul. How can one pray in the Church without first accepting the world on behalf of the Church? One prays by identifying oneself with the world (to 'overcome' it) and not by separating oneself from it (cf. PO 3): one prays by incarnation, death and resurrection. The eucharistic synaxis, as the 'centre of the assembly of the faithful over which the presbyter presides' (PO 5), is a local representation of the assembly of the peoples, summoned together by the word of the living God which it is the task of the presbyter to announce (cf. PO 4). Perhaps it is as the servants of God's eternal purpose to sum up all things in Christ that we shall find the sense of our apostolic ministry.[2]

---

[2] Besides the references given in the text, the following are also relevant: P. Franseñ, 'Priestertum', in *Handbuch Theologischer Grundbegriffe*; J. Lécuyer, *Le Sacerdoce dans le Mystère du Christ*, (Paris 1957); K. Rahner, 'Priestly Existence', *Theological Investigations III*, (London 1967, pp. 239–262); E. Schillebeeckx, 'Priesterschap' in *Theologische Woordenboek*.

## 15

## The Primacy of Peter: Theology and Ideology

I

It is now clear enough that the disturbance in the Catholic world caused by the publication of *Humanae Vitae* was a symptom of much deeper stirrings in the Church than a difference of opinion about contraceptive methods of family limitation. We have to recognize that a profound shift of Catholic consciousness had already begun to take place, and that the publication of Paul VI's encyclical served to precipitate this new consciousness and to make its protest against the old articulate.

The visible structure of the older Catholic consciousness is easily described: within the period between Pius IX and Pius XII, Catholics recognized their distinctive identity, especially in England, in terms of an explicit awareness of the Pope, Mary, eucharistic devotions as well as Mass, Friday abstinence and the unlawfulness of 'unnatural' methods of birth control. It is instructive to recall that the Pope who confirmed his predecessor's withdrawal of the discussion of contraception from Vatican II and who could not accept the recommendations of his theological commission is also the Pope who insisted on giving Mary the title of *Mater Ecclesiae* in his allocution of 21st November, 1964, at the close of the third period of Vatican II, although the title was after consideration excluded from the chapter on Mary in the constitution *Lumen Gentium* on the Church; thus Paul VI continued the tradition of Pius IX and Pius XII in associating Pope and Mary in a special relationship to the Church. Paul VI is also the Pope of the encyclical *Mysterium Fidei* on the Eucharist. We must recognize in the Pope Paul's utterances a deep anxiety to preserve the real values of the older Catholic consciousness; what we must ask is whether these values can only be preserved within a perspective which is structured in terms of those values alone, or whether, reintegrated into a more inclusive ecclesial consciousness, they may not continue to nourish and illuminate a newer mode of the Catholic mind in living coherence with other values which hardly became explicit in the older perspective.

The work of Vatican II may perhaps be best seen as a major effort to make explicit what I have elsewhere called the ecclesiological *a priori* of theology. It is Vatican II itself, and the preliminary studies of its theological architects, which have allowed us to review in terms of ecclesiology the theological consciousness which has found expression throughout the centuries of the history of the Church. Whereas it was quite recently common to maintain that there was no theological treatment of ecclesiology prior to the twentieth century (the word 'ecclesiology' itself is a newcomer), studies of the 'ecclesiology' of writers of all periods now proliferate. The fact is that the 'ecclesiologies' of these older authors have to be elicited by historical reconstruction as the unconscious *a priori* of their explicit theologies. One of the distinctive features of our own experience of the Church today is that in spite of the work of Vatican II many people in the Church are still unconsciously governed by an ecclesiological *a priori* which is not that of Vatican II and which only found expression in what might be called 'symptomatic' themes. The symptomatic themes of the unconscious ecclesiology prior to Vatican II have already been listed. These symptomatic themes are tenaciously clung to perhaps because it is obscurely felt, rightly, that their ecclesiological *a priori* would be recognized to be inadequate and would be dissolved once the themes are integrated into a more inclusive ecclesiological consciousness. The difficulties of our situation are only intensified by the fact that it is just those themes which are singled out for hostile attention by people claiming to speak out of new ecclesiological consciousness, although quite frequently they have never seriously investigated their own *a priori*s and merely assert new symptomatic themes with a naive arrogance.

The foregoing observations have been deliberately phrased in language reminiscent of depth psychology on the one hand and Kant on the other. This is partly to recognize that by undertaking to examine the theological sense of the papacy in the Church one is touching an extremely tender point in the life of the Church today. But it is also to draw attention to the possibility of practising ecclesiological studies in ontological, as well as psycho-analytic and epistemological, depth. I must also ask to be allowed to confess that like everyone else in the Church today, I am personally involved in the birth-pangs of a new consciousness, and that I cannot hope to have achieved the serenity of a mature contemporary ecclesiological consciousness. It may be shameful to have to admit it, but it is only in recent months that I have made any separate study of the history of the papacy, a study in which some attempt has been made to question the perspectives in which that history is commonly recorded by Catholic historians and commonly read by Catholic readers, including myself. Clearly such a study could only have been superficial; but I must record that the effect of this reading has been one of deep shock. This has very little to do with the notorious immoralities of an Alexander VI, or the abject irrelevance of the so-called *saeculum obscurum*, the papacy of the tenth century. It is not the depths to which the papacy has sunk but the heights to which it has climbed which raise the most searching questions for the Christian conscience. I have been bound to ask myself whether the papacy has not done more harm than good to the Church of Christ. From the time of Victor and the paschal controversy to the present day, with very few exceptions, a violent, intolerant dominativeness has been a characteristic mode of papal utterance and behaviour. Great, even saintly men, seem to have been the victims of a cruel, un-Christian system. No one who has not himself undertaken a study of this papal history, after to some extent freeing himself from an older *a priori*, should question the fairness of this description (a beginning might be made with the excellent papers of R. A. Markus and Eric John in their book *Papacy and Hierarchy*, Sheed and Ward, 1969), especially since a pious papalism of devotion (supported by a ruthless curial papalism of terror) has been the presupposition of Catholic consciousness in the era before John XXIII and Vatican II.

For someone like myself who firmly wishes to remain a Roman Catholic the Christian justification of the papacy becomes a matter of urgent and acute concern. This justification is not sufficiently to be found in large world-historical views which exhibit the role of the papacy in the emergence of Europe and the West, especially from the time of Gregory the Great and later Stephen II. The only satisfactory justification of the papacy lies in showing that it is an intrinsic element in the *mysterion* of God's eternal purpose for man in Jesus Christ. It seems to me that this involves providing a justification for the papacy in terms of a theological ontology, for it is only in these terms that one can adequately distinguish the theology of the papacy from its ideology, that ideology which has been the normal vehicle of the theology of the papacy for so many centuries.

Finally, it does not seem to me that many contemporary well-meaning attempts to 'place' the papacy within the apostolic or episcopal college and so to contain its saving or destructive power and energy are likely to lead very far. The claim which has consistently been made for the primacy of Peter and his successors is for a unique primacy in the Church of Christ, and this claim is not adequately met by any definition of a role, even that of head, within the apostolic or episcopal college. The Petrine claim is not merely an institutional, it is an ontological claim. The question is whether this ontological claim is a Christian one.

## II

There is very great need of an historical dictionary of theological terms, perhaps on the lines of Kittel's *Theologisches Wörterbuch zum neuen Testament*. One of the terms which would be dealt with in such a dictionary would be 'primacy', *primatus*. In the constitution 'Pastor Aeternus' of Vatican I it is laid down that the Apostle Peter received not merely a *primatum honoris* but a *primatum jurisdictionis* from Christ (DS 3055). The next chapter of the constitution goes on to speak of the perpetuity of this Petrine primacy in the Roman Pontiffs. It should be noted that this primacy of jurisdiction is spoken of as identical in the Apostle Peter and his successors, the bishops of the Roman See, whereas it is usually recognized that only some restricted part of the Apostolic office as such is transmitted to the successors of the Apostles, the bishops, since the Apostles, as Founders of the Church and immediate organs of revelation, share in the historically unique, 'ephapactic' character of the beginning, while their successors and continuers of their mission rest on their foundation and transmit their revelation. 'Whoever succeeds Peter in this chair (*cathedra*), receives Peter's primacy over the entire Church by Christ's institution' (DS 3057). This Petrine primacy is transmitted whole and entire.

It becomes all the more urgent to enquire whether this opposition of two sorts of primacy, one of honour, the other of jurisdiction, is in fact exhaustive; or whether there is not some other sort of primacy as well. It may be that the 'primacy of jurisdiction' is capable of analysis into ideological and theological parts, since the phrase is being used to exclude what is thought to be its only alternative, the primacy of honour. In what follows, we shall argue that there is a third kind of primacy, an ontological primacy, to be defined in theological terms, which has been consistently confused with an ideological primacy in the expression 'primacy of jurisdiction'.

Some indication of the kind of fluctuation in the early use of the term *primatus* may be found in the canons of the first four ecumenical councils and their Latin versions, though the exact sense of the expressions has been the subject of intensive scholarly discussion. The title of the sixth canon of Nicaea, in the Latin version of Dionysius Exiguus, runs 'de primatibus episcoporum', rendering *peri ton proteion* of the Greek (*Conciliorum Oecumenicorum Decreta*, ed. Jedin *et al.*, 1962, p. 8). In the text of the canon itself, *presbeia*, which is later to have *primatus* as its equivalent, is rendered by *privilegia*. The canon itself is concerned with the metropolitan or embryonic patriarchal authority of certain sees over ordinations in the neighbouring territory: the rights of Rome are referred to as an example. In the famous third canon of Constantinople, the bishop of Constantiople is said to have the *primatum honoris* (*ta presbeia tes times*) after the Bishop of Rome, since Constantinople is the new Rome (Jedin, p. 28). In what is thought to be the text of a Roman synod held under Damasus in 382, this canon is responded to in a very clear and peremptory way. It is said that although the Catholic Churches spread throughout the world form a single bridal-bed (*thalamus*) of Christ, the holy Roman Church is raised up above all other Churches, and not in virtue of any conciliar decrees; rather, it has received the primacy by the gospel word of our Lord and Saviour himself: 'Thou art Peter...' (I follow the text as given in the so-called 'Decree of Gelasius', DS 350. If the decree does in fact go back to Damasus, this is the first really clear use of the 'Petrine text', Matt. 16.18f., to justify the Roman primacy). This part of the decree concludes by establishing an order among the great sees, all in virtue of a relationship to Peter: first Rome, then Alexandria, consecrated by Mark in Peter's name, then Antioch, where Peter dwelt before coming to Rome.

Finally, in the equally famous canon 28 of Chalcedon (Jedin, pp. 75–6), a primacy (*presbeia*) is claimed for Constantinople, the new Rome. Whatever the precise sense of the claim, it is rejected by Pope Leo as an injury to the rights of Alexandria and Antioch (not of Rome), and also because it bases the claim on such secular grounds as the location of imperial authority, not on the divine grounds of Scripture (Ep. 104 *ad Marcianum*, *PL* 54, 995). The claim seems to be for the same kind of authoritative primacy as was spoken of in the sixth canon of Nicaea.

One final example of the use of *primatus* comes from what is now widely thought to be Cyprian's own first recension of his *De unitate Ecclesiae*, ch. 4. Here it is said that *primatus Petro datur,* in a sense of 'primacy' which it is argued could be interpreted at Rome as an authoritative primacy, but which by Cyprian himself is meant only as a 'seniority' (Bévenot) or a 'priority in time' (G. S. M. Walker, *The Churchmanship of St Cyprian*, 1968). It seems preferable to see this 'primacy' as an *originality*, a temporal priority which has the unique significance of being *first* (cf. Cyprian's language in this chapter of *unitatis originem* and the parallel text of the second recension, *exordium ab unitate proficiscitur*). From these few examples we may see tha the opposition of the *primatus honoris* and the *primatus iurisdictionis* is highly oversimplified. The primacy of jurisdiction itself was thought of primarily as a metropolitan or patriarchal right to supervise the ecclesiastical life of a territory adjacent to an apostolic see, and historically the patriarchal rights of the Roman See were confined to the West and what has now become the Latin Church. In both the *primatus honoris* and the Cyprianic sense of *primatus* as a source of the unity of the Church there seems to be an ill-defined sense of a more profound primacy, pointing perhaps in the direction of what was called above an 'ontological' primacy. It is in the sermons and writings of Leo the Great that we find what is still the most satisfactory articulation of the consciousness of this deeper primacy, overlaid (so it will be argued) by a juridical terminology which will serve the later papacy as the basis for a papal ideology of power.

III

There is at least one aspect of the famous sermons preached by St Leo on the anniversary of his episcopal consecration which does not seem to have been sufficiently adverted to; and that is that they are in fact anniversary sermons, and for that reason exhibit the same kind of temporal structure as the sermons preached by him during the course of the liturgical year. Thus, in a careful study by Dom Maria Bernard de Soos (*Le Mystère liturgique d'après St Léon le Grand*, 1958), the sense of the *Hodie* of many of the sermons for the liturgical seasons is shown to include by a kind of 'sacramental' identification the time of the originating event within the day in serial time on which the sermon is preached. Or as the translator of the *Sources Chrétiennes* edition of Leo's sermons puts it, the liturgical celebrations, 'while they recall the saving events of the Redeemer's life, make them really live again in their saving efficacity; they are 'signs', *sacramenta*, which re-present for believers the acts which the Saviour has accomplished once for all' (Dolle, in t. 1, p. 66, n. 1).

It is primarily because the time-horizons of Leo's anniversary sermons are the same as those of his seasonal sermons that Leo can make that 'sacramental' identification of himself with Peter which Jalland, for instance (*St Leo the Great,* 1941), found somewhat disconcerting. The 'event' of Leo's own ordination coincides 'sacramentally' with the 'event' in which the Lord institutes Peter in his *honor,* his office of dignity in the Church, and can be represented each year, such that Peter's institution persists in and sustains Leo's.

It is noteworthy that Leo takes up easily the traditional theme according to which it is Peter's faith that is crowned and confirmed by the Lord's institution. 'The solidity of Peter's faith is enduring; and just as what Peter believed abides in Christ, so there abides what Christ instituted in Peter' (Serm. 3; *PL* 54; 145). 'On this rock, Jesus says, I will set up an eternal temple, and the heights of my Church towering up into heaven will rise up upon the firmness of this faith' (s. 4, 150). The importance of this becomes clear from an absorbing study by J. Meyendorff ('St Peter in Byzantine Theology', in Meyendorff *et al., The Primacy of Peter,* 1963), who shows that the Byzantine theologians continued to speak in this tradition even after the schism because in the tradition, common to East and West, the Petrine text of Matt. 16, 18f., was not thought of as applying to the Bishop of Rome in particular but to all the faithful and especially to all bishops.[1]

Leo is perfectly clear that every Christian shares in the royal priesthood of Christ in virtue of his faith and baptism. In sermon 4 he insists that no matter what differences of office there may be in the Church, all are 'one in Christ' (Gal. 3.28) and all are attached to the head of the body:

> Thus in the unity of faith and baptism we have an undivided fellowship and a shared dignity, as the blessed Peter says: 'You are a chosen race, a royal priesthood, a holy nation, God's own people' (1 Pet. 2.9). For all who are reborn in Christ are made kings by the sign of the Cross, consecrated priests by the anointing of the Spirit; so that apart from that subjection in the ministerial service which is peculiar to us (Leo is referring to himself here), each and every spiritual Christian should understand and acknowledge that he shares in the royal dignity and the priestly office.... Now since by God's grace this has been made com-

---

[1] It is plausibly argued that it was Pope Stephen's use in a 'papalist' sense of Cyprian's reference to the Matthaean text which made Cyprian revise his original version of the *De Unitate Ecclesiae.* For Cyprian, the Matthaean text signifies 'the authority of the bishops, each in his own Church' (Bévenot). In general, see J. Ludwig, *Die Primatsworte in der altkirchlichen Exegese,* (1952), and F. Dvornik, *Byzance et la primauté Romaine,* (Paris, 1964).

mon to all, it is devout and praiseworthy for you to celebrate the day of our elevation as though it were your own honour and dignity, so that in the whole body of the Church a single sacramental mystery of high-priesthood (*pontificii sacramentum*) should be celebrated (4, 148–9).

This last sentence is especially significant. Leo sees the festival celebration of the anniversary of his elevation as a 'sacramental' *action* in which the 'sacramental' *participation* of all Christians in the high-priesthood of Christ is renewed; the consecrated ministerial priesthood of the Bishop of Rome is the 'sacramental' *representation* of the general priesthood of all believers throughout the Church.

It is in virtue of this inclusive 'sacramental' consciousness that Leo can go on in the same sermon to make daunting claims for himself as Peter's successor. Leo asks his hearers to celebrate this anniversary day in veneration of him who was flooded with such abundant streams from the very source of all graces (*charismatum*) that while he alone received so much no one else received anything except by participation in him. Leo refers this concentration of graces to the Incarnation itself. The Word made flesh was already dwelling among us, and all things in heaven and on earth were subject to him, nothing was beyond the power of a *sacramentum* which the unity of his own godhead and the Trinity were simultaneously enacting:

> And yet out of the whole this individual Peter is chosen and set at the head of the vocation of all peoples, of all the Apostles, of all the fathers of the Church; such that although there are many priests and pastors in the people of God, it is Peter who rightly rules them, ruled simultaneously as they are in the first place by Christ (*omnes tamen proprie regat Petrus, quos principaliter regit et Christus*). Beloved, the divine condescension has bestowed a great and marvellous association (*consortium*) in its power upon this man; and if it was its will that other leaders should have something in common with Peter, it was only through him that it gave whatever it did not deny to others.

Leo goes on to support this exposition of Peter's powers by an analysis of Matt. 16. It was Peter alone who spoke for the disciples in confessing the Lord's true dignity. The Lord is the unshakable rock, the corner stone, the foundation, who by calling Peter 'Rock', makes him share in the solidity of the Lord; so that what is by the Lord's authority proper to him, is to be shared with Peter by participation. So, in the words of a text already quoted, the temple of the Church towers up into heaven upon the basis of Peter's faith.

We may see foreshadowed in this conception what later showed itself in a terminological shift from *Vicarius Petri* to *Vicarius Christi*. It is however essential to see that in Leo's mind the extraordinary claims made for Peter (and his successor) are in exposition of a 'sacrament' enacted by the incarnate Word when he conferred upon Peter in response to his confession of faith a participation in his own unique dignity; now this 'sacrament' is the effectual symbol of a participation in Christ of all those who believe. It may seem from Leo's words that he is claiming for Peter (and his successors) a mediatorial role in the communication of all graces which has been committed to him by the Mediator Jesus Christ. This claim, even if it were a possible interpretation of Leo's words, must of course be resolutely rejected. But it is also possible to see that participation in Christ by faith, common to all believers, implies and requires a symbolic representation of that single and common participation, and that the Petrine office in the Church provides such a symbolic representation of the one faith of all believers. We may even go further and argue that if this symbolic representation of the one faith is rejected, a contradiction arises, damaging to the faith itself, between that faith and its public profession. Leo's view could then be interpreted in the public order of the Church, such that Peter's public confession of faith, continued in his successors, is the effectual symbol of the unity of the public faith confessed by the Church, remembering that a discontinuity between internal, subjective faith and communal, professed faith, is a more familiar possibility in our time than in Leo's.

It should now be reasonably clear that the continuance of Peter's profession of faith and its associated participation in Christ is seen by Leo as a 'sacramental' identity of Peter and his successors. But in recent years it has been forcefully maintained by Professor Walter Ullmann (see especially 'Leo I and the theme of Papal Primacy', JTS XI (1960), pp. 25–52; also *The Growth of Papal Government in the Middle Ages*, 2nd edn., 1962) that Leo, faced with the problem of establishing a continuity between Peter and his successors, found his solution by adopting Roman juridical categories, notably that of the *haeres*, according to which the heir continues the deceased, the latter is literally continued in the former: '*Haereditas est successio in universum ius*' (art. cit. pp. 33s.). Professor Ullmann also feels bound to insist that this juristic solution of the problem of identity is the only satisfactory one, and that no other solution is or was possible. This is not the place to discuss his claim, but it may be noted that although his great learning has thrown much light on a whole dimension of ecclesiological thinking, Professor Ullmann seems strangely insensitive to other dimensions of ecclesiology.[2] In his new synoptic work, *L'Ecclésiologie du haut Moyen-Age* (1968), which will clearly become a standard work for any ecclesiologist, Fr Y. Congar remarks:

> Nous croyons que l'idée institutionelle-juridique du pape comme vicaire de Pierre au sens de son successeur, ne suffit pas à rendre compte de ce qui s'exprime dans ces textes. Nous espérons montrer ailleurs que l'idée de *vicarius* comportait alors une valeur en quelque sort sacramentelle de présence opérante de Pierre sous et dans une autre existence historique (p. 189).

For the purposes of this article, it is sufficient to note the simultaneous presence, in Leo's consciousness of himself as Peter's successor, of sacramental and juridical motives and themes. What was to happen in succeeding centuries was a development and expansion of the juridical themes, while the sacramental themes became less and less distinct. Yet it may be suggested that the sense of sacramental continuity was the source of energy for what, in an inappropriate juridical idiom, became the monstrous claims of a Gregory VII or a Boniface VIII. In its 'sacramental' expression (in the pregnant sense of 'sacrament' for Leo) Leo's reflections on the papal office would seem to provide elements for a theology of what was earlier in this article called an *ontological* primacy of Peter; the decay of the sacramental consciousness led to a jurisdictional or 'political' theology of the primacy which was to find its most balanced expression in Vatican I. These are clearly massive oversimplifications of an exceedingly complex historical process; all that is offered here is an indication of the way in which a symbolic, sacramental or quasi-sacramental theology of papal primacy may better express the fundamental intentions of Vatican I and thus offer a different perspective in which to evaluate the place of the papacy in the Church today. (An essential complement to what has been said here is the fundamental article by L. Hertling, s.j., 'Communio und Primat – Kirche und Papstum in der christlichen Antike', *Una Sancta* 17 (1962), pp. 91–125.)

[2] See Professor Geoffrey Barraclough's note in his excellent book, *The Medieval Papacy*, (1968), p. 198. In general, on the growth of legal institutions in the Church, see e.g. Gaudemet's volume, *L'Eglise dans l'Empire Romain*, 1958, in the *Histoire de Droit et des Institutions de l'Eglise en Occident*, edited by Le Bras, and Feine's one-volume *Kirchliche Rechtsgeschichte*, 4th edn., 1964.

## IV

In the light of what has been said in the first part of this article, it may be useful to examine briefly the text of Matt. 16, 17–19. It is remarkable that most of the interesting exegesis of this passage has been the work of Protestant scholars, notably O. Cullmann in his *Peter: Apostle and Martyr,* and also J. Ringger, 'Das Felsenwort. Zur Sinndeutung von Matt. 16, 18, vor allem im Lichte der Symbolgeschichte' in Roesle-Cullmann, *Begegnung der Christen,* 1959, together with numerous articles on key-concepts by J. Jeremias now available in English in the translation of Kittel's *Theological Dictionary of the New Testament.* As to the propriety of looking at these verses in isolation, we may quote the remark of the Catholic exegete, W. Trilling (*Das wahre Israel,* 3rd ed., 1964): 'This language, dense with imagery, of a kind also found in the Qumran writings, is in itself foreign to Matthew' (p. 156). It may be that within the perspective of a modern jurisdictional theology of the primacy, the symbolic sense of the text was not easily accessible to Catholic scholars before Protestant exegetes opened the way to an understanding of it in some respects closer to patristic exegesis.

In summary, then, the whole passage is an instance of anticipated eschatology, in which the Messiah invests an individual with his own messianic powers over the messianic community.

v. 17. In response to his messianic confession, Simon is greeted with a 'beatitude' or 'macarism', for in him the eschatological event of the last times has been anticipated by 'apocalypse'. Without committing oneself to any view of literary dependence, one may note the parallelism to our present text of Gal. 1, 15–16, in particular the opposition of heavenly 'apocalypse' to 'flesh and blood' (see A. M. Denis, O.P., 'L'investiture de la fonction apostolique par "Apocalypse",' *Revue Biblique* 64 (1957), pp. 335–62, 492–515). Simon has not only confessed that Jesus bears the messianic title, he expounds the title to mean the Son of the living God; and it is God the Father of the Son who has revealed this.

v. 18. Simon too has a title, one which is conferred upon him by an authoritative act, and the content and functions of this title are now expounded. The Rock-man is to be a foundation upon which a building is to be built: the Messiah will 'build' or 'make a house'. In chapter 2 of 1 Peter, which many critics would be prepared to attribute to the historical Peter, we see the writer playing with the notion of 'stone' (*lithos,* not *petra*). He invites his readers or hearers to be 'like living stones built into a spiritual house' (v. 5). The play on words is easier for its antecedents in the Old Testament, for instance in the messianic prophecy of 2 Samuel 7. David proposes to build the Lord a 'house'; but Nathan speaks to David according to a vision by night and declares that the Lord will make David a 'house'. This 'house' is the royal descendance of David, his family and kingdom, as the Lord's 'house' is his temple (in all cases 'house' = *bayith*). We may also consider the appointment of Jeremiah to his prophetic office (*pqd*) 'to pluck up and to break down, to destroy and to overthrow, to build and to plant' (Jer. 1.10). 'Building' and 'planting' are the acts of the Lord who comes, and the acts of his emissaries, the prophets and apostles: for they are the 'foundation' upon which the household of God is built, 'Christ Jesus himself being the corner stone, in whom the whole structure is joined together and grows into a holy temple in the Lord; in whom you also are built into it for a dwelling place of God in the Spirit' (Eph. 2.20–22; various derivatives of *oikos*, house). The author of 1 Peter continues his play on the word 'stone' by recalling texts of Isaiah (28.16; 8. 14–15), bringing out the double character of this stone for faith. The first of these Isaian texts is perhaps specially attractive; it seems to offer an inscription for a foundation or corner stone: 'He who believes will not shake' (following the reading implied by the Targums and the Syriac versions).

A characteristic text from the Qumran hymns is instructive:

> The deeps resound to my groaning
> and [my soul has journeyed] to the gates of death.
> But I shall be as one who enters a fortified city,
> as one who seeks refuge behind a high wall
> until deliverance (comes);
> I will [lean on] thy truth, O my God.
> For thou wilt set the foundation on rock
> and the framework by the measuring-cord of justice;
> and the tried stones [thou wilt lay]
> by the plumb-line [of truth],
> to [build] a mighty [wall] which shall not sway.
>
> 1 QH VI, 24–27; trans. Vermes.

The parallels here to Matt. 16.18, already noted by Dupont-Sommer, would be still closer if instead of 'foundation' translating an emendation *yswd*, the original reading *swd* were retained, meaning 'circle of intimates' or 'mystery', that is, the Community as a group initiated into God's secret plan (see Carmignac in Carmignac-Guilbert, *Les Textes de Qumran*, I, p. 224, n. 90). The parallelism only illustrates, of course, the way in which certain biblical themes might have developed independently in two movements within post-biblical Judaism.

The *ecclesia* of Matt. 16.18, then, is the community of God's chosen People to be built upon the Rock-man. This People is never an unstructured mob; it is differentiated into tribes and camps, as the five thousand who were fed were made to sit in 'companies' (Mark 6.39), the city of Rev. 21. Another 'city', indicated by the 'gates' as part for whole, rises up against the *ecclesia*; this is the combined powers of the underworld, sealed and shut down by the sacred rock (cf. Rev. 20. 1–3). These are the powers of disorder and death; it is in virtue of the Resurrection that the Rock endures and is victorious over death.

v. 19. The keys provide another instance of multiple symbolism. Taken with the preceding verse and the city-gates image, they imply an authority to admit or to exclude, but they may also be seen as an authority of stewardship, as in Isaiah 22. 15–25. We may compare Paul in his role as Apostle in 1 Cor. 4. 1, asking to be regarded as servant of Christ and steward (*oikonomos*) of the mysteries of God. In this sense, Simon is being appointed 'Vizier of the Messiah' (Benoit); in no sense is he the 'porter' or doorkeeper (*janitor caeli*). In accordance with the general structure of each of these three verses, in which a theme is stated and then expounded in antithetic parallelism, the image of the keys is probably to be related primarily to the 'binding and loosing'. This expression, in its Rabbinic use, was applied primarily to doctrinal decisions, declaring things and actions forbidden or permitted, and only secondarily to persons (excommunication). Within the perspective of the inaugurated eschatology of the New Testament, Peter's authority as steward consists in his power to provide or withhold access to the mysteries of God, above all the mystery of the community of the Messiah and Son of Man, the anticipated sacramental realization of the reign of God, the *ecclesia*, the Church.

It is important to note that not all these assurances are proper to Peter alone. The beatitude of v. 17 is appropriate to Paul too, as we have already seen; and it appears from the 'hymn of praise' (Matt. 11. 25–27; Luke 10, 21–22) that the Son may choose to reveal his Father (and his sonship) to 'babes'. Again, in the 'rule of the Community' of Matt. 18, the power to bind and loose is solemnly declared to belong to the *ecclesia* (v. 18; cf. Trilling, p. 116), here the local community. Since this verse, addressed to 'you' in the plural, follows immediately upon two verses addressed to 'you' in the singular, it is difficult to see how its force can be confined even to the Twelve; it may be best to take it as addressed to the community *as a whole,* in which case the community as a whole

might be thought of as concentrating its own powers as steward in its personal steward, Peter. As Vatican I puts it, 'the Roman Pontiff ... enjoys that infallibility which the divine Redeemer wishes his *Church* to be equipped with in defining doctrine concerning faith or morals' (DS 3074; my italics).
There remains v. 18. What is promised here is assuredly as unique and personal as the proper name. But if it is proper as the personal name, is it communicable? We seem to be back at the problem discussed in the section on Leo. There can be no doubt at all that a Catholic must believe that at least something in Peter is in some sense communicable to his 'successors'. Is it, as Professor Ullmann would have us believe, a *ius haeredis*, or as Vatican I appears to assert, a *primatus iurisdictionis?*
The essence of the answer to this question, I suggest, consists in recognizing that while 'Peter' is a proper name, it is also a *title*. As personal name, 'Peter' is proper to the historical Simon alone; as title, it is communicable. Perhaps one might think of some English equivalent such as 'Mr Standfast'. What is communicated is the functions symbolically condensed in the title; and we have seen what these might be.
As far as the New Testament evidence goes we can say no more, it seems to me, than that communication of what is 'Peter' is *possible*. Even the idea of episcopal succession to part of what is involved in the Apostolic office is at best only hinted at in the New Testament. It is only in the evangelical *life* of the Church ('Tradition') that we can discover the evangelical sense of the Scripture.

V

The purpose of this article has been to suggest a possible perspective within which to see the place of the papacy in the Church. It used to be suggested that whereas Vatican I defined the place of the papacy in the Church, Vatican II defined the place of bishops in the Church. It has now been clear for some time that this is a misleading over-simplification. Not only do the affirmations about the Pope, taken over by Vatican II from Vatican I, stand out uncomfortably in their new context; but theological discussion since Vatican II, which has tried to interpret the papacy in terms of the 'collegial' categories of Vatican II, does not seem to have been notably successful. Nor can we dismiss the bearing of the famous *Nota Explicativa* to *Lumen Gentium*. It does not seem to me that the peculiar place of the papacy in the Church can be satisfactorily understood in terms of the headship of the episcopal college.

What has been suggested here is that we need to interpret Vatican I on the primacy in a wider ecclesiological context than the fathers of Vatican I allowed themselves to do (it will be remembered that under various pressures only one chapter of the much more comprehensive schema on the Church was discussed, what forms the present constitution *Pastor Aeternus*), or indeed even envisaged. Like everything else in this article, the suggestion needs far more detailed investigation than has been possible here. Nevertheless I believe that it is of the utmost importance that we should deliberately expose ourselves – at the highest pitch of sensibility to which we can screw ourselves (or perhaps by relaxing into the profoundest receptivity) – to every faint echo of an understanding of the Church, office in the Church, and the papacy in particular, which, while it has never been wholly lost, has for so long found inadequate expression that it is extraordinarily difficult to recover.

For instance, it seems to me that what is now frequently called a 'crisis of authority' in the Church is only a symptom of something a good deal deeper. If Gratian in his *Decretum* was the first to interpret the power of binding and loosing as 'the judicial authority of the ecclesiastical tribunals over the Church as a society' (Robert L. Benson, in an important book, *The Bishop-Elect*, Princeton, 1968, pp. 48-9 and the references there given), it is quite misleading to oppose this to a sacramental power exercised in the Church's *forum internum* (Benson, p. 48); 'private penance' and the theory of the internal forum are comparative late-comers in the complex history of 'sacramental' penance. The 'authority' exercised in exclusion from or reconciliation to the Church in what is now called the 'sacrament' of penance is neither simply 'sacramental' nor 'jurisdictional': at some deeper level this authority is an original unity which has been inadequately differentiated in later times. For this reason I cannot accept Robert Murray's thesis in what is otherwise a very valuable paper, that 'the institutional element in Christianity, by which I mean especially social structure and law, *is not part of the Gospel*' ('Authority and the Spirit in the NT', *Authority in a Changing Church*, 1968, p. 19; Fr Murray's italics). It may be that he is misled by an inadequate notion of 'institution' (see John Beattie, 'On the Notion of Institution', *New Blackfriars*, February 1969), but it seems to me also that he has been overreacting against a particular version of authority (as jurisdiction). The authority of Jesus Christ is neither simply 'sacramental' nor 'jurisdictional' (consider the healing miracles and the expulsion of demons), nor is it simply the authority of 'witness'. In some sense that authority has been transmitted, including powers to heal and to expel unclean spirits (Matt. 10.1, if not also Mark 16.17).

It is to this sort of original unity that we have been pointing in speaking about an 'ontological' primacy of Peter. Perhaps even in Leo we see the beginnings of a differentiation between 'sacramental' and 'jurisdictional' versions of this primacy, though Leo's use of *sacramentum* is much wider than that which became standard from the middle ages to our own day. At any rate we need to take simultaneously into account every clue to this original unity. What is more, in the providence of God, we have actually had an historical Pope in recent years, John XXIII, who has given us a personal expression of that original unity, perhaps because personal sanctity alone is the only valid means of discovering and disclosing it.

I believe that current discussions of 'authority and conscience' stimulated by *Humanae Vitae* tend more often than not to be constricted by perspectives in which the ontological primacy of Peter and his successors, in its original unity, *cannot* come to sight; this would be true of both parties to the controversy. It is characteristically unfortunate that the notion of the *magisterium* should so often serve as the focus of these discussions, since this notion saw its chief theological development in the nineteenth century, in connection with the jurisdictional primacy of the Pope. There is something both fascinating and depressing to watch in the contortions of so many writers, professional theologians and others, as they struggle to extend or contract the sense of this historically conditioned notion in current controversy. Perhaps it would be a good thing to stop using the word altogether for some years, as was suggested not so long ago for the word 'God'. If what has been proposed in this article is acceptable, the service of the Gospel in the Church by Peter's successors is not in the first place to be construed as a form of jurisdictional, dominative authority over 'private' consciences; it is in the first place being the foundation stone on which is inscribed, 'He who believes will not tremble' – though we have yet neither the institutional nor the theological forms in which to translate that symbolic perception of the original unity into everyday praxis.

# 16

## How to See an Angel

I have given this talk the title of 'How to see an Angel', partly because it is a funny title but also because I want if possible to look at the subjective conditions for talking about angels rather than at angels themselves. I take it that in one sense or another what has been said so far in this course of talks has really rather looked at the angels themselves, what I shall call, for the moment, objectively, their objective aspects, the angels 'out there'.

Now as I said the title 'How to see an Angel' is an attempt to look at the subjective conditions for any kind of awareness or knowledge of angels. The two terms 'objective' and 'subjective' are clearly open to criticism, and in fact criticism of them will be one of the points I hope to make towards the end of the talk. But let it stand for the moment, since I am interested more in the conditions for knowing angels, as it might be the *a priori* of our knowledge of angels, than in our knowledge of angels as such, although I hope that the discussion of the *a priori* conditions of the knowledge of angels will in fact bring out a certain amount about angels themselves. And perhaps I had better say right at the start that I do actually believe in angels. You may begin to feel a bit doubtful about this as we go on! But in fact I have no difficulty about angels at all. But while I have no difficulty about angels existing, I do have a certain amount of difficulty about the interest of angels. Frankly I don't spend a good deal of my time thinking about angels. This again is another feature which will I hope be discussed as we go along: Why angels are boring. Because in point of fact I can't get very worked up about angels unless I do a lot of things. The number of things one wants to do in order to get interested in angels seems to me to be part of the subjective *a priori* of the knowledge of angels. I don't think angels just drop into one's lap as it were, so that one can look at them. I think one has got to do a lot in order to see an angel and the fact is that we don't want to do much of this; it is rather tedious to go through all of this so we don't in fact see angels very much. Perhaps we shall succeed in having just a brief glimpse of one by the end of this talk.

What I would like to start by doing is considering extra-biblical parallels, if you like, to angels. I take it that you have heard quite a lot so far about angels in the Bible, and you have also had the metaphysical discussion of angels in St Thomas. I think it might not be wholly without use to look at the extra-biblical parallels to what we take to be angels in our history and biblical tradition.

One of the technical difficulties here, of course, is how one decides what is a parallel and what is not. But this is a general problem of comparative religion which I don't think one need go into, although we can say that there are in fact outside the Christian-biblical-Jewish tradition a number of phenomena of which one can say: Well don't these beings remind us in some ways of angels? Don't, for instance, the Homeric gods remind us somewhat of angels? The Homeric gods are the same kind of embarrassment to us, I fear, as angels are. It is not easy to take these Homeric gods (I am dealing specifically with the Homeric gods as opposed to whatever kinds of divinities one finds before Homer) very seriously in a way. Some of you may know the book of Charles Seltzman on the Homeric gods. It provides some rather attractive pictures but the discussion is on the level of, so to say, high facetiousness, which doesn't help very much. And of course in the Greek tradition itself the Homeric gods were treated with a certain amount of contempt. Plato hadn't much time for them. At the same time they do offer some parallels and one of the books I have here is by W. F. Otto (as opposed to Rudolph Otto), writing about the Homeric gods. It is one of the best accounts given because it is a creative attempt (and this again is actually important for our general purposes) to enter into the meaning of the Homeric gods. Otto belonged, in a loose way, to the circle round Heidegger. That is to say he was a classicist, a classical philologist in the German tradition, but one whose interests weren't confined entirely to literature but also to the life manifested in the literature. Let me just read one or two things here from the Introduction. He first of all talks about the way in which in Homer we find instances of the intervention of the gods, at certain critical moments where for instance, a decision has to be taken. We hear how the god whispers a saving device to a baffled warrior at the right instant. We hear that he arouses spirit and kindles courage, that he makes the limbs supple and nimble and gives the right arm accuracy and strength. But these are not the only occasions. Not only the flow of events with its critical moments, however, but also duration itself indicated the divine. In all large or small forms and conditions of life and existence the Greeks perceived the eternal visage of divinity. Taken all together these essences constituted the holiness of the world. In their world, the Greek world, the divine is not superimposed as sovereign power over natural events. It is revealed in the forms of the natural and is their very essence and being. For other people miracles take place. But a greater miracle takes place in the spirit of the Greek, for he is capable of so regarding the objects of daily experience that they can display the awesome lineaments of the divine without losing a whit of their natural reality.

You see in point of fact in one sense, one sense of that very, very, slippery word 'nature', gods are a manifestation of nature. And there are some very moving accounts of the individual gods in this book of Otto's, particularly about Apollo. All the emblems of Apollo and all his symbols are brought together by Otto to produce a very plausible kind of figure. I have always had rather an attachment to Apollo myself for various reasons and I find this account of Otto's instructive, the way in which Apollo is a kind of condensation or coalescence of various aspects of nature – nature manifesting itself in various ways and brought together in a poetic spirit, either Otto's, or Homer's before him, or the Greeks' – whichever you like to say; the various aspects are brought together in a poetic creative way in the personified (another very slippery word here) figure of a god – a revelation of natural forces or power. That is an instance taken from a particular kind of approach to something that might be taken as a parallel to angels, some sort of 'divine being'.

Another example I want to go on to, is again outside the biblical tradition, and was again studied by someone who stands outside the tradition he is examining. (Clearly Otto was not himself a Greek. Otto was a 20th century German of a highly sophisticated kind trying to practise the simple vision. This is part of our general methodology in this kind of thing. And here we have someone in the 20th century with a complicated mind looking at people long centuries before and trying to understand their particular appreciation of the divine.) The other instance I want to take is from a people belonging to our own times, a very different sort of people: a Sudanese tribe, the Nuer, as studied by Professor Evans-Pritchard in his classic work of social anthropology called *Nuer Religion*.

It first of all ought to be said that it was based on first-hand field study. Also it ought to be said that it is the result of reflection long after that field study had been conducted. The book I suppose appeared about ten years ago, but he hadn't been in the Sudan for a long time. He had been reflecting on this experience and then he wrote the book, and it wasn't just the record of first-hand experience. This doesn't diminish the interest of the book, but it does point to something, that it is in fact a sophisticated piece of work; it is something which the Nuer themselves could clearly not have written.

One of the features which we may start with (obviously I cannot go into the very complicated analysis in detail; I am not competent to do this) is the way in which one word 'Kwoth' occurs in their language. It is used on the one hand for some kind of supreme spirit, and *Kwoth* is in fact a word that can be used for the sound made by the siren of a Nile steamer, the blowing sound. *Kwoth* can be that, but it can be used also for this supreme spirit. But interestingly enough it also occurs in the plural in the form 'Kuth'. They talk about 'spirits'. And in fact a great deal of their religion is concerned with the relationship between *kwoth* which is just the transliteration given by Evans-Pritchard, and *Kuth,* the plural. And it is this relationship between *Kwoth* and *Kuth* which is part of what is interesting in their religion.

I remember a conversation with him in which he brought up the question of Sabellianism. Because he was interested in the way in which the Christian tradition of thought about God and creatures might help him to analyse his problem. In the Christian heresy known as Sabellianism, the persons of the Trinity are thought of as only differentiated by the relationships of the Godhead to the creature. Evans-Pritchard was interested in Sabellianism as a possible way of analysing the relationship between *Kwoth* and *Kuth* in Nuer religion. But in fact he doesn't adopt this Sabellian way of thinking because he finds something really rather more sophisticated. He talks about refractions, refractions of the divine. The kind of refraction he is particularly concerned with here is the way in which particular sorts of social organization or particular sorts of social interaction or particular sorts of social structure provide ways in which the Divine (with a capital 'D' you might say) is split up into particular localized kinds of divinity. This is the relationship between *Kuth*, in the plural, spirits, and the Spirit, and in itself this relationship is a reflection of the way in which partial social organizations are related to a total social organization. One can imagine the sort of way in which this can happen. What is interesting is to see the similarity between *Kwoth* and *Kuth* on the one hand and the patterns of social organization among the Nuer. So by talking about refractions of the divine we mean the way in which the 'personality' of God, of the single spirit, *Kwoth*, can be 'personified' in various subordinate or subsidiary ways in accordance with, and parallel with, the structures of social organizations. This relationship between, shall I say, in a general sense, politics and religion is also one which is going to concern us. And let us remind ourselves again that what we have here is a highly sophisticated analysis of what is conventionally called 'primitive' people, at least a non-technological people. That is to say, it is an attempt by a highly sophisticated 20th-century man, reflecting partly it may be on Sabellian theology and on parallels to Christianity, with a very considerable awareness of other styles of social organization, other primitive peoples, with all this awareness of differentiation of culture, to look at a very simple pre-industrial, pre-technological culture, examining it as far as possible from within, but also from without, and so to analyse the beliefs of this people, their approach to what we may call in some very generalized sense, the divine.

The point of insisting on the reflective or second-level character of this analysis is to bring out the way in which we are now in this position about angels too. We belong to the 20th century, not to any other century. We don't belong to the biblical world. It is a great mistake to suppose that we do. We belong to quite a different sort of world. And if we want in some way to enter into the biblical world we have got to go through a fairly complicated kind of process. We have got to do something to ourselves. As I said, angels don't fall into our lap. We don't find angels when we open the door and walk outside. We don't find them in the railway station, we don't find them in the road or the streets or when we switch on the television. (That is an interesting point that we might come back to, whether we do in fact find angels when we switch on the television.)

In the ordinary way we don't come across angels. There is one way of finding an angel which we might think of as ordinary, and that is if we go outside in this rather specialized kind of world of Hawkesyard and look at trees and things and then perhaps we might imagine we see an angel. But I think it is rather important that we are doing something rather specialized if we do this. Let us remind ourselves here of a text which I am sure is very familiar to you: it is from Wordsworth's 'Lines Composed a few Miles above Tintern Abbey'. Wordsworth was going through one of those rather tedious moments of reflection on his youth. I suppose we all, when we reach a certain age, tend to do this but Wordsworth tended to do it rather a lot. But it has an interest because, again, 'age and youth', 'sophistication and innocence', is one of the themes I want to discuss. Wordsworth is talking now about his own private individual life. He talks about the way in which he has changed.

> For nature then
> To me was all in all. I cannot paint
> What then I was. The sounding cataract
> Haunted me like a passion: the tall rock,
> The mountain, and the deep and gloomy wood,
> Their colours and their forms, were then to me
> An appetite; a feeling and a love,
> That had no need of a remoter charm,
> By thought supplied, or any interest
> Unborrowed from the eye. That time is past.

'That time is past' is one thing I want to emphasize. But he goes on with the often quoted passage:

> And I have felt
> A presence that disturbs me with the joy
> Of elevated thoughts; a sense sublime
> Of something far more deeply interfused,
> Whose dwelling is the light of setting suns,
> And the round ocean and the living air,
> And the blue sky, and in the mind of man:
> A motion and a spirit, that impels
> All thinking things, all objects of all thought,
> And rolls through all things.

I don't think I am cheating too much if I emphasize 'I felt a presence', the sense of a Presence through nature, the sense of being haunted by this natural world. This is the kind of thing I was talking about when I spoke of going out of the door and having feelings about nature at Hawkesyard. One can, I think, work up a feeling about trees and things – not when it is raining quite like this; one does need good weather on the whole to have this. But having actually just come from Devon it is very striking the way this hit me, the way in which mountains seem to look all right in any weather but this kind of country looks pretty dreadful in this sort of weather. But the thing to note is that this is the early 19th-century Romantic (with a capital R) approach to nature, not a Greek approach to nature at all, a very different kind. And yet you see it is an *approach* to nature, there is some possibility of going through some kind of transformation in order to respond to Nature with a capital N and to feel there a presence, a Presence you see, and a spirit, and a motion. What exactly of course this spirit is, is not a question one can decently ask of Wordsworth. I don't think he would have been able to say, and in his later stages he became orthodox, at least what he thought was orthodox, and he probably would have tried to interpret it in some Christian sense. In fact I don't think one *can* say; and one of the important things about angels happening is that one should not really be able to say very clearly anything about them. One should not be able to say very clearly just what they are. Perhaps that is a very rash thing to say. But anyway the kind of presence that one finds in Wordsworth here is I think extremely instructive about the way in which on the one hand we now are different from the Greeks. For Wordsworth it was important not to give a name except perhaps the name of 'Nature' to what this presence was, this 'something' far more deeply interfused. Of course the Greeks were prepared to give names and personify their deities, personify them in the sense of actually talking about Apollo or whoever. But Wordsworth did not do this.

Something else I want to get out of this text is Wordsworth's own awareness of historical change. We too might very well sit around like Wordsworth wringing our hands because we cannot respond to nature in this way any more. We might put it down to, diagnose our situation, simply in terms of age. We might see it in terms of *the* age, of belonging to the 20th century. You might feel for instance that what is really needed is a shot in the arm. LSD clearly is the thing. Why do people want LSD? Not for kicks, as they keep saying, but because they want a religious experience. And perhaps what we really need if we want to see an angel is big heavy regular doses of LSD. But there may be alternatives as well and we want to look at the alternatives first.

Even before Wordsworth, the systematic problem that we are concerned with is expressed very clearly by Blake. There is a classic bit of Blake about this, a text again that you are probably familiar with, which is found in notes which he wrote for a painting on the Last Judgment. It says: 'What, it will be questioned, when the sun rises, do you not see a round disc of fire somewhat like a guinea? On no, no, I see an innumerable company of the heavenly host crying Holy, Holy, Holy, is the Lord God Almighty.' And that you see is a systematic opposition here. Blake is quite explicitly rejecting the whole tradition starting from Locke, and for him summed up in Newton, that the scientific world, the world in which the sun looks a guinea and can be analysed of course, the world of commonsense experience, is the real world. The real world is the world provided in vision and in Blake's kind of prophetic vision, in this instance the presence of an innumerable company of the heavenly host crying 'Holy, Holy, Holy is the Lord God Almighty'. And that is a much more interesting world. For Blake it is vision, it is the life of creative imagination, which does deliver and manifest the real world. Not, in fact, the world of common experience shared by everybody, reduced as it were by negations to a common denominator, the world in fact of physical science; no, it must be this world ultimately revealed to the prophetic insight of the genius and the visionary. And of course, this is what produces those long interminable poems of Blake's which are almost unreadable because he keeps on having the vision.

Yet at the same time it is certainly a systematic question raised here by Blake. And for my purposes it is particularly useful to notice that he is in fact referring to Isaiah, chapter 6: Holy, holy, holy, Lord God of Hosts. This particular text is one of the key texts as far as we are concerned. If we are going to meet angels at all we will find them in fact where this text is constantly being recited, in fact in the eucharistic liturgy. Day after day we have this text of Isaiah, built up in various ways liturgically into what is called *Trisagion*, the *ter sanctus*, the thrice holy.

Here we have, it seems to me, a clear and fundamental locus for the presence of angels not simply as it were in literature but actually in action, because if we believe in angels at all this is where we are going to be able to see them.

Let us look at some of these liturgical texts. It is worth saying that this trisagion, or what we call the Sanctus, generally speaking occurs in one form or another in every known liturgy except, curiously enough, the earliest of these, the liturgy of the Apostolic Tradition of Hippolytus from the beginning of the third century, and also the one liturgy derived from it. But all the others, east and west, all have some form or another of the sanctus. Either they have a simple form, for instance in a text which I shall look at a little more closely, from the so-called liturgy of St Mark of Alexandria, or they have the fuller form with the *Benedictus qui venit*, blessed is he who comes, taken from the gospel accounts of the entry into Jerusalem.

But it has been very instructively pointed out that already here in all these texts we get in fact an amplification of Isaiah in the sense that not just the earth is full of God's glory but *heaven* and earth are full of God's holy glory. The seraphic hymn of acclamation is expanded in all Christian liturgical texts by saying it is not just the earth which is full of the glory but also heaven. This seems to be characteristic of the Christian version. I say the Christian version because there has been one attempt to show that this sanctus, as used liturgically in the Church, is really a borrowing from the synagogue worship where you have a similar kind of acclamation called the *Qadusha,* derived from *qadosh,* holy, in the text from Isaiah 6. In the synagogue form you have the *Holy holy holy, the earth is full of glory,* and you have something like Ezekiel 3, 12. 'Blessed is the Lord of glory from this place'. The point, made in a very instructive and a very fine piece of writing indeed by Erik Peterson, in a book recently translated called *The Angels and the Liturgy,* is that for a Christian the new Jerusalem is not any particular place. Ezekiel is distressed about the passing of the glory from Jerusalem but the point of course is, that for Christians the glory is concentrated in the body of the risen Christ and this glory is in heaven. So in point of fact the essential difference between the Jewish *Qadusha* and the Christian *Sanctus* is that heaven is introduced and heaven is the place where the glory is concentrated in the body of the ascended, risen Christ.

But let us look a little more at this particular text which is simply one among others, but perhaps more attractive in some ways. This text is obviously led up to in something like what we would call a preface; it is long, it is very much longer than anything we would be able to put up with in the West. 'Thou art above every principality and authority and power and dominion and every name you name not only in this world but also in that which is to come. Around thee stand thousand thousand and ten thousand times ten thousand armies of holy angels and archangels. Around thee stand thy two most honourable living creatures, the cherubim with the many eyes and the seraphim with six wings; with twain thereof they cover their feet and with twain they do fly and they cry aloud the one to the other with unresting mouths and unsilent praise the chant of the thrice holy hymn, singing, shouting, glorifying, crying aloud and saying to thy majestic glory. Holy holy holy Lord of Hosts.'

Now of course we know very well that prefaces in our ordinary Roman rite do actually make the point that the earthly liturgical worship is the place where we enter into the eternal heavenly worship of the angels; and the biblical text clearly behind this is the text which we find in Apocalypse 4, 5. You remember that the whole passage here is taken up again with the animals, these curious animals of Ezekiel, the throne-bearing animals. The idea here is of course the *Merkabah* of Yahweh, the idea that Yahweh has a throne which is supported by these four animals, these mystical animals, who go on saying night and day, they never stop singing, Holy holy holy Lord God Almighty, he was, he is and he is to come'. The worship also which is directed eventually to the Lamb.

It is fairly important to look at the detail of the worship simply to draw attention to the fact that this is in fact capable of being parallelled throughout by the emperor cult, the cult of the emperors. Peterson insists on the political character of the Christian worship in heaven. He uses the word 'political' here in a very large sense. I want to draw attention to that particularly at the moment because you may remember earlier on, talking about the Nuer, we talked about the parallel relationship between the social structure of these tribes and the structure of the divine for these tribes. Here again we are finding a kind of parallelism of the emperor cult and the cult in heaven.

The point for our purposes after all this is, what about us? We don't have emperors. We have a king, or a queen rather, but whenever the queen appears on television I have the impression personally that it is all rather a bit of a joke. And I don't think we have really got to the point yet where we can think of what is going on in heaven as being a bit of a joke. Or, if we have got to that point, then we probably won't stay Christian for very much longer. But the systematic point I want to make is that here, you see, with the help of liturgical studies, with the help of biblical studies, we can begin to appreciate the way in which angels do have their kind of function in a whole world-view which ultimately culminated in a vision of the divine. But we don't share this world-view. You see, once again we are, as it were, standing apart from it, reflecting upon it in the curious sophisticated way we have. We can draw attention to a relationship between the cult of the emperor and the incense and the processions, the prostrations, all this kind of thing; we can draw attention to that and to the worship thought of by the author of the Apocalypse as to what is going on in heaven and the heavenly throne. But having done this, then what? Do we abandon, as it were, our present 20th-century stance and try to become first-century Christians or first-century inhabitants of the Mediterranean area? No, we don't try to do this. We don't lose our own particular stance in time simply by becoming Christians. We have this double relationship to the past and to the present. And this again is one of the conditions of seeing an angel. We have the particular advantage here as Christians of being able to renew in a very special kind of way, liturgically by an anamnesis, a situation which is not just a literary one. That is to say in the liturgy we actually perform something, we actually do something, which creates a situation which is not simply that of, as it were, reflecting in our minds on something that has happened in the past. That is to say, the liturgical anamnesis does in some way or other reactualize the past.

But does it reactualize it in the sense of, as it were, creating a new consciousness? We are certainly brought once again in the liturgy into the real presence of Christ who suffered and rose again and ascended into heaven where he is surrounded by the angels. But we have still got to ask the question, are the angels here simply part of the poetic furniture? Could we in fact, without any serious loss whatsoever, simply drop the preface form with all that stuff about angels and simply have a kind of dinner table as it were as at the last supper? We are once more faced with this problem of how we can see an angel.

Let us just review what we have been trying to do so far, the kind of steps we have taken. The permanent question which is concerning us is what are the subjective conditions for knowledge of an angel. We have looked at some examples of the way in which highly sophisticated 20th-century people have recreated a simple, naive it may be, innocent sense of the divine in its multifariousness. Multifarious in the sense of being Homeric gods, multifarious in the sense of being social refractions of the divine. We have also examined to some extent characteristic Wordsworthian ruminations on what is meant by this early innocence and later sophistication. That is to say in a single mind, Wordsworth's mind, recalling his past he can think of a time when angels of some sort or another, some sense of the divine at least, some spirit, might have been manifested in nature, but now of course he cannot do this. And we are rather like this. And we have looked also briefly at Blake and the way in which the systematic difficulties for discovering angels are expressed in terms of Blake's own insistence that only by a kind of prophetic vision, only by a kind of LSD, so to speak, can we overcome this secularization of the world, this desacralized world brought in by Locke and Newton and by the industrial revolution which we find still more in our own times. We can see that the question of angels is part of the question of the secularized world in which we live. And we certainly are not going to find angels in a secularized world. That is, as I said, fairly clear. At least not in the form that we would expect to find them. There is this gap between the world, the ancient innocent world in which angels might walk with man, might appear at any moment, and our kind of industrialized world in which they cannot. At least they cannot in the form in which we would expect to find them if they were the forms of the innocent world. We cannot expect to find innocent angels in an industrial world. This is why they seem so peculiar to us. We may of course try to find an industrial angel in the industrial world. That is a possibility which we will have to examine in a moment.

I have also tried to suggest some of the difficulties in even the biblical texts presented to us. But even if we do recreate the sense of the eucharistic liturgy, of the Apocalypse and so on, still we are actually performing this fairly sophisticated thing in the head. Do we really get any closer to seeing angels just because we now know how to read the text of the Apocalypse and to talk glibly about the emperor cult? To be able to do this is quite interesting, but does it help us to see an angel? And even when this recalling, this anamnesis of the past world, is conducted in a very real sense in the eucharistic liturgy, does this take us any further, because after all what is the connection between the eucharistic world and the world in which we live? The important thing about the liturgy for us here is that it is at least something we do. At least in one sense or another, by simply performing the liturgy, by simply recalling angels, not simply by reading about them: we are at least creating here a kind of sphere, a kind of sacral area, in which an angel might very well appear. So this at least is a privileged place where angels might be accessible to us. Because it is not merely going through something in the head as a student of comparative religion might do, it is actually performing something. That is to say, part of the epistemological condition for seeing an angel is to do something. It is actually to create a kind of state in which an angel might appear. Because in the ordinary state which we have now made for ourselves in Western society angels are not going to appear. We have to create a special kind of state where angels might appear and we might in point of fact see an angel.

That is, as I say, a kind of review. The last step now, the final step which I want to take, is how else might we do this apart from liturgy? Because if we can say how else we might do this, we might be able to go back to the liturgical tradition and see how this need not be quite so odd as it appears at first sight. The last witness that I am going to draw on is the 20th-century German poet Rilke. He has a mind which I find very sympathetic. I don't know whether other people will really find it very appealing. If you are not already struck by him you may find him rather unpleasant, rather peculiar. Like so many people of the time and his own area, he was of course a lapsed Catholic. And for his own purposes and in his own way he played with the idea of angels in the famous collection of poems called the Duinese Elegies, begun in the Castle of Duino. The first words simply streamed out of him apparently, 'Who, if I cried, would hear me among the angelic orders' – in the famous translation I was brought up on. There is one particular passage which I would like to read, in the second Elegy, because it has a very different set of images for the angel which is quite a help in some ways, perhaps, for breaking down our own subconscious residual picture of angels, the biblical one, let alone the renaissance ones. I will read again the Leishman translation.

> Early successes, favourites of fond Creation,
> ranges, summits, dawn-red ridges of all forthbringing – pollen of blossoming godhead,
> junctures of light, corridors, stairways, thrones,
> chambers of essence, shields of felicity, tumults
> of stormily-rapturous feeling, and suddenly, separate,
> mirrors, drawing up again their own outstreamed beauty into their own faces.

That at least is a very different assembly of images from those to which we are accustomed in the Christian tradition. And the question of course is what Rilke's angels are supposed to be. I think a very brief answer might be that they are the symbol for Rilke of an achieved state of being which we ourselves are still only trying to reach. This achieved state of being is one of, as it were, containing the visible world within themselves. Our task, our role, our destiny, is to transform the visible world into the invisible. The angels are the symbols of this achieved transcendence. And I think the idea is instructive in view of what we were saying earlier about manifestation, the way in which the manifestation of nature has been taken in the innocent world as the manifestation of the divine. For Rilke the idea is that there is a kind of total process, which he calls that of transformation, in which humanity is involved. And humanity has a role here, a task of taking part in this transformation of the visible world into the invisible. By way of instance he will talk about certain specific ways, again nostalgically, in which say, poetry, or traditional art, has achieved this in certain forms of making; his awareness of the industrial world makes him sure that this kind of making is hardly possible any longer except in this Ditchlingesque way. There has got to be an interiorizing experience by which this total transformation is achieved. It is something that goes on slowly maturing until it is ultimately summed up in an act of praise. Because this is what the angels are doing. It is the activity of praise ultimately that is the supreme act of transformation, a taking up of this real world and its transformation into a complete act of praise. The point of history then is the transformation of the visible world into some fulfilled being that we can call invisible, anyway into a superior, higher kind of being.

The angel, at least as a symbol here for Rilke, is instructive for us, in the sense that we can now recognize that whereas in the innocent and primitive world the presence of the divine was simply acknowledged in the form of personified beings 'out there', we have now in this new version recognized the angels as something which, as it were, stands ahead of us. The angel is not something which we have to acknowledge or which is there, but it is a symbol of what we have to achieve, still in terms of a relationship with the visible world. Not as though in this case (in Rilke's vision the angel is embodied in nature) that it simply has to be allowed to show itself in the world. On the contrary we have got to take part in a process in which we are guided by a vision of the angels and in this sense we enter into a kind of angelic life.

Now, can we accept this in Christian terms? Rilke is quite explicitly rejecting the idea of a Christian angel when he talks like this. Can we ourselves say he wasn't rejecting really Christian angels, he is perhaps rejecting the renaissance angels, perhaps, sentimental angels? By way of summing up I should like to raise again the question about subjective and objective. Remember we started at the beginning by saying that by objective we meant an angel out there, the angel dropped into our lap, and by 'subjective' the epistemological conditions for knowing angels, the question, How do I see an angel? And what I am trying to draw attention to is that the angel can never be 'out there' any more than God can be. That is to say, if we want to know an angel, we don't know it, we can't know it, in the way in which we might know any kind of material object – clearly that is simple enough. Everyone will agree about that. That is what St Thomas says. There is no question of there being objective angels at all. There can only be subjective angels. That is to say they are 'subjects' just as much as we are, and in this sense we cannot come into contact with, cannot see an angel, except by sharing a community with angels. What we can do, and what has been done throughout the whole course of history, is to create artistically and otherwise objects in which we embody our vision of the angel, as Blake might do, for instance. Blake in the prophetic vision might create a picture, an engraving, or some sort of poem, in which his views of what an angel might be are embodied. But in point of fact that is only a kind of reflection of what an angel is. We cannot paint an angel in the sense even in which we can paint each other. Or talk about each other. The only way in which we can understand, or see, an angel is precisely by being *with* an angel, by sharing a community with angels. In this sort of sense, then, what we might try to say about how to see an angel is that we can share in a world of presences which, again in Christian terms, can be concentrated at a particular privileged point, the presence which is the eucharistic liturgy. The best way of seeing an angel is first of all to go through the process, the actual action of re-enacting a liturgy, re-enacting a liturgical cult. This is to create a dimension of the world which wasn't there until we actually elicited it, by actually doing something by performing something historically. In this way we can create a privileged place for seeing an angel and by doing this we can then at this point hope to share in the real presence of angels.

It is not any longer I think going to be in the sort of political form which was associated with the emperor cult. It is not I think at all insignificant that the notion of the 'people of God' is a very democratic-sounding expression. I am pretty certain myself that the interest in the phrase, the people of God, is not simply because people have got all worked up about the biblical and liturgical basis for it. I think the phrase 'the people of God' is attractive because it suggests a democratic non-organization which seems to be a much happier state of affairs than a hierarchical institution or a hierarchical body of angels for that matter. So we can create a privileged locus for meeting angels, and meet them there as sharing the common presence with us in the real presence of the glorified body of Christ in the sacraments; and we meet them there as it were on equal terms, not as hierarchical figures with whom we share in an emperor cult. We meet them in this kind of democratic way where we assemble, the people of God, around the risen Christ and there actually acknowledge with them the glory of the risen Christ.

# 17

# Wrestling with the Word

**The Sermon**

'No one has ever seen God'; this is the text which was read to us from the first Epistle of St John, and which also occurs at the end of the Prologue to St John's Gospel. 'No one has ever seen God': an appropriate text, perhaps, for the Sunday after the Ascension and before Pentecost, in that pause which the liturgy has contrived for our meditation between the departure of the Son as risen Lord and the coming of the Spirit, an experience of absence through which we may more profoundly recover an experience of presence – absence, presence, of what, of whom? Of God, whom no one has ever seen.

Let us recall what must be a familiar experience to all of us at some time in our lives: the sleeping city, the lights shining in the empty streets, oneself, the solitary watcher withdrawn from the human community of sleep, to which one is all the more deeply drawn. This is the before and after of all the active business of the day, the multifarious contradiction of human project, plan and purpose, the coming and going: all rises from and returns to sleep, movement back to stillness, the rising and falling of a single biological rhythm of breathing, unconscious, at rest. Are these sleepers dreaming their personal dreams, or are they united in the single impersonal dream of the world? Even those who do not sleep in this sleeping stillness, the sufferers awake in their white nights alone, the lovers involved in their private intimacy, aren't they too enacting in this universal dream a typical human destiny of pain and sex, death and procreation, sounding a ground bass of human existence? The sleeping city: a human community realized in a unity before and after, below if not above, the community of active function and conscious purpose: this underlying community finding itself in a deeper unity of typical man. And who or what sustains this deeper unity; is the dream of the world really impersonal, or does the dream unfold in some deeper dreamer? And is the sleeping city in the dark the deficient image of a waking community more deeply awake than any depth of sleep, caught up into the unity of a single radiance of light where the mystery of waking life finds its consummation and its sense, the heavenly city, Jerusalem? A peace, a tranquillity, a blessing, repose, *shalom*, more profound than the deep unconsciousness of sleep.

A modern translation of the opening of St John's Epistle brings out strikingly the force of the neuter pronouns there: 'It was there from the beginning; we have heard it; we have seen it with our own eyes; we have looked upon it, and felt it with our own hands; and it is of this we tell. Our theme is the word of life.' What is this 'it', or who is it? It is the expression, the declaration, annunciation, communication of the God no one has ever seen. 'No one has ever seen God, according to the Gospel prologue, but he alone God as Son at the heart of the Father, he has made him known'. It is Jesus who discloses the Father, for whoever has seen Jesus has seen the Father. But how do we see Jesus? According to the Gospel (12.20 f.) some Greeks came to Philip and said to him, 'Sir, we wish to see Jesus'. Philip went and told Andrew, Andrew went with Philip and they told Jesus. And Jesus answered them: 'The hour has come for the Son of Man to be glorified. Truly, truly I say to you, unless a grain of wheat falls into the earth and dies, it remains alone; but if it dies it bears much fruit.' So seeing Jesus means sharing the life of a seed, a neuter *it* (as much an *it* as flesh and wine, bread and blood), which dies and by dying bears fruit, initiates a communion, is no longer alone. We see God without seeing him, by entering into a communion of life with the Word of God which communicates life. The communion is so personal that it can only be talked about in neuters and abstracts: 'neuter' means *neither,* neither masculine nor feminine, neither male nor female, personal as ultimately, typically that in man which is image of God.

So no one has seen God except the Son who has departed in his Ascension; yet it is for our advantage that he goes away, so as to send us the sustainer, counsellor, advocate, Paraclete. 'No one has ever seen God; if we love one another, God abides in us and his love finds its completeness in us. By this we know that we abide in him and he in us, because he has given us of his own Spirit.' So the Epistle. The presence manifested by the visible Jesus is withdrawn: the substance of that presence – the communication of risen life – is to be manifested by the Spirit of life in the mutual love of those who have received the Word of life. The God whom no one has ever seen is to become tangible, felt, as a presence of love; for God is love. 'So we know and believe' – that is, it is our experience in faith – 'this love with which God brings himself forth in us. God is love, and he who abides in love abides in God, and God abides in him.' We feel our way into the God whom no one has ever seen, who is the ultimate sense of our personal lives, who is so deeply personal himself that we must refer to him by the abstract, Love.

'Love', of course, is a word of multiple application. Love as *eros*, 'erotic' love, was a god before Christianity and is a god, a universal force even now. 'Love makes the world go round' – so the pallid reminder of a view which saw eros reflected in the rotation of the spheres, the drift of the stars, the rise and fall of the tides, the cycle of the seasons, cosmic sympathy and human tenderness and warmth: eros articulate as lyrical excitement and tragic conflict. And love is the inarticulate bearing by a mother of her son, the connection in the womb which persists and endures through long years of erratic growth. This love has many faces and many masks, some of them grotesquely distorted; this love may be a god or gods: but is God this Love? And if not, why can we use the same word 'love' for the gods and for God? How strange that *agape* should be the word for love in the Greek translation of the Song of Songs in the Bible, and that Jewish and Christian mystics should find their vocabulary in this canticle of erotic love!

John offers us some criteria. 'By this we know love, that he laid down his life for us; and we ought to lay down our lives for the brethren. But if anyone has the world's goods and sees his brother in need, yet closes his heart against him, how does God's love abide in him?' The link between the eros-gods and the God who is *agape* comes out more clearly if we remember that what is here translated 'heart' is more literally and semitically 'bowels', bowels of compassion, the organ of human connection, sympathy, fellow-feeling. *Agape*-love is something to do with the flow and the bond of human connection, connection at the fine point of ultimate humanity, neither male nor female, where all men are or have to become *one*. *Agape*-love is the living sense of what is ultimately common to all men, the feeling sense of human community, human contact in the fragile and delicate flesh, contact become tangible at the point where each of us may be most intimately and searchingly touched. *Agape*-love is human communion as compassion. John is renewing in the sense of Jesus, the Son of Man, what Isaiah had said about the fast:

> Is it not to share your bread with the hungry,
>     and bring the homeless poor into your house;
> When you see the naked, to cover him,
>     and not to hide yourself from your own flesh? (58.7).

'To hide yourself from your own flesh.' *Agape*-love is shown up by its negation, that is, withdrawal from communion in the bare flesh of man-kind, a withdrawal in which the heart hides itself in deliberate insensibility, hides itself from itself, and turns to stone: 'Is there any cause in nature that makes these hard hearts?' This is the unkindness which denies human kinship, the oneness of man.

In Jesus's prayer before his Passion, he prays to his Father for the men whom the Father has given him 'that they may be *one* even as we, Jesus and the Father, are *one*'. Jesus, as the One who by dying and rising again becomes Many, is the manifestation of the God who is love, who is One in Father and Son and who seeks to include all men in the communication of this oneness; and we by being one in the love of God abiding in us, manifest Jesus by laying down our lives for the brethren, manifest the God who is love by being many in one, in a unity which is community.

What we are talking about is the ultimate point of human existence; and that is God whom no man has ever seen. We discover the invisible God in the context of human meaning inaugurated by the Word of God; we have seen it and felt it with the eyes and hands of apostolic witnesses and, in the medium of a sensibility made delicate by the Spirit, with our own eyes and hands; and we discover the invisible God in the presence of the Spirit initiating a human communion of divine consanguinity and consubstantiality, the blood of God's love. The invisible God has three witnesses: the Spirit breathing within us, the symbolic-sacramental water, and the irreducibly historical blood of Jesus. These three witnesses run together into one, God's Son, the Son of Man, who has become our light and life and truth, and who by stretching out his arms on the Cross has drawn us into the all-embracing unity of the God whom no man has ever seen: the one God whose compassionate love is manifested in the compassionate communion of mankind in the fine point of humanity, the extreme Passion of the Son of Man. For this one God of love whom no man has ever seen has made his own the one flesh of mankind and manifested his glory there, in a naked *Consummatum est*.

### The Preparation

The texts appointed for this Sunday, the Sunday after Ascension Day, were Acts 1.15–17, 20–26; 1 John 4.11–16; John 17.11b–19. I followed my usual practice and simply glanced at these texts some days before. I must confess that I regard this first moment in the genesis of the sermon as quite fundamental. This glance at the text is in no way a piece of conscious study, even when the texts are unfamiliar. In this case of course the texts were extremely, even painfully, familiar; glancing at them meant at the conscious level verifying that they were what they were and recognizing that they were about what is deepest in Christianity. At this conscious level, then, there was an ironic admission to myself that I should have either to evade them, to sidle up to them, as it were (this is something I had felt forced to do when confronted with the Prologue to St John's Gospel some months before); or, somehow, meet them head on with a kind of shock of collision, which would have to be registered later as a sort of broadside discharged at the congregation.

But what I regard as fundamentally important is allowing the texts to subside into the back of the mind for at least twenty-four hours, so that settled there, in that foyer of awareness just prior to consciousness where one's interest, one's life-concern, are in active process of taking shape (the meristem or growing point of the mind; I don't, therefore, mean some deep unconscious), they can offer a point of condensation and crystallization for these active concerns. My experience has been after a twenty-four-hour period of incubation like this, the texts begin to press for some kind of utterance, generate a restlessness which drives me to a variety of books in the attempts to formulate questions at the level of articulate consciousness and eventually find a focus, a perspective, for final communication, where an indistinct but quite firm sense of an audience, of a congregation as horizon, is now awake. The texts have 'fertilized' the life-interests, and assumed whatever vital density they have at the moment. I must also add that explicitly or implicitly and habitually there would be some invocation of the Holy Spirit at this stage, some exposure of texts and life-concerns together to a consecrating and equilibrating influence acknowledged to be beyond the reach of deliberate control. Basically, I believe, the sermon must be allowed to *happen,* to be an event in one's own process of growth in the Spirit; and this in turn involves the presence of some matured confidence in the receptive interests of the audience, some unspoken estimate of what it is prepared to take. In the present case a tradition of some three years of preaching by Dominicans to a congregation which has freely opted to take part in the evening Mass at Blackfriars allows of some measure of assurance that life-concerns are shared, over and above a general conviction that preaching must be a communication in the Spirit.

I am afraid that much of this must seem pretty pretentious, in view of what actually emerges and has actually emerged in this case; but it does represent the theological expectations at work in my preaching practice. In the case of the present sermon, the deliberate 'letting-be' of the texts in the back of my mind produced unexpected results, since I eventually felt compelled to begin putting down on paper what was emerging consciously; this is only the second occasion in some fifteen years of preaching that I have written out a sermon. I shan't, however, venture here to discuss the implications of preaching with or without a complete 'score', except perhaps to admit to a private distrust (for myself) of any attempt at formal coherence and tightness of organization in a sermon. Somehow, it seems to me, one oughtn't to *dare*: the sermon is inescapably *provisional*, as open-ended, at both ends, as any stretch of a human life ... which makes the present sermon all the more puzzling to me. And let me say quite frankly that I *am* puzzled by my own sermon; I don't quite trust it.

Quite clearly the set scriptural texts had on this occasion longterm interests to engage. I saw, without defining them, that the two Johannine texts had their manifest and hidden connections, while the text from Acts had a different kind of life, so that I tentatively decided to rest the sermon on the Johannine texts. The immediate front of interests encountered by the texts happened in fact to be Jewish mysticism, in particular for the light it seems to throw on the kind of imagination active in St John's Gospel. Apart from Scholem's remarkable book, *Aspects of Jewish Mysticism,* I should mention the fine novel by Patrick White, *Riders in the Chariot,* the title of which is in fact a translation of the *Yorde merkabah* of early Jewish mysticism. (I had read the novel some months ago when I was pursuing similar investigations on a somewhat broader front, but it was still in my mind.) I was also in the middle of a course of lectures on Sin and Grace.

Once the process of active questioning and search had begun, I noticed what, shamefully, no doubt, I have never noticed before: the sentence 'No one has ever seen God' occurred in the Gospel as well as in the Epistle, with a minor and insignificant difference in the Greek. I suddenly saw that this could be linked with the queerness of the Sunday, liturgically speaking, falling between Ascension and Pentecost, a non-Sunday, as it were, celebrating nothing but an interim, a pause; so absence, God's not being in the world. I hoped, without wishing to make too much of it explicitly, that the Johannine assertion, 'No one has ever seen God', could assume and allude to what is often thought to be a modern sense of God's absence from the world; then, to show how John's sense of the transcendence of God was sustained by the sense of his immanence (in Jesus, in the Spirit, in the community) would be to respond, by allusion at least, to this modern sense of absence as non-existence. This seemed to give me my main theme, or the perspective within which the texts could show themselves. What I had now to do was to face somehow the challenge of 'God is love'. My preoccupation became now to acquire a sharper awareness of 'the early Christian community', in particular John's community, so as to understand how an experience of community, an experience of God as love which showed in its immanence the transcendence of the God whom no one has ever seen. I spent some fairly fruitless hours turning over the pages of various books, most of which I had used before: commentaries on Acts, Schnackenburg's commentary on the Johannine epistles, Ratzinger's small book on Christian brotherhood, Warnach on *agape*.... None of these seemed really to connect.

While I was doing this I became more and more conscious of the relevance to what I was looking for of what had seemed a moment of insight some nights before, when, unable to sleep, I had looked out from my window at the top of the tower at Blackfriars over Oxford spread out before me. To speak of a moment of insight is perhaps rather pretentious; but there had seemed to be a valid glimpse of something – human community as exhibited in the community of a city – which on reflection and analysis brought up reminiscences of Wordsworth's Westminster Bridge sonnet, the night thoughts of Henry V in Shakespeare, passages in the early T. S. Eliot, as well as thoughts about the place of the city in early Near Eastern civilization and the writings of Lewis Mumford, linked with the Jerusalem-Zion theme in Old and New Testaments. The second paragraph of the sermon represents what became of these reflections, written down under some compulsion, without any very clear sense of just how this meditated experience was going to contribute to the sermon.

In fact, this registration of experience was a turning point, not only for what it seemed to be disclosing, but also because it initiated a certain style and rhythm of communication. If the congregation could swallow that kind of communication early in the sermon, we – they and I – could go on to explore 'God is love', and 'No one has ever seen God', in a style of communication which for want of a better word I could call 'poetic', meaning indirect and allusive rather than direct and declaratory. The rest of the sermon became an exercise in this style of indirect communication, the only way, it now seemed, in which reflections and half-intuitions of years past could be put into words.

It would be tedious and again pretentious to list the allusions which were drawn into the text of the sermon as it wrote itself. Of course they were not deliberately introduced, but as the words were put down on the page the allusions became more or less conscious – Dante, Aristotle (the *de Anima* on touch!) D. H. Lawrence, Shakespeare, Rahner on the Sacred Heart, apart from Scripture. The question remains in my mind as to whether this sort of sermon is a legitimate exercise, and beyond that what sort of communication is appropriate in theology generally. For instance, there is the play on the word 'naked', first in the Isaiah quotation and finally in the last words of the sermon; is this sort of ambiguity, whether or not creative in the sense of Empson's *Seven Types of Ambiguity*, appropriate to theological communication? I can't resist quoting here a text I came across while pursuing this question after preaching the sermon; it is a description of Mallarmé's conversation by a young poet-contemporary, which I found in Anthony Hartley's introduction to his Penguin *Mallarmé*:

> A pleasant voice. Ritual gestures. And inexhaustibly subtle speech, ennobling every subject with rare ornamentations: literature, music, art, life, and even news items, discovering secret analogies between things, communicating doors, hidden contours. The universe is simplified since he sums it up in dreams, as the sea is summed up by a murmur in a shell.

Should a sermon, a piece of theological communication, reach towards the summation of the universe in the dream-murmur of a shell?

# 18

# The Necessity of the Church in the Context of Non-Christian Religions

Of all the difficulties which emerge when one begins to consider the place of the Church in the context of non-Christian religions, the most immediate is the question of theological method. It is certainly true that the question of method in theology arises everywhere in theology today; and it may even be true that consideration of the particular problem with which we are concerned, since it is less closely tied to a long tradition of theological reflection than, say, Christology, may by the very nature of the problem demand a distinctive theological approach, thus as it were laying down in advance a solution to the question of method. It seems desirable, nevertheless, to offer some brief indications of the approach to be adopted here, if only so that readers may become aware of the theological presuppositions of the writer. This is to proceed *via disciplinae*; the *via inventionis,* I need hardly say, had to be traversed beforehand, and I regard this paper as merely a temporary halt on the way of discovery, sketching a provisional perspective. The paper will then begin with some remarks on method (1); go on to consider some of the terms of the question (2); and propose some provisional conclusions (3).

### 1. Method

The approach adopted in this paper is historical and hermeneutic. That is to say, it considers the particular question of the necessity of the Church in the context of non-Christian religions as a special case² of the general question: 'What is the meaning of this state of affairs in which I find myself involved?' This state of affairs is a particular historical conjunction, because it has its antecedents in the past and is open to a future; it is a state of affairs in which men have been, are, and will be involved, which interpretation and choice have shaped and will shape and reshape. The general question has been quite deliberately put in the first person singular, 'I', because I believe that there is a special need today for theological statements to be proposed as witness and testimony, backed by the speaker's or writer's at least provisional commitment, as an at least partial resolution of his own anxieties in the *krisis* which is laid upon us all.

To say, then, that the approach of this paper is historical is to indicate that the world of human meaning is its starting-point, its 'matter'; to say that it is hermeneutic is to indicate that its 'form', its level of discourse, is the analysis of human meanings, in their exchange and transmission. Negatively, this implies that cosmic or natural order has the value for theological discourse of a symbolic structure, as an historically ascertainable interpretation of human experience symbolically representing a different and mysterious order of divine purpose, the Meaning of meanings. Thus the general form of the answer to the general question, 'What is the meaning of this state of affairs...?' will run, 'It is God's will that...' *Fiat voluntas tua.*

For the theological character of this historical and hermeneutic exploration consists in displaying, as far as possible, the central meaning and significance of a given state of affairs by allowing it to become illuminated by the core of revealed meaning, the Gospel. This reference of the given state of affairs to the Gospel is of course reciprocal, a 'hermeneutic circle', such that the Gospel too becomes re-identified in the new idiom of each successive historical state of affairs. It is important to recognize that there is always a gap between the state of affairs and its theological interpretation. The gap may be regarded as a sign of the eschatological tension, implicit in human history, only partially accessible to Christian understanding. This partial understanding, and hence the gap between theological interpretation and the historical moment, is characteristic not only of our present theological effort but of any Christian theology, including the theological understanding offered in the Scriptures.[1]

---

[1] Further remarks on theological method by the present writer may be found in the relevant article in *Sacramentum Mundi*, vol. VI, and in 'A Preface to Theology', *Journal of the Anthropological Society of Oxford*, vol. II, n. 2 (1971). cf. Chapters 5 and 7.

## 2. The Terms of the Question

*(a) Church*

Clearly the most important term to be elucidated in our question is the term 'Church'. It might seem that after Vatican II there should be no special difficulty in providing an account of what we might mean by 'Church', since so many of the Council documents are concerned directly or indirectly with ecclesiology. In fact this does not seem to be the case, something which might provoke reflection about the nature of official ecclesiastical pronouncements. Without for a moment depreciating the value of the conciliar documents, it might be said, using the terms introduced earlier, that the ecclesiological utterances of Vatican II are neither historical nor, or only in a limited degree, hermeneutic. Their statements operate at a certain distance from what is or was historically the case, and the distance from the present moment makes it possible to assume a continuity with the past which is ideal rather than historically verifiable.

We may take a single example which is not irrelevant to our present concerns. At the beginning of the dogmatic constitution on the Church, *Lumen Gentium,* the Church is said to be 'in Christ as it were the sacrament or sign and instrument of intimate union with God and of the unity of the whole human race' (LG 1). Later, in a phrase recalled at the beginning of the decree on the missionary activity of the Church, the Church is called the 'universal sacrament of salvation' (LG 48; AG 1). Now these are admirable and encouraging phrases, and I hope to show their bearing for our present question; meanwhile it is not clear what they have to do with our actual, present or historical, experience of the Church. Take the word *sacramentum,* and the curious little explanatory parenthesis, *seu signum et instrumentum.* Without the parenthesis one might have thought that the constitution, in an archaizing use of the word, was evoking, say, Augustinian perspectives. It seems that in order to relieve neo-scholastic anxieties, the parenthesis has been added, however incongruously and still, of course, archaizingly. But more seriously, neither statement seems to bear closely on the empirical Church and its history.

To illustrate what might be meant by such an objection, let us remind ourselves that *Lumen Gentium* was promulgated in November 1964. In that same year Hans Küng addressed a Eucharistic Congress in Bombay[2], and Hugo Rahner published a

[2] 'The World Religions in God's Plan of Salvation', in J. Neuner ed., *Christian Revelation and World Religions* (1967). The German version of this paper, published separately in the series *Theologische Meditationen,* was, by a nice touch, dedicated to Hans Urs von Balthasar for his sixtieth birthday.

collection of his (admittedly earlier) articles in a volume entitled *Symbole der Kirche*. According to Küng, 'Church' means 'that community of baptized Christians, ordered upon the basis of the New Testament message, who believe in Christ the Lord, intend to celebrate the Eucharist, strive to live according to the Gospel, and wish to be known to the world as a Church' (p. 35). This is of course an *empirical* description of the Church, itself patently idealized (are all members of any Christian Church so enthusiastic as the description implies?). Given such a description of the Church, it is inevitable that Küng should prefer to relate the salvation of non-Christians not to the Church but to God's plan of salvation; we shall return to this point later.

By way of contrast, let us cite Hugo Rahner's preface to his collected articles:

> The 'great mystery' between the Church and Christ is in its depths a Trinitarian mystery, that contains in its maternal womb all the mysteries of divine Revelation. We may best express this relationship between the eternal Father and the Church, between the crucified Word and the Church, between the Spirit of glory springing up from the Cross, and the Church, in the words of Irenaeus: One God is the Father, who is above all and through all and in all. For the Father is above all and he himself is the Head of Christ. Through all is the Word, and this Word is the Head of the Church. In us all however is the Spirit, and this is that living water which the Lord pours out on all who rightly believe in him and love him.[3]

We may call this a *visionary* account of the Church, in the sense that it claims to render the deep meaning of the Church in a way which transcends its empirical appearance.[4]

Now it may seem that the empirical and the visionary accounts of the Church are simply incompatible, and that one or other alone must be the true account of the Church. And indeed it seems clear to me that if either account is taken exclusively, such that the Church is seen uniquely either as an empirical community or an archetypal assembly, then each view tends towards heresy (I use the word consciously), the heresy of extreme neo-Protestantism or of a spiritualizing gnosticism. For the one fundamental principle of Catholic ecclesiology is surely the coincidence without identity of

---

[3] *Symbole der Kirche,* p. 9. The beautiful essay, 'Die Arche Noe als Schiff des Heils', in this volume, pp. 504–47, is closely relevant to the topic of this paper.

[4] 'Visionary' should suggest Dante and Blake, as well as biblical and post-biblical prophets and seers. Cf. Chapter 16.

the empirical and transcendent Church, of the local, earthly ecclesia and the heavenly ecclesia. 'Triumphalist' ecclesiology tends towards the identification of empirical and transcendent Church; 'progressivist' ecclesiology tends towards their total dissociation. It is at just this point that the notion of 'sacrament' could have its part to play, if by 'sacrament' were understood, say, the anticipated real presence of an eschatological fulfilment. In this sense both the local Church, as well as the communion of local Churches in the great Church, would bear the sense and the reality of the fulfilment of God's promise to mankind in Jesus Christ, but bear that sense and reality as pledge of the future and its inadequate disclosure.

Yet to my mind ecclesiological discourse conducted in these terms tends, in virtue of its abstraction from the actual course of history and the immediacy of experience, towards the construction of a sort of artificial world for armchair theologians. What is surely needed is the detailed identification of particular instances where empirical and transcendent Church have coincided in the experience of believers, and the analysis of just how this coincidence has been formulated as the communicable meaning of such an experience. It would further be necessary to approach such a historico-theological investigation with at least some partially explicit presuppositions about the genesis of meaning in experience and of the diversity of styles in which meaning may be entertained and embodied. As regards this second requirement, it will have to be sufficient here to draw attention to the limitations of that sort of description which confines itself to a neutral empiricism, and to recall the place of poetic and visionary insight in the interpretation of experience; and further to point to the worlds of communicable meaning generated in liturgy and the plastic arts.[5]

As regards the first requirement, what seems to be needed is what I should like to call (alluding to some recent discussions in Christology) an ecclesiology 'from below'. As the Evangelical theologian Wolfhart Pannenberg describes the difference: 'For Christology that begins 'from above', from the divinity of Jesus, the concept of the Incarnation stands in the centre. A Christology "from below", rising from the historical man Jesus to the recognition of his divinity, is concerned first of all with Jesus' message and fate and arrives only at the end at the concept of the Incarnation.'[6]

---

[5] For the sake of some concrete reference here, see for example the account of 'theology in stone' in Françoise Henry's fine volumes on *Irish Art* (1965–70). Or consider the theology of ikons in the Eastern Churches.

[6] *Jesus – God and Man* (1968), p. 33.

For ecclesiology we may tentatively state the difference in terms which have already been introduced without much discussion. For ecclesiology that begins from above, the transcendent Church stands in the centre, and the empirical Church is only seen secondarily as the sacramental embodiment of the transcendent Church; an ecclesiology 'from below', rising from the historical Church and churches to a recognition of the Church as transcendent, is concerned first of all with the empirical and historical particularity of local churches, and arrives only at the end at a recognition of the transcendent Church.

The implications of this approach to ecclesiology 'from below' seem to me considerable. In the first place it would seem to situate in the particularities of history the abstract distinction between empirical and transcendent Church, and to relate them appropriately to each other. Whatever reserves one may have about the ecclesiology found in the writings of Küng, (and my own reserves are very considerable), it must be admitted that one of the essential functions of the Gospel, that is, its universal critique of all human religious forms, does find expression there. The appeal for evangelical simplicity, which must evoke a response in every Christian conscience, can find some partial satisfaction in an emphasis on the empirical Church, when this empirical Church is stripped down to what are idealizingly represented as its essential New Testament features and critically contrasted with an empirical Church of the moment where these features are obscured. Such an idealized version of an empirical Church can become a programme for reform of the Church. The radical and manifest weakness of such an allegedly evangelical account of the Church in empirical terms is of course that it leaves out an essential feature of every New Testament account of the Church, that this empirical group of believers is summoned by divine call and assembled by divine election. The empirical Church itself, that is to say, at the first moment of its autonomous existence, is sustained by a visionary awareness of its own transcendence.

A consideration of a second implication of ecclesiology 'from below' will perhaps bring this point out more clearly. For this version of ecclesiology, what I have called elsewhere[7] the 'genetic moment' in Christianity finds its permanent constitutive expression in the origin of the historical Church. This may be looked at in two ways. More fundamentally, as in Christology 'from below', ecclesiology 'from below' finds its permanent support in the resurrection of Jesus the Christ. The point is well made by the Evangeli-

[7] Cf. Chapter 3 above.

cal Church historian Leonard Goppelt: 'Jesus did not return to this world (as Lazarus did ...) but entered into the New World of God; he is its first-fruits. When the disciples spoke of the resurrection, they spoke of an event which, in keeping with the common Jewish conception, introduced the future Aeon, and so they spoke of an eschatological event.' Goppelt goes on to interpret the intention of the appearances of the risen Jesus: 'The disciples had forsaken him and had given up; he came and through forgiveness re-established fellowship with them. The first appearances came to the very one who had denied him. In that he offered himself anew to the disciples for fellowship as the Living One, he brought them into faith in that all the faith displayed on their part during the earthly ministry attained its goal, faith in the God who had raised him and exalted him to be Messiah.'[8] Ecclesiology 'from below' continually re-discovers the meaning of the Church in that genetic moment in which Jesus is transformed into the risen Christ and becomes the Way into the new Aeon, God's new world, establishing a continuity of the divine plan by way of the manifest discontinuity of the death of Jesus, and thus making the transcendence of God's plan and purpose visible to the faith of historical men, who themselves are now introduced by the risen Christ into God's New World.

A second way of looking at this genetic moment in ecclesiology from below is already apparent in what has just been said: it is in the terms of contemporary Jewish thought, above all, apocalyptic, that the meaning of the Church first disclosed itself and was formulated in the New Testament period. The transcendent meaning of what it was to belong to the congregation of Jesus found varied and developing expression by way of a self-understanding defining an identity differentiated from contemporary movements in Judaism, Palestinian and Hellenistic.[9] It is here that the other essential function of the Gospel made itself evident, that is, its function and

[8] *Apostolic and Post-Apostolic Times* (1970), p. 16; p. 19.

[9] This is of course an enormous area, industriously tilled by scholars in a variety of disciplines. I shall merely mention a few books I have found specially useful while preparing this paper. A. Toynbee ed., *The Crucible of Christianity* (1969; lavishly illustrated, with contributions by very distinguished scholars); Bo Reicke, *The New Testament Era* (1968). R. M. Grant, *Augustus to Constantine* (1971). P. Brown. *The World of Late Antiquity* (1971). H. Kosmala, *Hebraer-Essener-Christen* (1959). *Aux Origines de l'Eglise* (Recherches Bibliques VII, 1965). P. Richardson, *Israel in the Apostolic Church* (1969). R. J. McKelvey, *The New Temple* (1969). E. Werner, *The Sacred Bridge* ((1959). L. Ligier, 'De la Cène de Jésus à l'anaphore de l'Eglise', *La Maison-Dieu* 87 (1966). D. S. Russell, *The Method and Message of Jewish Apocalyptic* (1964). P. Vielhauer, in Hennecke, *New Testament Apocrypha*, II (ET. 1965), pp. 581–642. I have found E. Lohse's commentary on *Das Offenbarung des Johannes* (NTD 11, 1971) especially valuable.

efficacy not only as a critique but also as a transfiguration of human religious forms. An ecclesiology from below has to learn to read the New Testament as a collection of very varied witnesses to the experience of men who were attempting to express their experience of transformation into a mode of existence which transcended history, and thereby offering a set of paradigms for an experience of transformation, an experience of transcendence, at all times and in yet other idioms of expression. The genetic moment of the resurrection of Jesus is shared in by men who themselves undergo transformation in a genetic moment which Christians call the presence of the Spirit of Jesus. Visionary insight into the meaning of the Church is intrinsic to its historical, empirical character, and needs to be revived and re-formulated in every historical epoch, in every place and at every time.

A third implication of this ecclesiology from below is that it remains in principle open to fresh varieties of experience and new forms of association. An ecclesiology from above tends to impose traditional structures and church orders as metaphysical absolutes. Where the genetic moment in ecclesiology is duly appreciated, the varieties of structure and experience in the history of the Church can be creatively assimilated and allowed to suggest novel varieties of association and new interpretations of Church experience. For instance, it will be useful while studying the self-identification of the congregation of Jesus in the first century of the Church to remind ourselves of the sociology of sects, and hence to understand how the early Church was differentiated from the sectarian movement of the Essenes.[10] Sociological considerations of this kind also help to throw light on the 'rigoristic' application of the axiom *extra ecclesiam nulla salus*.[11] The missionary impetus of the early Church arose, not without challenge, from its sense of the inclusiveness of divine election and its universal scope, corresponding to its experience of the presence of God's transcendence in his New World; the sense of election was not in the first place interpreted in the exclusiveness of sectarian withdrawal from a sinful environment.

*(b) Necessity*
It is time to turn to another term of the question, 'necessity'. We should, I believe, remind ourselves that 'necessity' (for salvation) may be understood in two significantly different ways. The phrase

---

[10] Cf. e.g. Bryan R. Wilson, *Religious Sects* (1970), and the writings of the Church historian W. H. C. Frend.

[11] Literature on Cyprian in T. Camelot, *Die Lehre von der Kirche* (Handbuch der Dogmengeschichte III, 3b,1970), p. 12.

may firstly be understood as though salvation were a fixed goal or *finis*, such that the question bore on the means necessarily required to reach that end; the perspective is one of human purpose and choice, in a rationally ordered world. Or, secondly, the phrase may be understood within the perspective of divine purpose and choice, of God's plan for mankind, in an historical order which remains ultimately mysterious and cannot be reduced to a cosmic, metaphysical order. The second perspective is surely the biblical one (cf. Isa. 40–55).

The difference of perspective may be illustrated by a consideration of what has been called the *heilsgeschichtliches Muss*, the 'it must be so' which is disclosed in a human destiny, and typically disclosed in Jesus' way of the Cross; the term in the synoptics is *dei*. The 'necessity' here is one which is seen on the one hand as the external 'fate' imposed by the Father, and on the other hand as the internal and personal loving acceptance of a 'destiny' which actually brings about and reveals the mysterious plan of God. The *fiat* of the creature is the free expression of the mystery of God's love in his election and predestination; human freedom is assumed into the visible 'sacrament' of God's purpose in history – *sacramentum* is of course the Vulgate translation of *musterion* in the Epistle to the Ephesians. It will be important for our concluding reflections to bear in mind this sense of 'necessity', where human freedom helps to constitute the 'sacramental' disclosure of God's mysterious purpose and plan, the divine order of his providence in history.

For the moment, we should consider the place of the Church in this plan. As was remarked earlier, there is a way of describing the Church which seems to dissociate it from God's plan of salvation. I can only say that such a way of regarding the Church is utterly foreign to biblical revelation in its entirety. It is surely unnecessary to document this: the notion of 'covenant' is written into biblical revelation, even in the term 'testament', and even in the celebration of the Eucharist. The Church is the assembly of those upon whom 'the end of the ages has come' (1 Cor. 10.11; see Barrett, pp. 227f., and Conzelmann, pp. 198f., on this text); 'through the Church the manifold wisdom of God' is 'now made known to the principalities and powers in the heavenly places' (Eph. 3.10). The Church is the continuing revelation of God's *musterion*, the constitution of a new humanity, mankind, in the body of Christ. Theological wisdom consists in the pursuit of insight into the manifold wisdom of God displayed in Jesus Christ, and through Jesus Christ in his body the Church.[12] In this perspective, once again,

[12] On Ephesians I shall always be greateful for H. Schlier, *Brief an die Epheser* (2nd edn. 1959). By the same author, 'Die Kirche nach dem Brief an die Epheser,

'necessity', 'gift' and 'freedom' are not incompatibles.

*(c) Non-Christian religions*
It would be an impertinence in the present context for me to pretend to some didactic competence in the understanding of non-Christian religions. On the term itself, it seems to me that in a theological context, 'non-Christian' is an acceptable descriptive category, and further, that this context, given the ecumenical expansion of Christianity, provides a point of reference for a unified use of the word 'religion' which might otherwise be available to the comparativist study of 'religions' only if it adopts the dubious historical assumptions of *Religionsgeschichte*. I shall pursue a more modest course, and simply ask myself the question why, after nearly twenty-five years as a Catholic Christian, I should continue to find other religions than Christianity of often absorbing interest.

Perhaps I might approach an answer to this question by trying first to answer a similar question about, say, Beethoven's late quartets[13] or the tragedies of Shakespeare or Aeschylus – all those distinguished expressions of the human spirit from Palaeolithic cave art to the mathematical theory of sets. This is not the place to embark on a theological defence of beauty; here it seems enough to say that in such works one discovers the indefinitely extensive possibilities of growth of the human spirit, by which I mean that fine point of perception in oneself at which one can acknowledge kinship with all mankind in its capacity to disclose and articulate the sense of humanity. Now it seems to me that non-Christian religions, whether of pre-literate societies or those which transmit a millenial tradition through scriptures and their traditional oral interpretation, make their appeal to me in a similar way, as disclosing possibilities of the human spirit touched by the divine. This may take the form of a marvellously complex, interlocking web of religious symbolism, as in some African tribal religions,[14] or of the

---

*Die Zeit der Kirche* (2nd edn. 1958), pp. 159–185. See also J. C. Kirby, *Ephesians-Baptism and Pentecost* (1968). On wisdom, for the Old Testament, now G. von Rad, *Weisheit in Israel* (1970); for the New Testament, art. *sophia*, TWNT, VII (Fohrer-Wilckens). A. Feuillet, *Le Christ, Sagesse de Dieu* (1966).

[13] Perhaps I might be allowed to recall here the two mottoes appended by Beethoven to the last movement of Op. 135 in F major and attached to the motif of the Introduction and that of the allegro; 'Muss es sein?' and 'Es muss sein'. It is tempting to read these as an expression of something like a *heilsgeschichtliches Muss*.

[14] Cf. R. G. Lienhardt, *Divinity and Experience* (1961) or V. W. Turner, *The Drums of Affliction* (1968).

cultivated discipline of introversion into depths of the human spirit where it seems to become transparent to the divine,[15] or of the ecstasy of loving sympathy with the divine, whose only valid external symbol may be the dance.[16]

It seems to me as a Christian that there are inexhaustible riches to be explored here, in this field of play between the human and the divine; it seems to me that my Christian faith, shared with countless Christians from those first disciples reconciled to the risen Christ who is the Way into God's New World, elicits, from some point of personal being in myself beyond all words, a response of surrender to the divine in Jesus Christ which reaches deeper than any other religious exploration I can ever partially share in, and reaches deeper because it is the finger of God upon me touching me at my quick. I might even dare to say that the sense of this union of surrender in faith to the living God offers some remote inkling of the sense of union of his human spirit to the divinity in the total experience of Jesus himself; this could be one way of talking about adoptive sonship. Between that ultimate and definitive union of God and man in Jesus Christ on the one hand, and the historical empirical world of human experience on the other, there is an indefinitely broad and long and deep range of 'theandric' possibilities, to be assumed and integrated in some eschatological fulfilment of God's mysterious plan for mankind in Jesus Christ. It does not seem to me an illegitimate extension of Paul's phrase in 1 Corinthians to interpret his 'aeons', the end or ends of which have come upon us as we stand at the brink of God's New Aeon, to apply not only to the past ages of Israelite or Jewish history, but also to every age and epoch of human history, which God's New World relativizes and subordinates to its own transcendent fullness of new life. It is in the union of faith with the living God, the exemplar of which we find in the union of personal being in Jesus Christ, that we may find the strength of conviction we need to hold fast to the transcendence of the revelation of God in Jesus Christ.

### 3. The Necessity of the Church

At least one conclusion seems to stand out inescapably from the preceding examination of the terms of our question: that it is the

---

[15] Apart from M. Eliade's well-known book, *Yoga: Immortality and Freedom* (1958), also J. W. Hauer, *Der Yoga* (1958).

[16] Cf. H. Corbin, *Creative Imagination in the Sūfism of Ibn 'Arabī* (1969). G. van der Leeuw, *Sacred and Profane Beauty* (1963). Theological aesthetics in the massive work by H. U. von Balthasar, *Herrlichkeit* (1961-).

will and purpose of God that all men should be united with him in the single congregation and assembly of his Son, the transcendent Church of God's New World opened to history in the Resurrection. What this conclusion does not immediately bear upon is the mode of coincidence of the transcendent and the empirical Church at any given historical moment, and consequently the place of this empirical Church at any given historical moment in God's plan for mankind.

In my view, which is already at least implicit in what has gone before in this paper, the coincidence of transcendent and empirical Church is not open to some kind of absolute metaphysical definition; the coincidence is essentially historical. As has already been said, the New Testament may and should be read as a set of paradigms for an understanding of the way in which men are transformed in their history into participation in God's transcendent New World. The history of the Church offers a subordinate series of examples of the understanding of transformation, above all in the Mediterranean world and differently in the world of Celtic culture – this latter, unfortunately, much less studied.[17] The Mediterranean expression of transformation has exerted a kind of domination over Christian experience, the extent of which is being increasingly realized as it is being increasingly relativized. It should hardly be necessary for me to emphasize that of course I do not propose that the Church today should simply jettison its Mediterranean inheritance (any more than I should propose that we should stop reading Aeschylus). But it does seem to me that we should seriously endeavour to understand the history of the Church from New Testament times onwards *hermeneutically,* as paradigmatic and exemplary, as a history of failure as well as of success, thus as bound to this history and also free to extend it diversely into the future.

In this perspective, the necessity of the historical Church, its place in God's design at any given moment, is in an important sense provisional; above all, it is a 'necessity' which has to be *constructed.* If, as has been suggested, the secret of God's plan for mankind was definitively revealed in its free acceptance by Jesus, and if it is derivatively revealed in the Church, that derivative revelation needs to be continually re-enacted in the idioms appropriate to diverse historical epochs. And this must mean in terms of creative human freedom, since we are concerned with the revelation of God's elective love eliciting and sustaining human freedom. The historical self-identification and self-presentation of the

[17] See M. Dillon and N. K. Chadwick, *The Celtic Realms* (1967).

Church at any given time has to exhibit in terms of human freedom the necessitating character of God's love demanding the ultimate surrender of faith.

Now its seems to me that the Roman Catholic Church has been marked out by the loyalty with which she has presented the unconditional character of God's demand for the ultimate surrender of faith; and in this (if I may speak with some enthusiasm), I rejoice to be a Roman Catholic Christian. But it can hardly be said that in recent centuries Roman Catholic Christianity, in its official self-presentation, has shown much awareness of the need to disclose the necessitating character of God's elective love in the terms of an original, creative human freedom. To this extent I sympathize with some of the current attempts by Western theologians to crystallize the message of the New Testament in the gospel of freedom and liberation, even political liberation,[18] though I view with deep regret what seems to me the frequent blindness of some of these attempts to the visionary features of the Gospel. But in any historical conjunction, whether in the West or in the East, it is surely the responsibility of a local Church to make empirically visible the necessity-in-freedom of God's call in the fulfilment of his plan, in this sense to *construct* the necessity of the Church in its empirical self-presentation. It is in this sense that I would call the necessity of the historical Church in God's plan 'provisional'; this necessity depends on whether it has been visibly and empirically exhibited in appropriate historical terms. If it does not exist empirically, this necessity does not exist at all.

It is certainly the case that in the wide field of play between human and divine which, I have suggested, constitutes from a Christian standpoint the space within which non-Christian religions may be hermeneutically located, there will be empirically identifiable features within a given religious tradition which may serve as embodiments of a free surrender to God and acceptance by him into the body of his Son. But in East or West, in societies partially or dominantly affected by technological change, the missionary endeavour of the Church must at least in part consist in the actual identification of those features, and their assimilation and integration into the empirical life of the historical Church itself. It is only in the degree to which this actually happens, and continues to happen in continually changing historical circumstances, that one can speak of a necessity of the historical Church within God's mysterious plan for mankind in Jesus Christ.

[18] E.g. J. B. Metz. See his article, 'Political Theology', in *Sacramentum Mundi*, vol. V.

## Epilogue

In view of the schematic treatment of the topic offered in this paper, it hardly seems necessary to pick out items for possible discussion. But it may be felt that the paper has paid insufficient attention to some fairly recent approaches to the problem, for instance, the Rahner-Schlette view. In case this is so, it may be worthwhile to offer some remarks here, should anyone wish to take them up.

Perhaps my only reservation about this view concerns the kind of generality in terms of which it is proposed. Hegelian generality in terms of historical process seems to exercise a fatal domination over German thinkers of all kinds.[19] The present paper has also tried to offer views of some generality. But the generality here is meant to be that of a kind of hermeneutic space in which particular topics, above all particular historical situations, may be allowed to exhibit connections and continuities. As regards the salutary efficacy of a non-Christian religion, regarded as the traditional praxis of a society, it seems to me that one ought not to deal in general terms like 'primitive religion', Hinduism, or Buddhism, without detailed reference to the highly differentiated character of the traditional praxes in different local societies. And in scriptural religions, the gap between gnostic elite and common practice is often enormous, a gap which is frequently not appreciated by professional students of comparative religion, relying solely on their scriptures.[20]

After some communication prolonged into intimacy with some non-Christian, I may become sure that it is at least as likely that he is doing God's will as that I am; and I may make this sense the touchstone of my appreciation of the salutary efficacy of his religion and of other non-Christian religions. But that does not absolve me from the task of exhibiting in appropriate human terms just my sense of communication with my neighbour in Jesus Christ. My missionary responsibility seems to me untouched by general views about the salutary efficacy of non-Christian religions, because my real kinship with my neighbour in Jesus Christ still demands of me its concrete historical expression: the concrete historical expres-

---

[19] W. Pannenberg has some pertinent remarks on this in his important essay, 'Toward a Theology of the History of Religions', *Basic Questions in Theology*, vol. 2 (1971).

[20] This is what gives K. Klostermaier's *Der Hinduismus* (1965) a quite exceptional value. Cf. also in the same series, Hugo M. Enomiya, *Zen-Buddhismus* (1966).

sion of divine transcendence in the body of Christ here and now in our flesh and blood. Yet again, 'necessity' is a matter of freedom, realized in mutual human sympathy and love.

# 19

## The Vocation of Nature

There seem to me to be two sorts of contribution a Christian theologian might make to a series of lectures on 'The Limits of Human Nature'. In the first place, it is a matter of historical fact that the concept of nature has played a part in Christian theology, and, again as a matter of historical fact, Christian theology has helped in the past to shape many of our ways of thinking today. So a Christian theologian might make his modest but useful contribution by simply identifying some of the factors which have shaped some of our ideas about nature; it might turn out that merely by identifying these factors and indicating the way in which they interacted, connections might come to light which could help to explain the ways in which nature is problematic to us today.

In the second place, a Christian theologian might attempt to go further by trying to extend the Christian tradition of thought about nature so as to bring that tradition to bear on current discussions about nature. In this way a theologian might claim to contribute to the discussions not only as an historian of ideas but as a participant in an open discussion, the representative of a distinctive point of view. It is in this second sense that the present lecture is conceived, though the point of view it represents, by no means the only theological view possible, will have to be allowed to show itself by recourse to historical instances, with some fairly extensive quotation for the sake of particularity. The style will be historical, the aim constructive.

It should not be surprising that a discussion of nature and its limits should be offered in historical terms, even if one obvious sense of the word 'nature' contradistinguishes nature from history. Not so long ago Collingwood wrote an *Idea of Nature* in which he traced the history of the idea; and it is in any case obvious that 'nature' for Wordsworth was different from 'nature' for Pope, say. It isn't at all clear to me what defined use, if any, the concept of 'nature' might have for a modern natural scientist. As one turns the pages of J. Z. Young's impressive *Introduction to the Study of Man*, it is easy to pick out a familiar use of the word 'nature' in which it means no more than something like 'definite character', as in the phrase, 'an understanding of the origin and nature of this mechanism'. The phrase, colourless and unemphasized as it is, repays some attention.

Firstly, 'nature' is an object of understanding, not immediately evident, but prior to the activity of understanding. The world has its definite character or nature, which needs to be explored and can be ascertained progressively. Secondly, 'nature' is here coupled with 'origin', a peculiarly interesting conjunction, since it echoes etymological associations of both Greek *physis* and Latin *natura*, both of which are related (to put it cautiously) with birth and growth (*phuein, nasco*). It is clear that for Young the 'origin' is put somewhere in an evolutionary past, that the 'nature' to be understood is set in a history; and since the understanding looked for has its preordained schema such that this is the way and the only way in which the world of natures is to be understood, the particular nature is set in a universal history of 'Nature', or at least a general history of natures. Thirdly and most distinctively, the nature to be understood in Young's phrase is the nature of a 'mechanism', in this case the mechanism of homeostasis. It isn't only etymologically that 'mechanism' refers to a construction of human devising and ingenuity; it is central to the thesis of Young's book that 'mechanics', the immensely sophisticated mechanics of cybernetics and information theory, offers the most promising explanatory model for understanding the world and man as part of the world, in particular by the study of the brain (earlier books by Young, notably *A Model of the Brain*, have given special attention to this kind of explanation). All we need note here is that this 'model' (again an instructive notion of understanding) puts in question, to say the least of it, an older distinction between 'nature' and 'art', between what is prior to man and what he impresses upon it or elicits from it: a single style of particulate analysis is taken to be appropriate to both. If this view were to be pressed, it might seem that the limits of nature, including human nature, were those of combinatory analysis.

The point of this somewhat laborious examination of a casual remark in a recent book by a distinguished natural scientist was to suggest the historical dimensions implicit in any discussion of nature. The point could be made differently and perhaps more constructively. It is, I suppose, reasonable to assume that a discussion of the limits of nature is primarily concerned with human nature; and we might very well ask whether the concept of nature has any useful application in the consideration of man. Thomas Mann's phrase at the beginning of his great novel *Joseph and his Brethren*, where he speaks of mankind as a 'riddling essence', might I think help to pin down the inescapable ambiguity involved in speaking of man as 'nature', remembering that the 'essence' of the English translation stands for *Wesen,* a concrete nature. The whole passage deserves to be quoted:

> Very deep is the well of the past. Should we not call it bottomless?
> 
> Bottomless indeed, if – and perhaps only if – the past we mean is the past merely of mankind, that riddling essence (*Rätselwesen*) of which our own normally unsatisfied and quite abnormally wretched existences form a part; whose mystery, of course, includes our own and is the alpha and omega of all our questions, lending burning immediacy to all we say, and significance to all our striving. For the deeper we sound, the further down into the lower world of the past we probe and press, the more do we find that the earliest foundations of humanity, its history and culture, reveal themselves unfathomable.

And so on through the immensely leisurely and yet dramatic meditations of the Prelude. This human *Wesen* is mysterious in its *historical* being, interrogates itself as riddler and riddle, makes and poses itself as question. Its immediacy to the past is to be assessed not by the procedures of scientific archaeology but by an archaeology of the spirit, where origin and *arche* can be recalled by poetic celebration, *memoria* and *anamnesis*; even if Mann had not himself publicly declared his kinship with Freud, we should have been able to discern his sense of a living continuity with origins, the presence and pressure of a more than individual past. And it does not seem to be fortuitous that Mann should have allowed the question of man's 'nature' to arise in the evocation of a biblical narrative, the re-telling of a biblical story.

It is a matter of linguistic fact that biblical Hebrew has no equivalent for 'nature' (modern Hebrew uses *ṭb'*, which has the senses *coin, medal, impression on a coin, characteristic, substance, element, Nature, universe*). The registration of the fact ought, I think, to provoke an immense astonishment, to suggest vast perspectives in the history of ideas, and to raise in a new form the question of our self-identification. Once again, if Christian reflection has helped to shape reflection in the West, then the meeting of Jew and Gentile (Greek in particular) which is the proper setting of early

Christianity, is going to offer a privileged instance of the debate about the questionable 'nature' of man, where a search for understanding guided by a schema of *nature* has to try to come to terms with insights, revelation, about man and the world transmitted in quite other categories. It is certainly possible to examine the process of interdiffusion of cultures from the point of view of a sociology of knowledge, as a social anthropologist might try to present in a field study the categories of a preliterate society; only we should have to note that the sociology of knowledge itself is an instance of a historically-conditioned schema for the study of man. Again, the question about the nature of man is not one which necessarily admits a definite answer; it may turn out that the best we can expect to do is to provide a space in which we can go on asking the question.

The meeting of Jew and Greek had of course taken place centuries before the emergence of Christianity, after the conquests of Alexander the Great; the translation of the Hebrew Bible into Greek, the so-called Septuagint version, is a monument of this meeting. And in the greatest of the many Alexandrias founded by the conqueror, the Alexandria in Egypt, the process of Jewish self-understanding in Greek terms and the attempt to communicate this self-understanding as a contribution to Roman-Hellenistic culture reached its culmination in the writings of Philo, an older contemporary of Jesus Christ; there is no indication that Philo knew anything of his Palestinian contemporary. We can learn something of what is involved in the Greek interpretation of biblical revelation by looking briefly at Philo's commentary on the opening chapters of Genesis, *de Opificio Mundi*.

What we immediately notice is a lavish use of the word *physis*, in probably every one of the senses the word had acquired through centuries of Greek thought, and notably in the Stoic tradition. Philo himself could be described as a philosopher only in that very familiar sense of men of letters who find systematic philosophy distasteful yet sustain large philosophical views, often in the language of systematic philsophy, but on the basis of literary experience. In the context of the creation of the world, then, Philo adopts that use of *physis* which it seems not to have had before the fifth century BC, and speaks of Nature as immanent in the whole universe, the cosmos. Yet this world of Nature is administered not only by an immanent purpose but by the purpose of a transcendent Maker. To crown his creation, God made man 'and bestowed on him mind par excellence, life-principle of the life-principle itself, like the pupil of the eye: for of this too those who investigate more closely the nature of things say that it is the eye of the eye'. So the transcendent, god-like principle of intelligence animates this natural life of man, in a way compared by Philo to the natural scientist's or doctor's account of the pupil of the eye. Philo goes on to give reasons why man should have been created last, and one of these is worth quoting at some length.

> God, being minded to unite in intimate and loving fellowship the beginning and the end of created things, made heaven the beginning and man the end, the one the most perfect of imperishable objects of sense, the other the noblest of things earthborn and perishable, being, in very truth, a miniature heaven. He bears about within himself, like holy images, endowments of nature that correspond to the constellations.

Even in this poetic account, the transcendence of man is still being exhibited in cosmic terms. Man is a 'little heaven', whose natural endowments are like the stars in heaven, the sacred images in a *Greek* temple.

The next reason given by Philo to account for man's place in the order of creation is worth noting, not so much for its style, which is still naturalistic and psychological, but for what can be discerned through the style. Man is represented as king, as ruler or master 'by nature' of all other animals, all sublunar creatures: a 'governor subordinate to the chief and great King'. In fact this probably represents more accurately the point of view of the first account of the creation of man in Genesis, the so-called P-version. The underlying image of this version, an image common to Egypt, Mesopotamia and even the early Greek cosmogonies (perhaps derived from Oriental sources) is the emergence of an island mountain of dry land from a flood. This island is successively populated by vegetation and animals, and finally by man, 'monarch of all he surveys', if I may be permitted the anachronistic quotation. The sense of the enigmatic phrase 'in our image, according to our likeness' describing God's plan in creating man may then be explained by the purpose of the plan, that man should 'have dominion' over the earth. What makes man the image of God is his royal dominion over the earth and its fullness.

Philo's picture of archetypal man is taken over and developed by the Greek Christian Fathers. At the end of this tradition St John of Damascus, living under Islamic rule in the eighth century, sums up the teaching of his predecessors. Man is the link between visible and invisible natures, he says, quoting the fourth-century Cappadocian St Gregory of Nazianzus, and goes on:

> God, then, made man without evil, upright, virtuous, free from pain and care, glorified with every virtue, adorned with all that is good, like a sort of second world or microcosm within the great world, another angel capable of worship, compound, surveying the visible creation and initiated into the mysteries of the realm of thought, king over the things of earth, but subject to a higher king, of the earth and of heaven, temporal and eternal, belonging to the realm of sight and to the realm of thought, midway between greatness and lowliness, spirit and flesh. . . .

We might become so stupefied by this accumulation of contrasts as not to notice the sudden shift at the end of the passage, which concludes:

> Here, that is, in the present life, his life is ordered like that of any living thing, but elsewhere, that is, in the age to come, he is changed; and this is the utmost bound of the mystery, he is deified by merely inclining himself to God; becoming deified by participating in the divine radiance, not by being changed into the divine substance.

So man is presented as a paradoxical compound of two natures; and his destiny is to be transformed, deified by sharing in the divine radiance or glory; and this fulfilment of his destiny is open to him if he merely wills it. This last point is perhaps the most important: paradisal, archetypal man is in the image of God because he can freely choose to share in the deifying glory. Using a piece of Stoic vocabulary, Damascene calls man *autexousios*, in his own power; but the sense of the word has changed in Christian use. It is God above all who is *autexousios*, free with unbounded power; man is *autexousios* only in a limited sense, free with limited power, free to choose a destiny offered him by God. Over and above the paradox of his divided natures, the riddling essence of man is a finite freedom called to be transformed into a divine glory which transcends him, called to a transcendence which he must receive as gift.

It is interesting to see how this connection between God's unbounded freedom and man's finite freedom might be at least hinted at in the Genesis story. The Hebrew word *br'*, to create, is used there once in the opening sentence, once at the close, once to speak of the creation of living things, and three times in the sentence: 'And God created man in his image, he created him in the image of God, male and female he created them.' *Br'*, used only with God as subject in the Old Testament, is a word which by the time the Genesis account was written (the P creation-narrative of chapter 1 is a good deal later than the J narrative of chapters 2 and 3) had acquired considerable force in the writings contained in the latter part of Isaiah, chapters 40–55, where Israel in exile is consoled and comforted by having recalled to her over and over again the transcendent power of God. For example:

> For thus says the Lord who created the heavens (he is God!), who formed the earth and made it (he established it; he did not create it a chaos, he formed it to be inhabited!):
> 'I am the Lord, and there is no other.
> I did not speak in secret, in a land of darkness;
> I did not say to the offspring of Jacob, 'Seek me in chaos.'
> I the Lord speak the truth, I declare what is right.'

This Lord, who is 'doing a new thing' in history, recalls the exercise of his power in liberating Israel from Egypt and in creating heaven and earth; his power is unbounded by any man or by any other god; and it is this Lord of unrestrained freedom who is three times said to 'create' man in his image.

The Damascene passage is recalled by St Thomas Aquinas in the thirteenth century, at a crucial point in his *Summa Theologiae* where he is about to begin his treatment of man's return to God by the exercise of his moral freedom. Characteristically, all the poetic imagery is omitted, and only the abstract terms of Damascene's account are recalled. Man is said to be in the image of God, because like his exemplar he is *per se potestativus* (the Latin translation of Damascene's *autexousios*). Using an argument from Aristotle's *Eudemean Ethics* to show that human rationality alone is insufficient to explain freedom, Thomas endeavours to show that this human freedom is most perfectly realized as the responsive choice by man of a transcendent God who in his own freedom has initiated the human choice.

The mention of Aristotle should remind us that Thomas was writing in the middle of one of those Renaissances which have marked the history of European culture; if the rediscovery of Plato was a feature of the fifteenth-century Renaissance, the rediscovery of Aristotle was a marked feature of the thirteenth-century Renaissance. Among the newly-available works of Aristotle, his *Physics* was one of the most influential and controversial; and Thomas's theology of human nature is intelligible only as a rethinking of Aristotle's *physis*. Very briefly, and possibly misleadingly, it may be said that Thomas's understanding of Aristotle's *physis* is intermediate between the view of those modern commentators who hold (rightly, it seems to me, as far as the use of the word goes) that Aristotle never meant by *physis* Nature with a capital 'N', universal cosmic order; and the view of those modern commentators such as Heidegger, who see in Aristotle's *physis* a striking instance of his view that Being is a coming to light, disclosure, manifestation: there is some interest in the view of etymologists that *physis,* through the verbal form *ephun,* is cognate with German *bin* and English *being.* It must at least be said for Heidegger's view that Aristotle's account of *physis* formed part of his view of cosmic order, and that Heidegger's intuitive interpretation may be eliciting presuppositions which Aristotle himself never stated. For Thomas, all natures find their place in a hierarchical cosmic order: describable in modern terms as a total environment. What on any account of Aristotle has to be allowed, that his *physis* is an intrinsic dynamic principle, a principle of change in each thing which gives it its proper intelligibility, is accepted by Thomas too.

Now while human nature belongs to this total order of Nature, it also transcends the universal order in a distinctive way; for while all other natures merely imitate their exemplar (in a Neo-Platonic rather than an Aristotelian way) by being finitely what they are and so partially exhibiting the fullness of being of their source, human nature has an immediacy of presence to the exemplar and source which allows it to reflect the source universally. Further, the whole system of nature depends on the free creative act which brings it into being at all. It is these two basic principles – man's transcendence of the cosmic order and God's freedom in creating it – that allow human nature on this view to have a *history,* and in particular a history of fall and redemption. Thus human nature can have 'states' corresponding to epochs of history; it can be 'intact' before the Fall and 'wounded' after it, 'restored' by insertion into the redemption offered by Christ and 'transfigured' in the eschatological fulfilment of the Redemption. Finite human freedom, exercised in positive acceptance of its unbounded source or by negative withdrawal from it, leaves its mark on the nature whose calling to a transcendent fulfilment it can either consent to as destiny, or by negation reverse upon itself as fate and judgement. On this view, 'nature' is intrinsically limited by being what it is; but for human 'nature', what it is to be is to be called to transcendence.

It may help to particularize this rather sweeping account if we look at some remarks of St Thomas on death, by any account a limitation of human nature. First of all, perhaps, we should remind ourselves that when we speak of the Fall we are, to use Thomas Mann's words, looking into the deep well of the past, with Aeschylus and Shakespeare as better guides, it may seem, than archaeology and palaeontology. Second, we should also remember that human death can never be simply a biological phenomenon; I write this among the echoes of the Londonderry shootings. I shall attempt what is very nearly impossible, an account of Thomas's position without the technical terms of his theology.

What is distinctive about human creatures, Thomas says, is that they are capable of reaching a transcendent fulfilment, but not by the powers of their own nature, only by divine gift. He looks back again to primordial, archetypal man, and sees in him that combination of diverse natures which could sustain stability and equilibrium, even in this world, only with divine assistance. For Thomas, then, the gift of divine assistance is needed both so that human nature might transcend itself, and also so that it might simply be itself, 'intact', before the Fall. So for Thomas, following the Christian doctrine that death is a consequence of the Fall, human death is both natural and non-natural. It is nature, if we look at human nature abstractly, disregarding its destiny in God's plan; it is non-natural if we take that destiny into account and see human nature as called to transcendence. Archetypal man, on God's plan destined for transcendence, is preserved in stable equilibrium in spite of the innate tendency to dissolution of his nature; the Fall deprives human nature both of its due access to transcendence and of its stability against dissolution, so that our dying is the symptom of our alienation from transcendence. The interest of this account seems to me that it does try to do justice to our experience of death, while subjecting the notion of nature to what is perhaps intolerable strain.

I like to see St Thomas's theology as the classical moment in the history of Christian thought; but we do not live in a classic balance, and in fact it was not long before his views were succeeded by more discordant ones. Both his idea of 'nature' and his idea of the 'supernatural' were given a kind of rigidity which deprived them of their Christian sense as *gifts* of a free Creator and Redeemer. There can be no question here, even if I were capable of it, of tracing the further history of the idea of human nature and its limits; instead I shall deliberately select, as a point of departure for a final survey of the problem of the limits of nature as seen by a Christian theologian, the writings of William Blake, for whom it can be not too implausibly maintained that he is in a special sense the prophet of modern consciousness, not least for his awareness of the constraints of Newton's 'single vision'. In view of the sophistication of the modern Blake industry, I had better emphasize that my simple home-made observations are meant only as a means of recovering in our consciousness today some sense of the perspectives of early Christianity.

Broadly speaking, Blake-interpretation seems to fall into two streams, one interested in bringing out his place in the tradition of esotericism, the other in showing his place in the tradition of popular political revolt. E. P. Thompson, in *The Making of the English Working Class*, has well shown how, in certain circumstances, the life of the 'kingdom within' can seek liberation in the attempt to bring about a 'kingdom without', a kingdom of God as political liberation; and Thompson is surely right to see Blake in the context of English Dissent. On the other hand, as perhaps his treatment of Methodism shows, Thompson is not very well qualified to judge the quality of life in the 'inner kingdom' and of the ways in which it might find public expression in its own terms: vulgar Freudianism is not a particularly precise instrument with which to gauge the quality of the life of the human spirit. What remains true is that the tradition to which Blake was indebted was precisely esoteric, insufficiently exposed to the common light of shared civilization; while again, this common light was available only within areas of permissibility defined by the conventions of that civilization. Blake, that is, belonged to a psychological and sociological 'underground', and had to be rediscovered much later in the nineteenth-century when the conventions of English civilization had changed sufficiently to admit him to what Thompson calls the world of 'genteel culture'. It is perhaps appropriate and instructive to see a recent anthology of poetry of the 'Underground' in Britain, *Children of Albion,* edited by Michael Horovitz, placed directly under the patronage of Blake, and admitted to the genteel world of Penguin culture. Radicalism and respectability seem to need each other.

I am, then, proposing to see Blake's writings as a peculiarly significant expression of the 'riddling essence' of man, an expression which only rarely, above all in the *Songs of Innocence and Experience,* achieves an autonomy of poetic utterance and the pregnancy of contained ambiguity, but which elsewhere needs the kind of diagnosis offered by Blake-interpreters, the kind of diagnosis which sometimes illuminates man's riddling essence more tellingly than the symptom itself.

It may be useful to consider a couple of remarks made by Blake as marginalia to his reading of Lavater, himself described as a significant figure in the historical evolution of German Pietism on its way to *Aufklärung,* rational Enlightenment. The other direction in which Pietism evolved was of course Romanticism, well described as the 'apocalypse of the German soul', where the inner kingdom sought to interpret itself as the manifestation of immanent divinity, and so prepared the way for the secular eschatology of Marx, returning in this new guise to the light of common day and the public world.

On one of Lavater's peculiarly insipid aphorisms Blake remarks: 'Man is the ark of God; the mercy seat is above, upon the ark; cherubims guard it on either side, & in the midst is the holy law; man is either the ark of God or a phantom of the earth & of the water.' On another aphorism, in which Lavater, surely in terms of rational enlightenment, asks rhetorically, 'What nature will he honour who honours not the human?' (underlined by Blake), Blake declares: 'Human nature is the image of God.' Later Blake remarks, again on a depressingly insipid aphorism:

> It is the God in *all* that is our companion and friend ... God is in the lowest effects as well as in the highest causes; for he is become a worm that he may nourish the weak. For let it be remember'd that creation is God descending according to the weakness of man, for our Lord is the word of God & everything on earth is the word of God & in its essence is God.

It is obvious that an intuition of the holiness of everything that lives, but above all of man's inward being as the ark of God, can have political implications; but the intuition itself is surely the nerve of significance. It is almost inevitable that on this view a God who is discontinuous with his holiness in man, a Father-God, is seen as limiting the freedom of man's inward holiness to expand and be fruitful; it is precisely the human form that is divine ('the human form divine' is Blake's expression).

There would seem to be no future, certainly not here and now, in trying to say exactly what Blake meant by 'God' and 'divine'; the words are meant to be read not denominatively or referentially but as the exploratory, prophetic reactivation of a tradition of language, the opening up of a space in which the words 'man', 'God', can be released into new possibilities of semantic relationship. It is in this sense that I see Blake both as our contemporary and as making freshly accessible the tradition in which he stands: a tradition of Dissent, certainly, of vision suppressed or repressed, a tradition which leads us back to an epoch in which visionary experience was offered as the only key to the perplexities of human history. The origins of Blake's tradition are in fact clear enough; they lie in that period of history documented in the later strata of the Old Testament, in the New Testament, and in a quantity of literature now known as 'apocalyptic', the name being derived from its purest New Testament exemplar, the Apocalypse or Book of Revelation (*apokalypsis* is the Greek word for 'revelation'). The intermediate stages of Blake's tradition need not concern us here; in some ways it is more profitable to look back at the beginnings from our own time, say from the point of view of a very remarkable novel (with an epigraph from *The Marriage of Heaven and Hell*) by Patrick White, *Riders in the Chariot*. (Perhaps it might be mentioned here that the title of the novel is meant to render the Hebrew *yordê merkabah*, an expression belonging to the first period of Jewish esotericism, prior to medieval Kabbalism, in which speculation and vision were playing with the chariot-throne of Ezekiel's vision; recent investigation has suggested that this throne and chariot speculation can be seen as a transposition into visionary terms of the liturgical cult centred on the ark – cf. Blake's note on Lavater quoted above – in the Jerusalem temple).

Let us for a moment suspend our everyday expectations and suppose that we too, like Patrick White's characters, are waiting for the manifestation of the glory, for a transfiguration latent in the world of our experience. How would a Christian of the first century have waited for the glory? The answer to this question is in essence extremely simple, and it brings us to the heart of Christian understanding of the limits of nature. The early Christian would have waited for the manifestation of the glory as the final expression of the Resurrection and Transfiguration of Jesus Christ.

Some hint of the implications of this identification may be found by looking at the uses, not very numerous, of *metamorphoo*, the Greek word for 'transfigure', in the New Testament. The most obvious set of uses is found in the three parallel accounts in the Synoptic Gospels of the Transfiguration of Jesus. In Mark's version we have:

> And after six days Jesus took with him Peter and James and John, and led them up a high mountain by themselves; and he was transfigured before them, and his garments became glistening, intensely white, as no fuller on earth could bleach them. And there appeared to them Elijah with Moses; and they were talking to Jesus.... And a cloud overshadowed them, and a voice came out of the cloud, 'This is my beloved Son; listen to him.'

Some modern scholars would argue that this account is a projection back into the life of Jesus before his Crucifixion of a post-Resurrection appearance; that it is at any rate offered as a disclosure of the divine glory of Jesus is clear. The overshadowing cloud is an unmistakable reference to the manifestation of God's glory as this is recounted in the Old Testament, what in later Jewish writing was known as the *Shekhinah,* the abiding presence of God. It can be shown fairly convincingly that the scene is conceived of as the advent (*parousia*) of the mysterious Son of Man from chapter 7 of the book of Daniel, a typically apocalyptic portion of the Old Testament, and at the same time the enthronement of the messianic King. But this King is not a king in the political sense. In the eschatology of contemporary Jewish apocalyptic, one can distinguish a political eschatology, where the Messiah is meant to overthrow the enemies of the Jewish people and introduce a victorious reign over all the world; and a transcendent eschatology, where God's new world transforms and transfigures the old. Early Christian eschatology, generally speaking, sees the first emergence of God's transcendent new world in the transfiguration of the risen Jesus.

But other uses of *metamorphoo* in the New Testament seem to evoke the kind of associations the word had in the pagan mystery religions. In the *Metamorphoses* of Apuleius, for instance, better known as the mildly salacious *Golden Ass,* Lucius is not only changed into an ass; at the end of the book he is also transfigured by initiation into the mysteries of Isis, and as such exhibited to the devout worshippers assembled in the temple. A great deal of rather dreary controversy has gone on about whether this so-called 'Hellenistic' sense of transfiguration can be accommodated to the allegedly pure Hebraism of the New Testament. We need to bear in mind the place of Christianity in the Hellenistic world of the Mediterranean, and the sense of Christianity as a transposition of revelation, apocalypse, from the Jewish to the Gentile world. In that rich and multivalent passage of the Second Letter to the Corinthians, where Paul has been commenting on the passage in Exodus in which Moses is described as wearing a veil over his face to conceal its blinding irradiation from the weak eyes of the children of Israel, Paul contrasts the condition of Christians: 'We all, with unveiled face, beholding [or reflecting] the glory of the Lord, are being *transfigured* into his image from glory to glory.' It is not necessary to go into the complex exegetical problems raised by this passage to see that the essential point here is the *communication* of the Christian believer in the transfiguration of Jesus into glory. The transcendent glory of God is made accessible to man in Christ, made accessible in the sacramental transformation of baptism, where the limitation of death is anticipated and overcome in the death and Resurrection of Jesus. For the Christian, metamorphosis is exhibited in symbolic action, anticipating the transfiguration of the world of experience already achieved in the nuclear entry of God's new world through the risen Christ.

The passage from 2 Corinthians just quoted is introduced by the general statement: 'Now the Lord is the Spirit, and where the Spirit of the Lord is, there is freedom.' In the immediate context, this freedom can consist only in freedom of access, openness to the transcendent glory of God; and it is the freedom of those who have been chosen with infinite freedom to be the sons of God, liberated into communion with transcendent freedom. There is no longer the danger of being consumed by the fire of the Lord; his consuming fire has been made a purifying fire in the death of Jesus, into which the believer enters. The disfigured are transfigured by death and resurrection.

The Christian hope is the conviction of the need for, and the possibility of, a transfiguration of a disfigured human nature. The riddling essence of man is to be interpreted as the enigma of this need and possibility. His 'nature', if the word is to be used at all is the irreducible constant of an historical vocation to transcendence, a vocation which is identified primarily as anticipated transfiguration, secondly as the dark shadow left by the failure to accept it. We cannot precisely delineate the contours, boundaries, limits of this constant 'nature', any more than we can define the transcendence ('God') to which it is called, because the mystery of our being is one of finite freedom called, destined, to communion with an infinite freedom. Finite and limited, we cannot say just how we are limited. To quote the first letter of St John: 'Beloved, we are God's children now; it does not yet appear what we shall be, but we know that when he appears we shall be like him, for we shall see him as he is.'

# Index of Names

Aeschylus 219, 221, 232
Albert, St 59, 63
Alexander VI 173
Anawati, G. C. 72 n.
Anselm, St 19
Ansermet, Ernest 108 n.
Apuleius 237
Aristotle 2, 9, 12, 18–19, 47, 63, 74, 81, 83, 107, 131, 209, 231
Aubert, Roger 105 n., 126 n.
Augustine, St 5, 9, 73 n., 93, 108

Balthasar, Hans Urs von 42, 126 n., 160, 212 n., 220n., 234
Bañez, Domingo 104
Barraclough, G. 180 n.
Barrett, C. K. 218
Barrie, J. M. 152
Barth, Karl 78, 126 n.
Baum, Gregory 44
Beattie, John 185
Beethoven 219
Benoit, Pierre 99 n., 164, 183
Benson, R. L. 185
Béraudy, Roger 166
Berdyaev, N. 3
Betz, J. 66 n., 111 n.
Bévenot, M. 176, 177 n.
Blaise, A. 160
Blake 4, 91, 150, 193–4, 197, 213 n., 233–6
Boethius 47, 63 n., 67, 108, 138
Bonaventure, St 7
Bonhoeffer, D. 90 n., 94
Boniface VIII 180
Borgnet, A. 63
Botte, B. 166
Bouillard, H. 126 n.
Box, H. S. 115 n.

Braun, F. M. 122
Brown, Peter 216 n.
Bultmann, R. 57 n., 90 n., 121, 141
Bussche, H. van den 106 n.
Butler, B. C. 123
Buytendijk, F. J. J. 27

Calvin 122
Camelot, T. 217 n.
Campbell, J. 111 n.
Carmignac, J. 182
Caruso, Igor 27
Chadwick, N. K. 221 n.
Chenu, M. D. 63 n., 64 n., 69 n., 167
Chevallier, Ulysse 62
Chomsky, N. 54
Coleridge 44
Colish, M. L. 66 n.
Collingwood, R. G. 82, 225
Colson, J. 164
Congar, Yves 138, 162, 167, 180
Conzelmann, H. 218
Coppens, J. 99
Corbin, H. 71 n., 220 n.
Cornélis, H. 143
Cornford, F. M. 65 n.
Cullmann, O. 181
Curtius, E. R. 66 n.
Cyprian, St 166, 175, 217 n.
Cyril of Alexandria, St 125

Dante 209, 213 n.
Darlap, Adolf 143
Darwin 84
Davis, Charles 133 n.
Denis, A. M. 168, 181
Descartes 127, 135
Dillon, M. 221 n.

Dionysius the Pseudo-Areopagite 4, 9, 35, 57–73
Dionysius Exiguus 175
Dodd, C. H. 72 n.
Dolle, R. 176
Dondaine, H. F. 64 n.
Dupont, J. 129 n.
Dupont-Sommer, A. 100 n., 182
Durrant, M. 69 n.
Dvornik, F. 177 n.

Ebeling, G. 33, 57 n., 61 n., 83, 126 n.
Eberle, R. 72 n.
Eckhart 92
Ehrenburg, Ilya 3
Eliade, M. 55, 111 n., 220 n.
Eliot, T. S. 208
Eltester, F. W. 66 n.
Empson, W. 209
Enomiya, Hugo M. 223 n.
Erasmus 37–8
Eriugena, John Scotus 62, 64, 66
Euclid 68
Evans-Pritchard, E. E. 5, 70, 189–90
Evans-Wentz, W. Y. 31
Evdokimov, Paul 125 n.

Fabro, C. 62 n.
Farrer, Austin 119–22
Feine, J. 180 n.
Feuerbach, L. 90 n.
Feuillet, A. 122, 219 n.
Fink, Eugen 79, 90 n.
Fletcher, Angus 73 n.
Flew, A. G. N. 135
Fontaine, J. 144
Foucault, M. 72
Fransen, P. 170 n.
Franzelin, J. B. 130
Frege, G. 13
Frend, W. H. C. 217 n.
Freud 55, 90, 227
Fries, H. 105 n.
Fuchs, Ernst 33, 83

Gadamer, H. G. 57 n., 84
Galot, J. 121 n.
Gandillac, M. de 59 n., 64 n.
Gardet, L. 72 n.
Gasser, V. F. 130
Gaudemet, J. 180 n.
Gaulle, C. de 13
Geach, P. 69 n.
Geiger, L. B. 62 n.

Gödel, Kurt 54
Gonda, Jan 39
Goppelt, L. 216
Graham, A. C. 40, 141
Grant, R. M. 216 n.
Gratian 185
Graves, Robert 31
Gregory the Great, St 173
Gregory VII 180
Gregory of Nazianzus, St 229
Grelot, P. 164
Griffiths, Bede 156

Hartley, Anthony 209
Hauer, J. W. 220 n.
Hegel, 90 n., 132, 223
Heidegger, M. 2, 5, 20, 26–7, 57 n., 74, 84, 87–8, 90–1, 108, 126 n., 140, 232
Hengel, M. 72 n.
Henry, F. 214 n.
Hertling, L. 180 n.
Heschel, Abraham 71 n.
Hester, M. B. 70 n.
Hindemith, Paul 108
Hippolytus, St 194
Hölderlin 26
Homer 188–9
Hommes, J. 90 n.
Hopkins, G. M. 70 n., 134
Horowitz, M. 234
Hume, R. F. 39
Husserl, E. 108 n.

Ignatius of Antioch, St 164
Irenaeus, St 142

Jalland, T. G. 177
Jaspers, Karl 126 n.
Jeffries, Richard 31
Jeremias, J. 49, 74 n., 181
Jerome, St 164
John XXIII 147, 173, 186
John Damascene, St 229–31
John, Eric 173
Joyce, James 98
Jung 90, 151

Kant 47, 108, 140
Kelly, J. N. D. 33
Kierkegaard 3, 135
Kilwardby, Robert 8
Kirby, J. C. 219 n.
Kittel, G. 174
Klostermaier, K. 223 n.

Knight, G. Wilson 69, 72 n., 74
Koch, K. 74 n.
Kosmala, H. 216 n.
Kraus, H. J. 72 n.
Kremer, Klaus 62 n.
Küng, Hans 118, 212–15
Kuttner, S. 139

Lacombe, G. 63 n.
Lacombe, O. 39
Laing, R. D. 31
Las Casas, B. de 137
Laurentin, R. 115 n., 117–18
Lavater 234–5
Lawrence, D. H. 87, 209
Leavis, F. R. 44
Le Bras, G. 139, 180 n.
Lécuyer, J. 170 n.
Leeuw, G. van der 220 n.
Lefèvre d'Etaples 63
Le Guillou, M. J. 42
Leishman, J. 199
Leo the Great, St 175–80
Léon-Dufour, X. 57 n.
Lévi-Strauss, C. 11, 52
Lienhardt, R. G. 219 n.
Ligier, L. 102, 216 n.
Locke, John 193, 197
Lohse, E. 216 n.
Lorenzen, Paul 54
Löwith, K. 90 n.
Lubac, H. de 143
Ludwig, J. 177 n.
Luther 122, 149
Lyons, John 54

Maimonides 72
Mallarmé 209
Mann, Thomas 227
Marcion 130
Markus, R. A. 173
Marrou, H. I. 66 n.
Martin, Raymond 137
Marx 127, 151, 235
Mascall, E. L. 115 n.
Mauser, U. 71 n.
Maximus, St 64
McCabe, Herbert 133 n.
McKelvey, R. J. 216 n.
Merleau-Ponty, M. 27, 84
Metz, J. B. 222 n.
Meyendorff, J. 177
Minio-Paluello, L. 63
Moerbeke, William of 63

Montagnes, B. 68 n.
Morris, A. 119
Mouroux, J. 105 n., 107 n.
Müller, A. 125 n.
Mumford, L. 208
Murray, Robert 185

Neufeld, V. H. 32–3
Newman 3
Newton 193, 197
Nicholas of Cusa 20, 37
Nietzsche 90 n.

Otto, R. 90 n., 188
Otto, W. F. 90 n., 188–9

Pannenberg, W. 214, 223 n.
Pasolini 169
Paul VI 139, 171
Pears, David 53
Pera, C. 59
Peterson, Erik 195–6
Philo 51, 71, 72 n., 228–9
Picasso 98
Pinborg, J. 69
Pius IX 171
Pius XII 117, 166, 168, 171
Plato 2, 9, 12, 19, 62, 65, 72, 73 n., 90, 127, 188, 231
Pöggeler, O. 126 n.
Pope 225
Proust 31

Quintilian 63

Rad, G. von 219 n.
Rahner, Hugo 212–13
Rahner, Karl 4–5, 41, 66 n., 111, 126 n., 142, 143, 170 n., 209, 223
Ramsey, A. M. 89, 94, 96
Ratzinger, J. 42, 208
Reicke, Bo 216 n.
Richardson, P. 216 n.
Ricoeur, Paul 52, 55, 57 n.
Rilke 198–200
Rimbaud 31
Ringger, J. 181
Robinson, J. A. T. 5, 89–96
Roques, R. 59 n.
Rousseau, H. 13
Russell, Bertrand 13
Russell, D. E. S. 216 n.

Satgé, John de 119

Schillebeeckx, Edward 41, 46, 97 n., 98 n., 128, 170 n.
Schlette, H. R. 142, 223
Schlier, H. 100 n., 218 n.
Schmaus, M. 112 n., 166
Schnackenburg, R. 113, 142, 208
Scholem, G. 207
Schopenhauer 13
Schulz, W. 19
Searle, John 52
Seckler, M. 105 n.
Seltzman, Charles 188
Shah, Idries 31
Shakespeare 208, 209, 219, 233
Sheldon-Williams, I. P. 62 n.
Simon, P. 59 n.
Soos, M. B. de 176
Stenius, Erik 17
Stephen I 177 n.
Stephen II 173
Stevens, Wallace 12, 75
Stiker, H. J. 69 n.
Stravinsky 98
Strawson, P. F. 10
Suenens, L. J. 41

Talmon, J. L. 169
Taylor, John V. 146
Teilhard de Chardin 84
Tempels, Placide 146
Tertullian 130
Thomas Aquinas, St 2, 4, 7–12, 18–20, 26, 47, 56, 57–75, 83–4, 103–7, 138–40, 162, 231, 232–3

Thompson, E. P. 234
Thurian, M. 115 n., 118–119, 121–3
Tierney, B. 139
Tillard, J. M. R. 97 n.
Tillich, Paul 90, 92, 93
Toynbee, Arnold 216 n.
Trilling, W. 181
Turbayne, C. M. 72 n.
Turner, V. W. 219 n.

Ullmann, W. 179–80

Vermes, G. 182
Victor I 173
Vielhauer, P. 216 n.
Vitoria, F. de 137

Walker, G. S. M. 176
Warnach, V. 208
Watt, W. Montgomery 72 n.
Waugh, Evelyn 98 n.
Werner, E. 216
White, Patrick 207, 236
White, Victor 5
Wilson, Bryan R. 217 n.
Winch, Peter 25
Wind, Edgar 37
Wittgenstein, L. 2, 5, 13–27, 53, 70 n., 84, 133
Wordsworth 191–3, 197, 208, 225

Young, J. Z. 226

Zaehner, R. C. 31, 39
Zwingli 122

# Analytic Index of Subjects

Angels:
    subjective conditions for seeing 187 ff.
    and Isaiah 6, 194 f.
    Rilke's angels 198 ff.
    in the liturgy 200 f.
Apocalyptic:
    matrix of early Church 216
    Blake and A. 235 f.
    Christianity as transposition of A. 237
Apostolic ministry:
    ministerial priesthood 159 ff.
    dynamic transcendence of Christ 161 f.
    Catholic priest as emblem 162
    Vatican II provides new approach 162 ff.
    Apostolic office as re-presentation 164
    threefold office 166 f.
    priest as figure of Christ 168 f.

Being:
    intelligibility of 11, 18
    logic of 18 f.
    and 'Earth' 27, 88
    question of 84
    communion in 133
    manifestation of in Gospel 136
    *Seinsgeschichte* 85, 143, 155

Christianity:
    consecration of genetic moment 34 f.
    pneumatic power to transform 35
    reality of 158 f.
    consecration of revolution 169
Church:
    linguistic community 27
    institution and communion 78
    as sacrament 111
    Mary as figure of 122 ff.
    opposition to world 128
    figure of transcendence 159 f.
    sacrament of reign of God 183
    empirical and visionary accounts of 212 ff.
    continuing revelation of *mysterion* 218
    necessity of 221 f.

Death:
    St Thomas on 232 f.
Dominican vocation:
    life of study 149 ff.
    service of Word 150
    contemplative engagement 151
    preaching 202 ff.

Ecclesiology:
    ecclesiality of faith 78
    alternative emphases 111 f.
    as seminary course 137 ff.
    as ontological *a priori* of theology 139
    unconscious ecclesiology 171 ff.
    empirical and visionary 212 ff.
    'from below' 214 f.
Ecumenism:
    by fulfilment rather than anathema 81
    as search for the whole 118
Eucharist:
    as normative gesture of faith 110 f.
    representation of the peoples 170
    and angels 194 ff.
    and 'people of God' 201
European consciousness:

Oriental religions and 31
European Christian identity 147
Existence:
   and nature 130 ff.
Experience:
   Christian experience of genetic moment 34 f.
   theological critique of 47 ff.
   experience of transcendence 217
   Mediterranean inheritance dominates Christian experience 221
   visionary experience in Blake 235 f.

Faith:
   transcendence through 39
   as illocutionary act 52
   presupposition of theology 78 f.
   St Thomas on faith 103 ff.
   as communion with God 121
   and reason 133 f.
Figure:
   Mary as 'figure' of the Church 122 f.
   reigning pope as 'figure' of Peter 123
   Church as 'figure' 159 f.
Five Ways, the:
   readings of experience 9
   God as maximum in *Quarta Via* 19
   other 'ways' to be looked for 74
   and 'certain knowledge of God' 133
Freedom:
   transcendent freedom of God 36 f.
   and faith 51 f.
   human freedom and necessity 218
   gospel of 222
   finite 230
   finite and infinite 238

God:
   as maximum 19 f.
   Wittgenstein's account of 20 ff.
   presence-in-absence 26, 36, 207
   *Deus absconditus* 27, 35 f., 101 f.
   the word 'God' 50 f.
   as 'will' 51
   literal and metaphorical talk about 71 ff.
   the really real 73
   as Meaning of meaning 79, 156
   God's self-presentation in Christ 106 f., 109, 111, 114
   knowledge of by reason 130 ff.
   the invisible 203 ff.
   God's purpose in history 218
   glory of 237 f.

Gods:
   Heidegger's gods 27
   Yahweh displaces 50
   Homeric 188
Gospel:
   variety of terms for 33
   as manifestation of mystery of Being 136
   and sacrament 167
   as critique 215
   as transfiguration 217
   as liberation 222

Hermeneutics:
   for Ricoeur 55
   hermeneutic theology 57 f.
   hermeneutic locus of theology 83 f.
   hermeneutic approach 211
   hermeneutic reading of Church history 221
Humanism:
   emergence of acosmic humanism in St Thomas 73

Jesus Christ:
   what is unique to Christianity 9
   central affirmation of Christian faith 32 f.
   crucified Christ as paradigm of the hidden God 36
   'Jesus is the Christ' 48 f.
   centre of revelation of God 74 f.
   revelation of ultimate meaning 75
   an absolute beginning 79
   ontological meaning of history 86
   seems to vanish in classical theology 106
   Lord of the *mysterion* 114
   God-Man 130
   victory of Christ over world 159 f.
   'Christ-Event' 161
   the One who becomes Many 205
   see under Resurrection
Jurisdiction:
   theory of 'powers' in ministry 164
   papal 'jurisdiction' 174 ff.

*Kwoth*:
   Nuer God-term often predicate but seldom subject 51, 70
   singular and plural forms compared with Sabellianism 190

Language:
  Wittgenstein's picture-theory 14 ff.
  as form of life 21
  as event of truth 26
  Christianity as 'language-event' 33
  St Thomas on 68 f.
Limit:
  Wittgenstein's notion of 14 f.
  thinking limits from outside 20
Love:
  central Christian experience 37
  *agape* 204 f.

Mary:
  English Catholic attitudes to 115 f.
  Marian theology 117 f.
  an ecumenical problem 118
  Austin Farrer's argument 119 ff.
  as figure of the Church 122 ff.
  Marian piety today 125
Meaning:
  the central problem of philosophy 20
  as common and public world 20 f.
  as various as life 21
  as nativity of the word 27
  general presuppositions about 52 ff.
  for Lévi-Strauss 52 ff.
  not structure or source but praxis 55
  gardening as metaphor for 55
  Jesus 'maps' origin of meaning 56
  and Resurrection 75
  Meaning of meaning, God 79
  archaic theory of meaning in St Thomas 83
  investigations into 84
  musical meaning 108
  presence of ultimate Meaning amongst us 156
*Merkabah*:
  Jewish mysticism of Ezekiel's chariot-throne 195, 207, 236
Metaphor:
  St Thomas on 66 ff.
  'extended metaphor' 69
  dualism in literal/metaphorical distinction 71
  word 'God' prior to literal/metaphorical distinction 74
  Resurrection as 'metaphor' of world 75
Metaphysics:
  St Thomas as metaphysician 9 f.
  'descriptive' and 'revisionary' 10
  the old metaphysical search 23
  as sketching space for reflection 48
  non-historical metaphysics 143
Monastic code:
  in Dominican life 154 f.
Music:
  metatheology passes into 86
  and time 108 f.
*Mysterion*:
  God's hidden purpose according to St Paul 37
  ultimate meaning of history 51
  Pauline notion explained 98 ff.
  God with us 106
  and sacraments 110 f.
  and contemplation 151
  papacy as intrinsic element in 173
  'sacrament' of God's purpose 218

Natural theology:
  as seminary course 126 ff.
  four types distinguished 134 f.
Nature:
  connaturality of nature and human nature in St Thomas 18
  no word for 'nature' in biblical Hebrew 50 f., 227 f.
  and existence 131 f.
  Wordsworth on 192
  J. Z. Young on 226
  human nature as 'riddling essence' 227
  Philo on 228 f.
  St Thomas on Aristotle on 231 f.
  Heidegger on Aristotle on 232
  Blake on 234 f.
Necessity:
  in God's purpose 217 f.
Negation:
  in St Thomas 18 ff.
  in Wittgenstein 22 f.
New Testament Christianity:
  profitably investigated as 'language-event' 33
  transformation of languages already in use 33
  genetic moment in 34 f.
  NT witness as illuminating event 81
  as 'concentration of multiple meanings' 141
  idealized versions of 215
  NT as collection of paradigms for an experience of transformation 217
Nonsense:
  Wittgenstein on not necessarily

unimportant nonsense 14 f.
an *Alleluia* as significant nonsense 23

Object:
  how God becomes one 91 f.
  Existentialist 'dropping of the object' 92
  knowledge as objectification in St Thomas 103 f.
Ontology:
  logic of Being 19
  ontological interpretation of divine names 74
  trying to retain an ontology of meaning 75
  the 'ontological comparative' 79
  God-question as search for ontological meaning 84
  ontological dimension of truth 86
  this musical ontology of time 109
  Catholic Christianity implies an ontology 133 n.
  theological 139, 173
  the sense of 'ontological' defined 140
  an ontology of *Heilsgeschichte* 142
  history comprehended ontologically 143, 155
  Petrine claim is ontological 174 ff.

Petrine ministry:
  Peter's saving significance partly continued 123
  theology to be distinguished from ideology 171 ff.
  papalism 173
  justification of papacy in theological terms 173
  president of college not enough 174
  primacy of honour and of jurisdiction 174 ff.
  St Leo the Great's self-understanding 176 ff.
  examination of Matt. 16 181 ff.
  'Vizier of the Messiah' 183
  'Peter' as title as well as proper name 184
Philosophy:
  problems set for theology by Wittgenstein 13 ff.
  English 25, 31
  in seminaries 126 ff.
Pluralism:
  multiplicity of Christian meanings 79
  truly generous recognition of 145 f.
  varieties of structure and experience in the Church 217
Politics:
  Church's concern for 146
  'political theology' 222

Religion:
  as a family-word 28
  comparative as genteel theosophy 29 f.
  interrogation of Christianity by world religions 30 ff.
  gap between articulate doctrine and lived religion 39, 144, 223
  religions not static entities 144
  non-Christian religions 219 f.
Resurrection of Christ, the:
  paradigm case of worship of God the Father 34
  post-Resurrection Christ attracts to himself whole spectrum of religious concern 49 f.
  ultimate 'metaphor' of the world 75
  as cult and worship 95
  the genetic moment in Christianity 215 f.
  and Transfiguration 236

Sabellianism:
  Evans-Pritchard compares S. with Nuer religion 190 f.
*Sacra doctrina*:
  gospel tradition organized as discipline 47
  the 'science' which St Thomas discusses 58 ff.
  natural theology an abstraction of 135
Sacraments:
  and archetypes of saving history 95
  as particular realizations of *mysterion* 109 f.
  sacrament of Order 159 ff.
  a quasi-sacramental theology of papal primacy 176 ff.
Self:
  metaphysical concept of the self 23 f.
  self-understanding and theology 30
  and prayer 95
  as possibility of transcendence 160
Spirit, the Holy:
  new dimension of pneumatic life 34
  the Church in the power of *Pneuma* 88 f.

sponsal presence of Christ's Spirit 124
life in the Spirit as religion 162
preaching as growth in the Spirit 206
presence of the Spirit of Jesus 217
Structure:
   a primary explanatory concept 53 f.
Subject:
   the subject-object schema in epistemology 103
   subjective conditions of knowledge 187 f.
   angels can only be subjective 200
Substance:
   orientation to 'substance' necessary in Catholic theology 132
Symbol:
   Ricoeur's notion of 55
   in Pseudo-Dionysius 64 ff.

Theology:
   according to St Thomas 8 f.
   theology as Christian self-understanding 30 f.
   as critical praxis 43
   and 'concreteness' 44 f.
   'Jesus is the Christ' as centre of concern 48
   theology sketches a space at origin 56
   hermeneutic theology as theology of meaning 57 f.
   method 76 ff.
   theological epistemology 76 ff.
   as an encounter between Church and world 77
   every Catholic life a 'theology' 79
   theory and practice in St Thomas 83
   general perspectives for 83 f.
   the schema of God as Meaning of meaning 84 f.
   meta-theology 85
   history of theological meaning 85
   a new theological perspective 98
   types of natural theology 134 f.
   ecclesiology as *a priori* of theology 139 f.
   as 'culture' rather than 'science' 144
   as engaged contemplation 151 f.
   and ideology 171 ff.
   theological ontology 173
   theological communication in preaching 205 ff.
   theological statements as witness and testimony 211

Time:
   St Thomas on 107
   and music 108 f.
   Christian meaning of 151
Transcendence:
   of God for St Thomas 19
   no longer opposed to finitude in later Wittgenstein 24
   God's transcendence revealed in history 27
   and faith 38 f.
   Christianity as experience of dynamic transcendence 159
   as an experience of love 207 f.
   empirical and transcendent Church 212 ff.
   New Testament as an experience of 217
   as gift 230
   human nature and historical vocation to 238
Transformation:
   genesis of Christianity as transformation of languages 33
   force of Christian language 39
   as praise in Rilke 199
   and Resurrection of Jesus 216
   New Testament as a set of paradigms for understanding T. 221
   and transfiguration 236 f.
Truth:
   as revelation of being for St Thomas 10 f.
   Yes-No character of 81
   ontological dimension of 86
Vatican I:
   on 'certain knowledge of the existence of God' 130 ff.
   on papal primacy 174 f.
   a jurisdictional or 'political' theology of the primacy 180
Vatican II:
   and Marian doctrine 115
   Declaration on non-Christian Religions 140 ff.
   Decree on Missions 145 ff.
   victory of generation of 1940s 147
   valuable treatment of apostolic ministry 162
   Dogmatic Constitution on the Church 162 ff.
   a whole ideology of priesthood set aside by Council 165

Decree on the Ministry 166 ff.
profound shift of Catholic consciousness since Council 171 f.
ecclesiological utterances insufficiently historical 212

Worship:
Resurrection as paradigm case of 34
Christian cult as destruction of the Temple 88 f.
the 'object' of 89 ff.
participation in new life of the Lord 94 ff.
Christian worship refers itself to the source 111
not in the head but transfiguring the body 153
Christian life as 162
eucharistic liturgy as locus for presence of angels 194 ff.

www.ingramcontent.com/pod-product-compliance
Lightning Source LLC
Chambersburg PA
CBHW051633230426
43669CB00013B/2289